United States
Department of
Agriculture

Forest Service

Southern
Research Station

General Technical
Report SRS–106

Celebrating Minority Professionals in Forestry and Natural Resources Conservation:

Proceedings of the Symposium on the Tenth Anniversary of the 2 + 2 Joint Degree Program in Forestry and Natural Resources Conservation

Tallahassee, Florida
September 17–20, 2002

I0411472

DISCLAIMER

The use of trade or firm names in this publication is for reader information and does not imply endorsement by the U.S. Department of Agriculture of any product or service.

PESTICIDE PRECAUTIONARY STATEMENT

This publication reports research involving pesticides. It does not contain recommendations for their use, nor does it imply that the uses discussed here have been registered. All uses of pesticides must be registered by appropriate State and/or Federal agencies before they can be recommended.

CAUTION: Pesticides can be injurious to humans, domestic animals, desirable plants, and fish or other wildlife if they are not handled or applied properly. Use all pesticides selectively and carefully. Follow recommended practices for the disposal of surplus pesticides and their containers.

Papers published in these proceedings were submitted by authors in electronic media. Some editing was done to ensure a consistent format. Authors are responsible for content and accuracy of their individual papers and the quality of illustrative materials.

February 2008

Southern Research Station
200 W.T. Weaver Blvd.
Asheville, NC 28804

Celebrating Minority Professionals in Forestry and Natural Resources Conservation: Proceedings of the Symposium on the Tenth Anniversary of the 2 + 2 Joint Degree Program in Forestry and Natural Resources Conservation

Edited by

Oghenekome U. Onokpise, Don L. Rockwood,
Dreamal H. Worthen, and Ted Willis

Sponsored by

College of Engineering Sciences, Technology, and Agriculture (CESTA)
Florida A&M University

Florida Department of Agriculture and Consumer Services—
Division of Forestry (FDACS-DOF)

Ford Foundation
(Institute for International Education- IIE)

School of Forest Resources and Conservation (SFRC)
Institute of Food and Agricultural Sciences (IFAS)
University of Florida

USDA Cooperative State Research, Education, and Extension Services
National Research Initiative (CSREES-NRI)

U.S. Forest Service
Southern Research Station

REVIEWERS

Rory Frazier
Center for Forestry and Ecology
Department of Plant, Soil, and
 Environmental Sciences
Alabama A&M University
Normal, AL

William G. Hubbard
Cooperative Extension Service
School of Forest Resources
University of Georgia
Athens, GA

James I. Muchovej
Division of Agricultural Sciences
Florida A&M University
Tallahassee, FL

Fulbert Namwamba
Department of Urban Forestry
Southern University
Baton Rouge, LA

Oghenekome U. Onokpise
Forestry and Natural Resources
 Conservation Program
Florida A&M University
Tallahassee, FL

Donald L. Rockwood
School of Forest Resources and Conservation
University of Florida
Gainesville, FL

Wayne Smith
Institute of Food and Agricultural Sciences
University of Florida
Gainesville, FL

Tamara Walkingstick
Cooperative Extension, Forestry
 Environmental & Natural Resources
University of Arkansas
Little Rock, AR

Marcus Warwell
Rocky Mountain Research Station,
Forestry Sciences Laboratory
U.S. Forest Service
Moscow, ID

Carl Wilmsen
Community Forestry Research
College of Natural Resources,
University of California
Berkeley, CA

We are particularly grateful to our reviewers who spent several months reviewing many manuscripts at the same time. Their diligence and attention to details have resulted in a refereed proceedings containing papers in diverse disciplines of forestry and natural resource conservation, information that is rarely found in other publications, making this a very unique proceedings.

CONTENTS

SESSION I—FORESTRY AND NATURAL RESOURCES EDUCATION, UNDERGRADUATE RECRUITMENT, RETENTION AND EDUCATION

The History and Background of Urban Forestry Education at Southern University 3
Fulbert Namwamba, Daniel J. Collins, Kamran Abdollahi, Zhu Ning, Yadong Qi, and Rodney Stone

Recruiting, Retaining, and Educating Minorities in Natural Resources and Forestry: Florida A&M University—University of Florida 2 + 2 Joint Degree Program in Natural Resources 7
Oghenekome U. Onokpise, Donald L. Rockwood, and Ted Willis

SESSION II—GRADUATES IN THE WORKFORCE AND GRADUATE SCHOOL

Encouraging Minorities to Enroll and Graduate in Urban Forestry and Related Disciplines at Southern University 15
Fulbert Namwamba, Daniel J. Collins, Kamran Abdollahi, Zhu Ning, Yadong Qi, and Rodney Stone

Revitalizing Agronomic and Natural Resources Education at Florida A&M University 19
Oghenekome U. Onokpise, Robert B. Bradford, Cassel Gardner, S. Reed, and Odemari S. Mbuya

SESSION III—WOMEN IN NATURAL RESOURCES

You Don't Have to Spit and Chew 25
Denise McCaig

We Need Women of Color to Save the Planet 27
Louise Fortmann and Dreamal Worthen

SESSION IV—TITLE VI AND DELIVERY SYSTEM

The Future Starts Now! 31
Eurial Turner

SESSION V—GRADUATES OF THE FAMU 2 + 2 JOINT DEGREE PROGRAM

FAMU/UF Joint Degree Program Graduates: Where We've Been and Where We Are Now...........37
Marcus Warwell, Stephanie Steele, and Terrence Campbell

Review of Ecological Adaptation in Temperate and Boreal Forest Tree Species...........................41
Marcus Warwell

SESSION VI—FIRE IN THE URBAN/WILDLAND INTERFACE

Florida's Wildland Fire Risk Assessment Analysis....49
Jim Brenner, Jim Karels, Sue McLellan, Kass Green, and Julie Coen

Exploring Social Foundations that Support Community Preparedness for Wildfire...................55
Shruti Agrawal, Martha C. Monroe, Pamela Jakes, Erika Lang, Kristen Nelson, Linda Kruger, and Vicky Sturtevant

SESSION VII—FOREST PRODUCTS/FOREST EXTENSION/FOREST ECONOMICS

Highlights of Wood Products Research Activities at USDA Forest Products Laboratory 61
Irene Durbak

Celebrating Minority Involvement in Extension Forestry Opportunities...64
William G. Hubbard and Ben D. Jackson

The Role of NAFTA in International Trade of Forest Products..68
Zacch Olorunnipa

Minorities, an Under-Realized Market Segment in Natural Resource-Based Recreation: Potential Economic Returns to Directed Marketing.............71
Michael Thomas

SESSION VIII—URBAN AND COMMUNITY FORESTRY

Educational Opportunities in the Application of Geographic Information Systems in Urban and Community Forestry..................................77
Tommy L. Coleman, Wubishet Tadesse, and Teferi D. Tsegaye

Forest Service's Approaches to Urban Forestry...84
Ed Macie

The Role of Geographic Information Systems and Remote Sensing in Urban Forestry Education at Southern University..........................86
Fulbert Namwamba

Session IX—AGROFORESTRY SYSTEMS AND INTERNATIONAL FORESTRY

Integrating High Value Horticultural Crops into Agroforestry Systems in the Tropics with Focus on Alley Cropping 93
Manuel C. Palada, Stafford M. Crossman, and James J. O'Donnell

Agroforestry to Enhance Land Productivity and Environmental Protection 102
James L. Robinson

Opportunities Agroforestry Provide Minority and Limited Resource Landowners 104
Rory Frazier

Protecting the Ecosystem through Religion: A Case of Religious Groves in Ondo, Nigeria 108
Olugbemi Moloye

PREFACE

In 1992, Florida A&M University (FAMU) and the University of Florida implemented a 2 + 2 joint degree in Forestry and Natural Resources Conservation (FNRC). This program has been largely funded by the national initiatives of the U.S. Forest Service (USFS). The year 2002 marked the tenth anniversary of what is now considered one of the most successful of the national initiatives of the USFS. The purpose of the symposium was to highlight the program and its contribution to increasing minority professionals in forestry and natural resource conservation. The tenth anniversary symposium brought together graduates of the program, current students and officials from the universities, the USFS, other agencies, and private industry. It also offered an opportunity for FNRC professionals, especially minorities from public and private industry, to interact and educate future professionals. The theme of the symposium was "Education, Training, and Diverse Workforce." Two field trips were undertaken during the symposium. The first one was conducted in the Apalachicola National Forest, while the second one covered the canopy roads of Tallahassee, Leon County in North Florida.

Symposium sponsors included the College of Engineering Sciences, Technology and Agriculture (CESTA), Florida A&M University; Division of Forestry, Florida Department of Agriculture and Consumer services (DOF-FDACS), Institute for International Education (IIE), Ford Foundation; School of Forest Resources and Conservation (SFRC), University of Florida; USDA Cooperative State Research, Education, and Extension Services, National Research Initiative through a competitive grant; and USFS, Southern Research Station.

Proceedings of the symposium have been published in two volumes. Volume I contains peer reviewed papers published by the USFS, Southern Research Station, as a general technical report. Requests for manuscripts went out immediately after the conclusion of symposium activities. The second set of manuscripts were received 12 months after manuscripts had been requested. To ensure a complete review of the manuscripts, as much as 18 months were allowed for reviewers to complete the process. Each paper published in this proceeding was reviewed by three independent reviewers. Although a total of 37 papers were presented at the symposium, only 22 papers are being published. Volume II was published in 2005 as a pictorial publication by Florida A&M University.

We wish to thank everyone who made the symposium an overwhelming success. Thanks to the Communication Unit of the USFS, Southern Research Station, for publishing this unique volume of the symposium proceedings.

Oghenekome U. Onokpise

Donald L. Rockwood

Dreamal Worthen

Ted Willis

ACKNOWLEDGMENTS

SYMPOSIUM SPONSORS

College of Engineering Sciences, Technology and Agriculture, Florida A&M University
  Division of Forestry, Florida Department of Agriculture and Consumer Service
Ford Foundation (Institute for International Education)
School of Forestry Resource Conservation, Institute of Food and Agricultural Sciences, University of Florida
USDA Cooperative State Extension and Education Service, National Research Initiative
U.S. Forest Service, Southern Research Station

COMMITTEES

NATIONAL ADVISORY COMMITTEE

Terrence Campbell, Center for Disease Control (CDC), Atlanta, GA
Daniel Carraway, International Paper Company, Bainbridge, GA
Kim Davis, Florida Department of Environmental, Protection, Tallahassee, FL
Dixie Erenreich, University of Idaho, Moscow, ID
Kecia Hill, Quincy Chartered High School, Quincy, FL
Denise McCaig, U.S. Forest Service, Albuquerque, NM
Oghenekome Onokpise, Florida A&M University, Tallahassee, FL
Don Rockwood, University of Florida, Gainesville, FL
Stan Rosenthal, University of Florida, Gainesville, FL
Ron Smith, Tuskegee University, Tuskegee, AL
Stephanie Steele, U.S. Forest Service, National Forests in Florida, Oxford, MS
Verian Thomas, Florida A&M University, Tallahassee, FL
Marcus Warwell, U.S. Forest Service, Moscow, ID
Ted Willis, U.S. Forest Service, Florida A&M University, Tallahassee, FL
Dreamal Worthen, Florida A&M University, Tallahassee, FL

LOCAL ORGANIZING COMMITTEE, COLLEGE OF ENGINEERING SCIENCES, TECHNOLOGY AND AGRICULTURE

Registration and Facilities:
Josie Gaines
Cressie Wilson
Dreamal Worthen

Publications and Media:
Marian Gibbons
Pamela Hunter
Katherine Milla
Oghenekome Onokpise

Graduate Students:
 Yolanda Bassie
Hamilton Dueberry
Joyet Moody
Leroy Whilby

Awards and Appreciation:
Betty Hudson
Pamela Hunter
Shirlene Jordan
Ted Willis
Dreamal Worthen
Oghenekome Onokpise

Transportation:
Ron Gilmore
Oghenekome Onokpise
Ted Willis

SPECIAL ACKNOWLEDGMENTS

Field Trip Coordinators:
    Field trip on the Canopy Roads of Tallahassee:
      Stan Rosenthal, Leon County Extension Office
      David Marshall, Leon County Extension Office

    Field trip within the Apalachicola National Forests:
      James Hart, National Forests in Florida
      Ivan Green, National Forests in Florida
      Ted Willis, National Forests in Florida

Florida A&M University, School of Journalism—for symposium logos and banners:
    Ann Wead Kimbrough
    Quinetra Cromuel
    Andre Campbell

Florida A&M University, Biological and Agricultural Systems Engineering—for wording on logo:
Charles McGee

Florida Department of Agriculture and Consumer Services, Division of Forestry:
    Ray Mason
    Charles Maynard
    Earl Patterson
    Tom Gilpin

Florida A&M University, School of Business and Industry—for word processing support, before and during the symposium:
    Kecia McCulloch
    Dzifa Biga
    Eric Adu-Gyasi

Special thanks to all our keynote speakers, panelists, moderators, and all symposium participants. Finally, thanks to all the speakers who wrote manuscripts and participated in the rigorous review process.

Thanks to Nadine Bradley, Elizabeth Ramirez, and Christina Harper, College of Engineering Sciences, Technology and Agriculture, for assistance with formatting and word processing in assembling the symposium proceedings, volume 1.

SESSION I

Forestry and Natural Resources Education:
Undergraduate Recruitment, Retention, and Education

Presiding Moderator:

Pamela Hunter
Florida A&M University

THE HISTORY AND BACKGROUND OF URBAN FORESTRY EDUCATION AT SOUTHERN UNIVERSITY

Fulbert Namwamba, Daniel J. Collins, Kamran Abdollahi, Zhu Ning, Yadong Qi, and Rodney Stone[1]

Abstract—This paper discusses the vision, history, and milestones of Southern University's Urban Forestry program. Southern University's Urban Forestry program is highlighted as a successful program for training minorities in Forestry and Natural Resources. In recent years minorities have become a majority in major cities. With this reality, there is a compelling case to involve minorities in environmental stewardships in urban areas. Urban forestry and its benefits are important to minorities. This paper examines the definition, ramifications, and benefits of urban forestry. It highlights the relationship between minorities and urban forestry and underscores the need to provide minorities with high-level training in urban forestry.

INTRODUCTION

Southern University, Baton Rouge (SUBR) pioneered the Nation's first Urban Forestry program. Urban Forestry is an issue that is very relevant to minorities, and more minority representation of Forestry and Natural Resources (FNRC) professionals augurs well for minority perception of FNRC.

When Tuskegee University ventured to facilitate the entry of minorities into careers in professional forestry in 1968, there were few efforts in place that offered encouragement, opportunities, or role models to motivate those minorities wishing to choose forestry and natural resources as career choices.

In 1992, the proposal to establish a degree-granting program in urban forestry at Southern University was funded by the U.S. Forest Service for $650,000 for 5 years. Abdollahi (2001) states that the program was conceived to accomplish the following objectives:

To provide professional training in urban forestry to students from a wide array of backgrounds in the planning and management of urban forest resources so that they may make meaningful contributions to the physical, social, and economic well-being of urban societies

To provide minority professionals with training in urban forestry in order to meet the demand for ethnic diversity in the workforce

To augment the department's capacity to provide student experiential learning activities to enhance the urban forestry training program.

Keeping with the land grant mission of the university, the program has three pivotal goals:

(1) education, (2) research, and (3) outreach.

WHAT IS URBAN FORESTRY?

Definition
The Society of American Foresters (2002) defines urban forestry as the integrated biophysical management of urban forest ecosystems for improving the quality of life. This includes the art, science, and technology of managing trees and forest resources as an integral part of urban community ecosystems for physiological, sociological, economic, and aesthetic benefits.

Hence, urban and community forests are made up of trees and associated vegetation within the environs of populated places—from the smallest villages to the largest cities. Such forests involve trees along streets, within greenbelts, greenways, parks, public spaces, residential yards and neighborhoods, municipal watersheds, and other areas. There are 70 million acres of such forests in the Nation in communities where 80 percent of our citizens live, work, and play. The unique demands on urban forests, their location within heavily populated and developed areas, and their potential as a medium to educate and engage the public in natural resource issues requires unique management approaches. A recent assessment by the U.S. Forest Service indicated the extent and importance of our Nation's urban forests (Dwyer and others 1992).

Benefits of Urban Forestry
Urban forests provide multiple benefits (SAF 2002). The first major benefit is the reduction of energy costs by the provision of shade in the summer as well as winter wind protection (Akbari and others 2001, McPherson and Nowak 1993, Laverne and Lewis 1996). Studies of summer trends indicate a 1°F to 2°F (0.5°C to 1.0°C) decrease in temperature for every increase of 10 percent vegetation cover (Nowak 2000). Residences with tree shade require 4 to 25 percent less energy for cooling compared to those residences in the open. Wind-sheltered homes report winter heat savings of as much as 10.3 thousand BTUs or approximately $52 annually (Nowak and others 1994). Energy savings accrued from urban trees diminish future needs for fossil fuel as the impacts of global climate change occur.

A most important benefit of urban forests is slowing and reducing storm water runoff, flooding and erosion, thus reducing adverse effects of excessive water quantity and nonpoint source pollution. Tree foliages serve as natural air filters of particulate matter and pollutants such as ozone, nitrogen oxides, ammonia, and sulfur dioxides (Abdollahi and others 2000). Foliar filtration can be considered synergistically combined with carbon dioxide intake and of oxygen production during photosynthesis, and the natural cooling effects of evapotranspiration. This synergy can have a significant effect on smog; reducing air pollution in the process. Tree driven cooling effects help reduce the need for utilities to augment power generation capacity to meet peak

[1] Fulbert Namwamba, Assistant Professor, Daniel J. Collins, Associate Professor and Interim Program Leader, Kamran Abdollahi, Associate Professor of Urban Forestry, Zhu Ning, Associate Professor, Yadong Qi, Associate Professor, Southern University, Urban Forestry Program, Baton Rouge, LA; and Rodney Stone, U.S. Forest Service Liaison Officer, Southern University, Baton Rouge, LA.

energy load demand. This benefit also leads to less CO_2 production with the public accruing energy savings (Abdollahi and others 2000). In the United States, between 400 and 900 million metric tons of carbon are sequestered in the country's urban forests (Nowak and others 1994). Additionally urban and community forests directly enhance property values, therefore, making communities more attractive to tourists and industry (Morales 1980).

Why Should Minorities Be Involved with Urban Forestry?
Minorities should be involved with urban forestry because minorities are becoming a majority in major urban areas (Kuhns and others 2002). For the first time, nearly one-half of the Nation's 100 largest cities are home to more blacks, Hispanics, Asians, and other minorities than whites. As a result, non-Hispanic whites are now a minority of the total population living in the 100 largest urban centers (Schmitt 2001).

"The most important factor for public officials to be aware of in the next 10 to 20 years is that the vitality of cities will depend on their ability to attract and be a hospitable environment for minorities," said John R. Logan, director of the Lewis Mumford Center for Comparative Urban and Regional Research at the State University of New York at Albany (Schmitt 2001).

Creating opportunities and meeting the wishes of communities to improve their natural resources and forest environments will help engage and educate the public to improve the quality of life for all citizens.

It should be noted, however, that minorities are not sufficiently involved with natural resource conservation. Observations done in the cities in the State of Connecticut (Ricard 1997) indicate that some minorities feel alienated or ignored by the "environmental movement" and perceive it to be mainstream and exclusive. Such cities are examples of places where people of diverse cultural backgrounds live, yet the State's demographic richness is often not reflected in community programs. As a black forester observed, "If America's minority population remains uninvolved, urban forests have little chance of thriving in the future." There is a strong need for academic programs that successfully boost diversity in FNRC careers.

SUBR'S URBAN FORESTRY PROGRAM

Undergraduate Program
The undergraduate curriculum at Southern University offers a B.S. degree in Urban Forestry with concentrations in urban forest management and urban forest science. Abdollahi (2001), reports that the curriculum evolved through a series of national curriculum workshops with leading urban forestry professionals and others. The curriculum was subsequently reviewed by SUBR faculty to ensure relevance to the changing needs of society. The curriculum was designed to train and produce experientially prepared graduates with a liberal education exposure for entry-level jobs with private industry, state and federal agencies, and municipalities and entry into graduate school. The existing curriculum consists of 130 credit hours plus three credit hours of summer internships. Keeping with the land-grant mission of the university, the program has 3 pivotal goals namely (1) education (2) research, and (3) outreach.

Student enrollment rose during the first 7 years of the program's existence. By 2001, the program had graduated a total of 35 students. Approximately 35 percent of the graduates were attending graduate school, 55 percent were in the workforce, and 10 percent were engaged in personal businesses.

To boost retention, funds have been obtained for students to attend various conferences, workshops, and symposia. An urban forestry club was established to involve the students in outreach and volunteerism. The club was inaugurated in the spring semester of 1993. The club held fund-raising activities and participated in tree planting activities of various local communities and organizations. The club comprises the first International Society of American Foresters chapter in the South.

Experiential training is a major component of the program. Urban forestry students are required to participate in at least one summer internship during their matriculation. Students have participated in the summer internship program with both the private sector and governmental agencies. Sponsors of the internship program include the U.S. Forest Service, the City of Milwaukee, and the Louisiana State Department of Agriculture and Forestry. In addition, several students have been directly involved in research projects with their mentors or have undertaken research as a class project.

Graduate Program
In 1993, the Louisiana State Board of Higher Education selected the urban forestry program to host a graduate program due to its uniqueness and success in the State and in the region. Abdollahi (2001) reports that the MS degree program proposal and its strategic plan were developed in 1995. The Southern University Board of Supervisors approved them in November 1996. The Board of Regents' review team conducted an on-site review of the proposed MS program in urban forestry in October 1997. Based on the review report, the Board of Regents gave its final approval on March 18, 1998. The curriculum consists of two options: non-thesis option with a capstone project (30 credit hours) and thesis option with a thesis (30 credit hours).

Teaching and Research Infrastructure
In 1992, construction of the Greenhouse/Headhouse Complex was completed. The complex houses seven laboratories for instruction and research. Construction of the Center for Small Farm Research is now complete and houses part of the urban forestry research facility.

Survey instruments introduce students to state-of-the-art surveying. Instructional versions of computer software for GIS, tree inventory program (e.g., Tree Keeper), benefit-cost analysis package (e.g., QuantiTree), and math programming (LINDO) are available and accessible to all students.

The program has acquired modern scientific equipment including a gas and liquid chromatograph, stereo microscopes, ultra microtome, autoclaves, UV-VIS spectrophotometer, atomic absorption spectrophotometer, automated wet chemistry analyzer, N-analyzer, pH meters, analytical balances, Portable Photosynthesis System, Thermocouple Psychrometer, and Sap Flow-Meter. Various soil testing instruments and lab ware are also in place.

The program has three state-of-the-art GIS and remote sensing laboratories. The laboratories are boosted with 14 Trimble GPS units. Computers are also available at the College Computer Learning and Resource Center allowing computerized multimedia instruction. Students utilize the computer facilities for data analysis using SAS, MS Office Suite, and other urban forestry related software.

The University's main library has obtained funds for establishment of a unique forestry collection now housed at the University library.

Outreach
The faculty and students of SUBR's urban forestry program continue to be actively involved with profit and non-profit organizations which host activities pertinent to urban forestry. Activities include lectures and/or workshops in community/neighborhood tree planting. An agreement with the city of Baton Rouge to develop the city's urban forest as a training lab for students has been worked out and implemented.

The program continues to work with Baton Rouge Green, a non-profit organization in promoting tree planting in the city. Members of SUBR's Urban Forestry faculty sit in the National Urban and Community Forestry Advisory Council (NUCFAC), the Louisiana Urban Forestry Council, and the Society of American Foresters. The program maintains its links with the city of Baton Rouge, involving its students with tree planting projects, as well as other environmental initiatives.

FUTURE DIRECTIONS

Long Term Goals
NUCFAC (1998) reports that Section 1219 of the 1990 Farm Bill entitled "Urban and Community Forestry Assistance" amended the Cooperative Forestry Assistance Act (16 USC 2105) to fundamentally change this Nation's approach to managing urban and community forests. The 1990 Farm Bill created a 15 member National Urban and Community Forestry Advisory Council (NUCFAC) to provide advice on urban and community forestry to the U.S. Secretary of Agriculture. NUCFAC draws members from all levels of government, citizen action groups, industry and trade associations, educational institutions, and non-profit organizations. An SUBR urban forestry faculty member represents academic organizations in this council.

Southern University is committed to maintaining a high quality urban forestry program which will adequately meet the needs of students and the community in the next millennium. Abdollahi (2001) outlines the following long-term goals in the program's strategic plan:

- To become a regional urban forestry clearing house for academic, research, and outreach program thrusts

- To develop an international urban forestry component that can address forest health protection and global change related problems

- To establish partnerships with nontraditional entities

- To provide service to small and limited resource communities

Abdollahi (2001) points out that while the program works toward these goals, it will continue to meet the University's enduring commitment to:

- Prepare a dynamic group of graduates for professional employment in Urban Forestry or entry into graduate schools

- Strengthen Southern University's ties with urban and conventional forestry programs within the State and the Nation through university linkages

- Establish a state-of-the-art teaching, research, and outreach program in urban forestry

- Integrate quality research and experiential learning at the undergraduate and graduate level

Strategies to Achieve Goals
Abdollahi (2001) outlines the following strategies to be implemented to achieve the long-term goals. SUBR's urban forestry program will:

- Continue the urban forestry summer institute as a recruitment tool for high caliber high school students

- Establish partnerships with the U.S. Forest Service Job Corps centers and the U.S. Department of Labor for training students on technical aspects of urban forestry

- Maintain the U.S. Forest Service urban forestry liaison officer at Southern University to coordinate recruitment, counseling, internships, job placement, and collaborative projects

- Maintain the state-of-the-art urban forestry computer laboratory including GIS, remote sensing, GPS and others

- Obtain additional student cooperative internships with private industry, the U.S. Forest Service, and other governmental agencies

- Fund post-doctoral researcher(s) in the graduate program

- Identify and secure funding for the program

THE BIG PICTURE

Initiatives Relating to Civil Rights
Southern University in collaboration with the Civil Rights unit of the U.S. Forest Service and other partners has hosted the first National Urban and Community Forestry (UCF) Minority Outreach and Education conference and will publish and distribute its proceedings. The goal is to increase the involvement of minority and underserved populations in UCF programs. Specific goals are to: (a) educate minority sectors in the care and stewardship of urban forests where they live, work, and play, (b) create a strong network of minority communities, non-profit UCF organizations, federal agencies, and private industries to better target the needs of the communities, and (c) provide information on educational, funding, and career opportunities in UCF.

Society of American Foresters' Position
The Society of American Foresters (SAF) believes actions and practices that strengthen and improve the urban and community forestry discipline within the broader profession of forestry are vital to the social and economic well being of the Nation (SAF 2002). The SAF strongly supports activities and funding levels that promote the establishment, maintenance, and sustainability of healthy urban forest ecosystems for all urban communities. The SAF supports integrating the science and art of urban forestry into urban land use planning systems and related commitments. Urban

and community forestry is a viable and complementary component of managing the Nation's forest ecosystems and a viable part of urban ecosystems. Urban forestry also improves the quality of life in urban areas. Prior to the establishment of an urban forestry program, a socioeconomic analysis of the area and community involved needs to be done. The ultimate success of such programs will also depend upon the efforts of individual citizens from all ethnic and socioeconomic levels who, on a voluntary basis, participate with local, state, and federal governments to ensure program objectives are met.

CONCLUSIONS

Southern University has risen to the challenge as the Nation's first urban forestry program. Urban forestry is a critical issue to minorities in urban areas as they become a majority in the Nation's major cities. Southern University's urban forestry program has fit well into the niche of its original objectives and remained a leader in training minorities in urban forestry. The program has been critical in promoting diversity in Forestry and Natural Resource careers. The success of the program can be attributed to a commitment to a clear vision. The program has developed a curriculum that addresses urban forestry education. It also continues to maintain focus in research related to urban forestry by acquiring state-of-the art research facilities. The program has performed as required in urban forestry outreach activities. Faculty members from the program continue to be active in national urban forestry organizations. Its students are making an impact at national and local levels. Ten years after its inception, the program has served well in its designed role.

ACKNOWLEDGMENTS

The authors express their gratefulness to Dr. Oghenekome Onokpise of Florida A&M University and the Ford Foundation.

REFERENCES

Abdollahi, K.K. 2001. International Society of Arboriculture, Southern Chapter Publication.

Abdollahi, K.K.; Ning, Z.H.; Appeaning, V.A. 2000. Global Climate Change and The Urban Forests. Franklin Press Inc. ISBN: 1-930129-62-9. Library of Congress Card Number (LC): 00-103362.

Akbari, H.; Pomerantz, M.; Taha, H. 2001. Cool surfaces and shade trees to reduce energy use and improve air quality in urban areas. Solar Energy 70(3): 295-310.

Dwyer, J.F.; McPherson, E.G.; Schroeder, H.W.; Rowntree, R.A. 1992. Assessing the benefits and costs urban forest. Journal of Arboriculture. 18(5): 227-234.

Kuhns, M.; Bragg, H.; Blahna, D. 2002. Involvement of women and minorities in the urban forestry profession. Journal of Arboriculture 28(1):27–31.

Laverne, R.J.; Lewis, G.M. 1996. The effect of vegetation on residential energy use in Ann Arbor, Michigan. Journal of Arboriculture 22:234-243.

McFarland, K. 1994. Community forestry and urban growth: a toolbox for incorporating urban forestry elements into community plants. Washington State Department of Natural Resources. Community Forestry Program Publication.

McPherson, E.G.; Nowak, D.J. 1993. Value of urban greenspace for air quality improvement: Lincoln Park, Chicago. Arborist News 2(6):30-32.

Morales, D.J. 1980. The contribution of trees to residential property value. Journal of Arboriculture 6(11).

Ning, Z.H.; Abdollahi, K.H. 1999. Global climate change and its consequences on the Gulf Coast region of the United States. Baton Rouge, LA: Franklin Press, Inc. and GCRCC: 98 p.

Nowak, D.J.; McPherson, E.G.; Rowntree, R.A. 1994. Chicago's urban forest ecosystem: results of the Chicago Urban Forest Climate Project. U.S. Forest Service. 1994. U.S. Forest Service Gen. Tech. Report NE-186. Chicago, IL.

Nowak, D.J.; O'Connor, P.R., comps. 2001. Syracuse urban forest master plan: guiding the city's forest resource into the 21st century. Gen. Tech. Rep. NE-287. Newtown Square, PA: U.S. Department of Agriculture, Forest Service, Northeastern Research Station. 50 p.

Nowak, D.J. 2000. Impact of urban forest management on air pollution and greenhouse gases. In: Proceedings of the Society of American Foresters 1999 National Convention; 1999 September 11-15; Portland, OR. SAF Publ. 00-1. Bethesda, MD: Society of American Foresters: 143-148.

Nowak, D.J.; Crane, D.E. 2002. Carbon storage and sequestration by urban trees in the USA. Environmental Pollution. 116:381-389.

National Urban and Community Forestry Advisory Council (NUCFAC). 1998. Community forest systems: Living and working among trees. NUCFAC Action Plan.

Phills, B.R. 1992. Proceedings of the Society of American Forests Natural Conservation, Bethesda, MD. : The Society, 1985-1992. p. 488-493.

Ricard, R. M. 1997. How important are minorities to tree programs? Urban and community forestry . West Hartford Extension Center Publication. West Hartford, CT http://www.canr.uconn.edu/ces/forest/fact10.htm.

Schmitt, E. 2001. Minorities becoming majorities in cities. New York Times, April 30, 2001.

Society of American Foresters (SAF). 2002. Urban forestry: The position of the society of American Foresters. (SAFB2WG2002). http://www.safnet.org/policy/statements.htm#UrbanForestry.

U.S. Department of Agriculture Forest Service. 1990. Benefits of urban trees. USFS Southern Region Forestry Report R8-FR17.

RECRUITING, RETAINING, AND EDUCATING MINORITIES IN NATURAL RESOURCES AND FORESTRY: FLORIDA A&M UNIVERSITY—UNIVERSITY OF FLORIDA 2 + 2 JOINT DEGREE PROGRAM IN NATURAL RESOURCES

Oghenekome U. Onokpise, Donald L. Rockwood, and Ted Willis[1]

Abstract—Since 1992 when Florida A&M University (FAMU) and the University of Florida (UF) established a 2+2 joint degree program, recruitment and retention have been critical to educating minorities in natural resources and forestry (NRF). Among the recruitment efforts implemented are the annual summer programs organized by FAMU for targeted high school students and the identification and selection of middle and high school students to attend a one-week "Forestry 2000" summer program organized by UF and several public and private agencies. Critical to our recruitment efforts have been the involvement of the U.S. Department of Agriculture Forest Service liaison officer and college recruiter at annual career fairs held at FAMU and heavily attended by freshmen and sophomores who were undeclared majors; invitation letters, and phone calls to incoming freshmen with GPAs of 3.0 or better to consider NRF careers. While scholarship and tuition waivers have been important for student retention, several ingredients have been crucial for our retaining and graduating minorities in NRF: internships eventually converted to student cooperative education programs (SCEP), the provision of laptop computers to students as long as they maintained a minimum GPA of 3.0 and stayed in the NRF programs, an Academic Success Workshop (ASW) that enhances student skills and awareness when they transfer from FAMU to UF, and the awarding of an Associate in Arts (AA) degree when students complete the FAMU portion of the NRF program. Students are also encouraged to participate in professional clubs related to NRF such as Minorities in Agriculture, Natural Resources and Related Sciences (MANRRS), the student chapters of the Society of American Foresters (SAF), and the Wildlife Society (WS). These, coupled with advising and mentoring services at both FAMU and UF, have been largely instrumental in the successful completion of academic programs by minorities in NRF.

INTRODUCTION

There are limited numbers of minorities in Natural Resources and Forestry (NRF). Whether from lack of interest or lack of encouragement in NRF, agriculture, and related sciences, the relative number of minorities in degree programs in these disciplines is extremely low. Consequently there are very few minorities in the NRF professions. African-Americans comprise 3.1 percent of professional foresters, for example, women, African-Americans and Hispanics constitute only 10 percent, 0.42 percent, and 3.9 percent, respectively, of the more than 18,000 members of the Society of American Foresters (SAF) (Personal Communication. Kollinson and others 1995, Anderson and others 1996, Geihrgen 2002). Similar proportions have been reported for other natural resource-related societies like the Wildlife Society of America and the Ecological Society of America. White non-Hispanic, African-American, and Hispanic persons (70.9, 12.9, and 12.5 percent of the U.S. population in 2001) received disproportionate shares of the B.S. degrees in Agriculture and Natural Resources (87, 2.8, and 3.6 percent, respectively).

Recruiting and retaining blacks and other minorities in NRF has always been very difficult (Anderson and others 1996; Ehrenreich 1996; Heard 1995; Mobley 1996; Onokpise and others 1997, 2004; Zink 1998). During the past decade, a number of private and public agencies put mechanisms in place to enhance minority participation in forestry and natural resources. The successes of these programs are now being reported in many publications (Onokpise and others 1997, Lineham and others 2000). This symposium, Celebrating Minority Professionals in Forestry and Natural Resources Conservation, represents the success achieved in the past 10 years, for the program initiated at Florida A&M University (FAMU) as a partnership with the U.S. Forest Service, Southern Research Station (SRS), the College of Agricultural

and Life Sciences, the University of Florida (CALS-UF), and the College of Engineering Sciences Technology and Agriculture, FAMU (CESTA-FAMU). This initiative, started in 1992, is a 2+2 joint degree program in Forestry and Natural Resources Conservation (FNRC) (Onokpise 1995). The students spend their freshman and sophomore years at FAMU and their junior and senior years at UF. Students who excel in their junior year by maintaining a 3.75 GPA or better, enroll in the 3+2 program and take advanced classes in their senior year in an accelerated M.S. degree program after obtaining a B.S. in Forest Resources and Conservation. While the SRS has provided a majority of the funding for the program through a tuition financial assistance and capacity building grant, other sources of funding have been obtained through competitive grant proposals. These include U.S. Department of Agriculture Cooperative State Research, Education and Extension Services (USDA-CSREES), the Multicultural Scholars Program (MSP), and the International Paper Company (IP) summer internship programs. This paper reports on the successes achieved in recruiting, retaining, and educating minorities in NRF as part of the celebration of minorities in the FNRC professions. Recommendations are also made for additional efforts for continued success of the program, even as we celebrate the tenth anniversary.

Recruitment Activities

The "non-glamorous" nature and the stereotypes associated with FNRC professions have made the recruitment of minorities quite difficult. Besides symbols and images, there is competition for minorities with other universities, other disciplines, and other scholarship programs and grants (Heard 1995). Therefore, we have used several approaches including (a) annual summer programs, (b) annual career fairs, (c) establishment and/or utilization of existing Web sites,

---

[1] Oghenekome U. Onokpise, Professor; Florida A&M University, Tallahassee, FL; Donald L. Rockwood, Professor, University of Florida, Gainesville, FL; and Ted Willis, U.S. Forest Service Liaison Officer, Florida A&M University, Tallahassee, FL.

(d) traditional brochures and flyers, and (e) invitational letters and phone calls to parents of upcoming freshmen to ensure success in our recruitment efforts.

Annual Summer Programs

FAMU organizes summer programs that target ninth to twelfth graders. For example, the Forestry and Conservation Education (FACE) summer program targets students who are in high schools in Gadsden, Jefferson, and Leon counties that have very high minority populations in North Florida. The students receive lectures, participate in field trips, and work with experienced NRF professionals. The objective of the three-week program is to expose these students to NRF professionals in order to stimulate their interests in NRF, with potential for enrollment at FAMU in the 2+2 joint degree program. The Raising and Training Literate Rattlers (RATLR) program targets eleventh and twelfth graders who have been admitted and are in the process of gaining admission to FAMU. Qualified middle and high school students were identified and selected to attend "Forestry 2000," a one-week long orientation to careers in forest resources. This is cosponsored by UF and several public and private agencies and organizations.

Since 1999, FAMU has been hosting a Forest and Conservation Education (FACE) summer program targeted at the four high schools in Gadsden County (Shanks high school, Havana high school, Greensboro high school and Chattahoochee high school). The objective of the three-week FACE program is to expose minority students from the eighth to twelfth grade to FNRC professions. Students undertake field trips to various sites, receive lectures from different professionals and conduct specific FNRC projects. The Washington Office for Civil Rights funded the project under the USFS Black Colleges and Universities Comprehensive Program (BCUCP). Interesting topics like forest fire management and the utilization of GIS and GPS for ecosystem and natural resource management are covered. These annual summer programs continue to be valuable avenues for recruitment. Closing ceremonies for FACE have been held at a church in Gadsden County in order to encourage parental involvement in the summer program.

Annual Career Fairs

The participation of the U.S. Forest Service liaison officer and college recruiter at annual career fairs held on FAMU's campus has enhanced recruitment efforts. This is because freshmen and sophomores, most of whom are undeclared majors, heavily attend these fairs. Discussion of the FNRC curriculum and related professions, plant the seeds in the minds of these students to consider Forestry and Natural Resource Conservation when they eventually declare a major.

Web sites of FAMU, UF and USFS

In keeping with new technology, both FAMU and UF have placed the curriculum for the 2+2 joint degree program in FNRC on their web sites http://www.cals.ufl.edu and http://www.famu.edu/acad/college/cesta. Thus, as students search these web sites, the curriculum appears, and interested students get the chance to check out what FNRC actually means. This often leads to additional inquiry with the potential for enrolling in the 2+2 joint degree program. Although it is too early to determine how much this approach has contributed to recruitment success, utilization of the Web site presents a great potential.

Traditional Brochures

Brochures and fliers were designed, updated, and distributed to high schools throughout the Southeast, especially adopted high schools in nearby counties in Florida. Through subsequent contact with high school counselors, interested students were identified and encouraged to apply for admission and tuition assistance. Parental participation has also been sought to assist with their children of high school age becoming interested in the FNRC professions.

Invitation Letters and Phone Calls

One unique method that we have adopted for recruitment is the distribution of invitation letters and placement of phone calls to incoming freshmen with GPAs of 3.0 or better to consider careers in FNRC. Working with the office of admissions, both the USFS liaison officer and the FNRC coordinator obtain a detailed printout, and phone calls are then made to the parents and incoming freshmen to enhance our recruitment efforts. Letters, phone calls, and career fairs have been the most successful methods for recruiting students into the program over the past 10 years.

Retention Activities

While recruitment is critical to the existence of an academic program, it is retention which eventually leads to graduation, the key to program success. Thus, major components of our retention efforts have been the award of scholarships, tuition assistance funds, and tuition waivers to qualified minority students. Under the USDA-CSREES Multicultural Scholars programs, both FAMU and UF have received competitive grants, which have provided several scholarships to a number of students over the past 10 years. Similarly, through its national initiatives the USFS has not only provided funds for tuition assistance to our students but also provided capacity building for laboratory improvement in order to facilitate experiential learning for the students. The provision of tuition waivers for out-of-state students has been instrumental to their effective retention in the program. As part of tuition assistance, students receive laptop computers during the second semester of their sophomore year to enhance their academic skills and class performance. This has become not only a strong retention incentive but also an excellent recruitment tool. Students have to maintain a GPA of 3.0 or better in order to keep scholarships, tuition assistance, or continue to receive waivers.

We have enhanced student retention through internships (IS) and student cooperative education programs (SCEP). Students enter IS and SCEP at the end of their freshman and junior years, respectively (table 1). Students receiving the USFS tuition assistance must participate in internships and cooperative education programs during their tenure in FNRC. Apart from enhancing student retention, the IS and SCEP local units, ranger districts, and research stations, enable students to gain hands on experience in several areas ranging from forest fires to utilizing geographic information systems (GIS) and global positioning systems (GPS). Over 70 percent of student interns have already earned certification as firefighters by the time they return to campus.

Table 1—Student internships[a] and Cooperative Education and Employment Programs (IS & SCEP) 1997–2002

Name	Location
Baker, Terry	Apalachicola National Forest, National Forests in Florida, Tallahassee, FL
Bruner, Joseph	Clearwater National Forest, Orofino, ID
Davis, Antoinette[b]	CEOP Intern, USDA Forest Service, Alabama A&M University, Normal, AL
Dixon, Tedrick	Ocala National Forest, National Forests in Florida, Ocala, FL
Flowers, Audria	Black Hills National Forest, Custer, SD
Gainous, Felicia	Apalachicola National Forest, National Forests in Florida, Tallahassee, FL
Hart, Byron	Apalachicola National Forest, National Forests in Florida, Tallahassee, FL
Hazelton, Daniel	Olympic National Forest, Olympia, WA
Humes, Tyrone	Ocala National Forest, National Forests in Florida, Ocala, FL
Lamar, Cory	Beaverhead-Deerlodge National Forest, Dillon, MT
Law, Jada	Mt. Hood National Forest, Sandy, OR
Mapps, JaTanisha	CEOP Intern, USDA Forest Service, Alabama A&M University, Normal, AL
Parson, Kimberly	Mt. Hood National Forest, Sandy, OR
Roberts, Travis	Chattahoochee and Oconee National Forests, Gainesville, GA
Robinson, TiAnna	USDA Forest Service, Forest Products Laboratory, Madison, WI
Steele, Stephanie[c]	Beaverhead-Deerlodge National Forest, Dillon, MT
Warwell, Marcus	USDA Forest Service, Rocky Mountain Research Station, Moscow, ID

[a] Internship was a requirement for all students receiving the U.S. Forest Service Tuition Assistance funds; no such requirement for USDA multicultural scholars.
[b] Also interned with the USDA National Resource Conservation Service (NRCS), Gainesville, FL.
[c] Also interned at the Osceola National Forest, Lake City, FL.

We have taken advantage of the mentoring and support services at FAMU and UF, respectively. Students are encouraged to use available tutorial classes in Calculus, Physics, Statistics, Chemistry, and Biology. During the summer session in which students transfer to UF, in addition to taking the required Dendrology course, they enroll in an Academic Success Workshop course for a six-week period. This course provides students with skills needed to succeed on a much larger and more diverse campus than FAMU. Other retention activities undertaken at both campuses include participation in the student chapters of professional societies and organizations such as The Society of American Foresters (SAF) and the Minorities in Agriculture, Natural Resources and Related Sciences (MANRRS). Very often funds are provided for selected students to attend the annual meetings/conventions of SAF, MANRRS, and the Association of Research Directors, Inc. (ARD) symposium. Students are encouraged to present oral and poster papers at these meetings.

Additionally, new courses have been introduced. This includes "Forestry in Rural and Urban Environments" which combines "Introduction to Forestry" and "Introduction to Urban Forestry" into one holistic course. Thus, the rural-urban forest interface is covered as a means of introducing forestry to new students while preparing them for advanced forestry courses. Many students enrolled in the joint degree program came from urban settings and had not been previously exposed to forestry and natural resources environments. Stereotypes remain critical in the mindsets of incoming freshmen and need to be addressed early in their education.

Finally to encourage retention, the Associate of Arts degree is awarded to qualified students as they transfer from FAMU to UF. This ensures that students do not have to take general education courses when they arrive at UF. Similarly, students receive the B.S. in Agricultural Sciences in the summer following their B.S. in Forest Resources and Conservation. These approaches were implemented in order to ensure that students remain in the program until graduation.

Graduates

This paper would be incomplete without mentioning the graduates. At this symposium, three of the graduates (fig. 1) from the 2+2 joint degree program presented an excellent paper that was very well received by the audience. Graduates (table 2) now work in a variety of disciplines in FNRC. The graduates produced since 1996 are high quality professionals who have contributed immensely to enhancing workforce diversity within the U.S. Forest Service (Personal Communication. Peter Roussopoulos, Station Director, U.S. Forest Service, 200 W.T. Weaver Boulevard, Asheville, NC 28804) and beyond. However, even as we celebrate minority professionals in FNRC, student enrollment still remains low

and the task of recruiting, retaining, and educating minorities in Forestry and Natural Resources remains very challenging. Funding from public and private sources is needed to sustain these fledgling programs.

ACKNOWLEDGMENTS

Funding received from the U.S. Forest Service (USFS) under its national initiative, and the USDA-CSREES through its Multicultural Scholars program are gratefully acknowledged. Special thanks are extended to the USFS Southern Research Station and the National Forests in Florida for the effective management and timely release of resources for the project. Thanks are extended to the administrators, faculty, and staff at FAMU and UF who have directly or indirectly been associated with the program, for their support and cooperation that have contributed to the success of the 2+2 joint degree program in FNRC.

Stephanie Steele

Marcus Warwell

Terrence Campbell

Figure 1—Three of the graduates of the 2 + 2 joint degree program.

Table 2—Graduates of the Florida A&M University and the University of Florida 2 + 2 Joint Degree Program in Forestry and Natural Resources Conservation (FNRC) (1997–2002)

Name	Degree	Location and professional employment
Campbell, Terrance[a]	B.S. NRC 1997; B.S. Agric. Sci. 1998	Centers for Disease Control, Atlanta, GA
Davis, Antoinette	B.S. Agric. Sci. 2001	Forester, USDA Forest Service, Ranger District in South Carolina
Evans, Maurice	B.S. FRC 1996; B.S. Agric. Sci. 1997	Fire Management Specialist, USDA Forest Service, Deschutes National Forest, Bend, OR
Orville, Fitz-Henley	B.S. NRC 1999; B.S. Agric. Sci. 2000	Botanist, Teacher, San Diego, CA
Robinson, TiAnna	B.S. NRC 2002; B.S. Agric. Sci. 2002	Environmental Pre-Law, Chicago, IL
Socias, Hector	B.S. FRC 1999; B.S. Agric. Sci. 2000	Forester, USDA Forest Service, Ranger District in Arkansas
Steele, Stephanie	B.S. NRC 2002; B.S. Agric. Sci. 2002	Wildlife Biologist II, USDA Forest Service, Ocala National Forest, Ocala, FL
Warwell, Marcus	B.S. FRC, 1999; B.S. Agric. Sci. 2000; M.S. Forest Genetics 2002	Research Geneticist, USDA Forest Service, Rocky Mountain Research Station, Moscow, ID

NRC = Natural Resource Conservation; FRC = Forest Resource and Conservation; Agric. Sci. = Agricultural Sciences.
[a] Also worked for the USDA Forest Service, Region 8, State and Private Forestry Unit, Athens, GA, as a forester from 1997–2002.

REFERENCES

Anderson, S.; Daley-Laursen D.; Stocker, L. 1996. Improving natural resources decision making. Journal of Forestry 94 (11): 14-19.

Ehrenrich, D. 1996. Documenting progress: the women in natural resources journal. Journal of Forestry 94 (11): 8-12.

Heard, M.S. 1995. A plan for improving cultural diversity in the workforce: chainlinks for successful and effective diversity and inclusion. In: S.H. Kollison, Jr., W.A. Hill and J. Yancey eds. Embracing diversity in the natural resources workforce: a blueprint for success. Tuskegee University: 7-19.

Ifju, G. 1996. To secure the future of the wood science and technology profession. Wood and Fiber Science. 28 (2): 145.

Mobley, S.M. 1996. Barriers to my participation in SAF. Journal of Forestry. 94 (11): 16.

Lineham, P.E.; Miller, D.L.; Jose, S. 2000. Developing an off-campus natural resources conservation program. Journal of Forestry 93(11): 24-29.

Onokpise, O.U. 1995. Increasing the pool of African-Americans and other minorities in forestry and natural resources conservation: A USDA-FAMU financial partnership. In: S.H. Kollison, Jr., W.A. Hill and J. Yancey, eds. Embracing diversity in the natural resources workforce: a blueprint for success. Tuskegee University: 35-37.

Onokpise, O.U.; Rockwood, D.; Willis, T. 1997. Graduating blacks: some joint programs show early success. Women in Natural Resources 19: 28-31.

Onokpise, O.U.; Bradford, R.B.; Gardner, C. 2008. Revitalizing agronomic and natural resources education at Florida A&M university. [This proceedings].

Zink, A.G. 1998. Elements of a successful undergraduate recruiting program. Women in Natural Resources. 19(3): 9-11.

SESSION II

Graduates in the Workforce
and Graduate School

Presiding Moderator:

Wayne Smith
University of Florida

ENCOURAGING MINORITIES TO ENROLL AND GRADUATE IN URBAN FORESTRY AND RELATED DISCIPLINES AT SOUTHERN UNIVERSITY

Fulbert Namwamba, Daniel J. Collins, Kamran Abdollahi, Zhu Ning, Yadong Qi, and Rodney Stone[1]

Abstract—Low minority student enrollment in urban forestry and natural resource-related fields continues to be a concern in land-grant institutions. Students are reluctant to pursue these disciplines due to poor public perceptions, and lack of academic preparation for success at the collegiate level. This problem is evident in government agencies trying to increase ethnic diversity in their workforce. In 1992, the first B.S. degree in urban forestry in the Nation was established at Southern University. In 1998, the Master of Science degree was added to the curriculum. Since its inception, the program has awarded approximately 60 baccalaureate degrees and 20 masters degrees. About 80 percent of the graduates have secured employment in urban forestry or natural resource-related fields. Others are pursuing graduate degrees at major institutions. Plans are underway to add the Ph.D. degree program. Success is attributed to unique and creative recruitment techniques, merit-based financial assistance, and effective mentoring programs for recruitment and retention.

INTRODUCTION

When Tuskegee University ventured to facilitate the entry of minorities into careers in professional forestry in 1968, there were few efforts in place that offered encouragement, opportunities, or role models to motivate those minorities wishing to choose forestry and natural resources as career choices. Collegiate minorities' enrollment has come a long way since then.

Diversity in the federal Forestry and Natural Resources Conservation (FNRC) workforce is still below expected levels, based on diversity of the civilian workforce. Nowhere in the federal government are diversity problems more pronounced than at the U.S. Department of Agriculture (USDA), an organization whose roots reach deep into rural America. Much progress has been made over the years.

A report from the USDA says that its workforce looks more like America than ever and the Department's hiring practices have increased diversity (Schultheis 2000). In 1999, minorities represented over 20 percent of USDA's total employment compared to 17 percent equivalent representation in the private sector. Minorities accounted for one out of four hires the Department made in 1999. While 20 percent of USDA's employees are minorities, whites hold 91 percent of the senior management positions.

The 1890 land grant institutions have made a big contribution to increasing minority professionals in FNRC. As minority FNRC professionals in public and private industry network and interact, it is important to take stock of obstacles to recruitment and retention.

Southern University pioneered the Nation's first Urban Forestry program (Abdollahi 2001). This paper outlines the strategies undertaken by the program to recruit and retain minorities whose future constitutes a major impact on the steadily rising numbers of minorities in FNRC. Urban Forestry is an issue that is very relevant to minorities, and more minority representation of FNRC professionals augurs well for minority perception of FNRC.

Rapid advances in technology demand a revolutionary change in educational systems. Institutions of higher learning have to closely evaluate their programs and the strategies they use to attract high quality students. Innovativeness of institutions of higher learning should not only be reflected in the curriculum, but also in recruitment strategies. These strategies should take advantage of current technological advances in communication.

Vastly expanded outreach efforts have paid off, according to the report. More elected minorities and women are serving and voting on USDA's County Committees. From 1998 to 1999, the number of women and minorities elected to committees increased by 28 percent and 30 percent, respectively. In addition to these elected members, USDA appointed nearly 1,675 women and minorities to County Committees in 1999.

ABOUT SOUTHERN UNIVERSITY, BATON ROUGE (SUBR) URBAN FORESTRY PROGRAM

The University

Southern University and A&M College, established in 1880, are committed to the land-grant mission. The university strives to provide quality education to conduct research and to provide service to the community. SUBR has over 9,000 undergraduate students and over 1,200 graduate students. The academic and research entities comprise 11 colleges and schools and 8 major research centers. SUBR is accredited with the Southern Association of Colleges and Schools (SACS). Eighty-three percent of eligible degree programs are accredited professionally.

History of SUBR Urban Forestry Program

The Urban Forestry Program is the first 4-year B.S. degree-granting program in the Nation (Abdollahi 2001). It was established in 1992, with $650,000 grant seed money as well as a 5-year grant from the U.S. Forest Service. Phills (1992) outlines the vision of the program. Keeping with the land-grant mission of the University, the program has 3 pivotal goals: (1) education (2) research, and (3) outreach. Student enrollment rose during the first 7 years of the program's existence. By the year 2001, the program had graduated a total of 35 students. From the graduating classes, approximately 35 percent of the graduates were attending graduate school, 55 percent were in the workforce, and 10 percent were engaged in personal businesses.

The undergraduate program offers a Bachelor of Science in 2 options, Urban Forestry Science and Urban Forestry

[1] Fulbert Namwamba, Assistant Professor, Daniel J. Collins, Associate Professor and Interim Program Leader, Kamran Abdollahi, Associate Professor of Urban Forestry, Zhu Ning, Associate Professor, Yadong Qi, Associate Professor, Southern University, Urban Forestry Program, Baton Rouge, LA 70813; and Rodney Stone, U.S. Forest Service Liaison Officer, Southern University, Baton Rouge, LA.

Management and Policy. The graduate program offers a Masters of Science Degree in Urban Forestry. The Urban Forestry program is primed for upgrading to provide Ph.D. graduate studies. The program has positioned itself to provide service to the community and to prepare quality graduates to fill the growing need for professionals in the environmental management field by training students for careers across a multidisciplinary thrust.

Since the inception of the program, 61 degrees have been awarded. Approximately 34 percent of the graduates are pursuing graduate studies at major U.S. institutions. At present, approximately 100 students are pursuing degrees in Urban Forestry. The program has a diverse body of six faculty members and six staff members, who are strongly committed to continued improvement of academic and research programs. This can be evidenced through the successful grantsmanship efforts of the faculty members who have secured funds in excess of $2.7 million.

Funding sources include USDA Capacity Building Grants, U.S. Forest Service USDA/CSREES, Environmental Protection Agency (EPA), and the International Society of Arboriculture (ISA). The potential for research efforts in the Urban Forestry program have been recognized and resulted in the award of Departmental Excellence through Faculty Excellence (DEFE).

MINORITIES BECOMING MAJORITIES IN CITIES

Schmitt (2001), reports that for the first time, nearly one-half of the Nation's 100 largest cities are home to more blacks, Hispanics, Asians, and other minorities than whites. This data is evident from an analysis of the latest census figures. While the population of the country's fastest growing cities increased in all racial and ethnic categories, the vast majority of American cities—71 of the top 100—lost white residents. As a result, non-Hispanic whites are now a minority of the total population living in the 100 largest urban centers.

"The most important factor for public officials to be aware of in the next 10 to 20 years is that the vitality of cities will depend on their ability to attract and be a hospitable environment for minorities," said John R. Logan, director of the Lewis Mumford Center for Comparative Urban and Regional Research at the State University of New York at Albany. "At the moment, minority populations are perceived largely in terms of potential problems in providing public services, or for their potential for creating new political divisions, instead of in terms of the contributions they're making to the vitality of the city" Mr. Logan said.

Challenges in Recruiting Minorities to Natural Resource Programs

Observations done in the cities in the State of Connecticut (Ricard 1997) indicate that some minorities feel alienated or ignored by the "environmental stewardship movement" and perceive it to be mainstream and exclusive. Through careful surveys, the United Way learned that minorities and women would not volunteer for any program if it gives them an uncomfortable sense. Connecticut's cities are examples of places where people of diverse cultural backgrounds live, yet the State's demographic richness is often not reflected in community programs. As a black forester observed, "If America's minority population remains uninvolved, urban forests have little chance of thriving in the future." A hospitable environment would be very helpful in strengthening the quality of life among urban communities. Sullivan and Kuo (1996) argue that tree corridors in cities create activities that lead to reduction in domestic violence.

According to the same studies, minorities' perception about participating in natural resources conservation can be summed as follows: (a) they feel that they are mere "tokens", (b) the programs are viewed as "all talk and no action", (c) they feel isolated from other minorities and women (d) the programs seem irrelevant to their concerns, (e) they cannot communicate effectively with others because of language differences, (f) attitudes or behavior are discriminatory or perceived to be discriminatory, (g) they lack the qualifications to serve in a "high-powered" capacity, (h) what they have to say is not taken seriously, (i) they feel that they are being intimidated, (j) there are no real benefits to serving, and finally, (k) they feel that there are no role models. Hence, there is a strong case for collegiate programs that target minorities for high level training, exposure and experiential learning as FRNC professionals. Southern University's Urban Forestry program perfectly fills this niche.

Agricultural sciences continue to face a formidable task of overcoming stereotypes associated with the profession. Agriculture professionals are viewed as farmers and the jobs are perceived as "farming only" and "boring". Little value is therefore placed on agricultural production. The stereotypes, however, do not reflect the true nature of forest and natural resources.

Another important consideration is the overall under-representation of minorities in professional jobs requiring a college education. The representation is even lower when considering the number of African-Americans with Ph.D. degrees. In 1993, the percentage of African-Americans holding Ph.D. degrees in all subjects was 3.2 percent. Of all the doctoral degrees awarded in all U.S. universities since 1984, there was a very low percentage awarded to African-Americans. Recruitment and retention of African-American students in the universities will lead to an increase in the number with terminal degrees. These people will serve as role models for younger people to follow the same path.

SUBR'S RECRUITMENT AND RETENTION STRATEGIES

The importance of a diverse workforce was emphasized once again in the February 1997 Civil Rights Action Team Report of the U.S. Department of Agriculture. This report and its recommendations are the result of an audit of civil rights issues facing USDA; its agencies, partners, senior managers in program delivery, employment practices, and workforce diversity issues. SUBR's Urban Forestry program has an aggressive recruitment program that is managed with a multi-prong approach. The recruitment program centers around the U.S. Forest Service liaison officer on campus. It involves faculty, students, and alumni.

To attract sizeable numbers of high quality students, the program offers annual scholarship awards and work study opportunities. This is coupled with state-of-the-art hands-on research opportunities. The program avails quality internships and placement opportunities. Finally, the program has collaborative ventures with other universities. The program is made exciting and interesting by highlighting existing students at national, regional, and local conferences. To attract the best high school students the program offers two summer programs: (1) the Beginning Agriculture Youth Opportunity Unlimited (BAYOU) program, and (2) the Urban Forestry Summer Institute. The College of Agriculture and Family and Consumer Sciences (CAFCS) at Southern University has a firm commitment to developing innovative approaches of recruitment and retention of high quality students. One existing highly successful recruitment program is the BAYOU program.

Scholarship, Financial Assistance, and Work-Study Opportunities

SUBR's Urban Forestry program maintains an excellent liaison with the U.S. Forest Service. This has enabled it to secure scholarships and work-study opportunities through several initiatives. The scholarship programs has been the single most important retention strategy and has led to many students transferring to Urban Forestry from other departments on campus. The program has awarded merit-based educational assistance in the amount of $386,750 to 44 students in the form of 31 scholarships and 13 undergraduate assistantships. The U.S. Forest Service was the primary funding source. These funds resulted in the leveraging of additional support from the USDA 1890 Institution Capacity Building Grants Program.

State-of-the-Art Research Opportunities

Many of the Urban Forestry research grants at SUBR have budgeted research positions for both undergraduate and graduate students. Being the only graduate program in agriculture, the program offers many research opportunities for students. The program applies current technology to solving problems facing society today. The research positions create attractive opportunities both as student funding but also as experiential opportunities for students.

Internships and Placement Opportunities

Student internships have been a key component of experiential learning. The highest number of available opportunities for internships are from the U.S. Forest Service. In recent years SUBR Urban Forestry students have spent their summers at the U.S. Forest Service regions 1, 3, 5, 6, and 8, as well as, at the U.S. Forest Service headquarters at Washington, DC. Cities and universities that have offered SUBR students internships in Urban Forestry include Milwaukee, WI, Baton Rouge, LA, Plymouth, MN, Savannah, GA, Hot Springs, AR, Lafayette, LA, New Iberia, LA, Colorado Springs, CO, Juneau, AK, Cincinnati, OH, and Chattanooga, TN. Private industries and nonprofit organizations which have also extended internships to Urban Forestry majors include: Davey Tree Experts, Entergy, Virginia Power Co., and the Country Club of Louisiana. Nonprofit organizations that have offered internships include American Forests, Baton Rouge Green, the National Arbor Day Foundation, Tree Trust of Minnesota, and Louisiana the Beautiful.

Collaborative Ventures with Other Universities

Universities that have offered internships opportunities include Purdue, Auburn, Ohio State, Michigan State, UC-Berkeley, Syracuse, Colorado State, and Pennsylvania State.

Local, National, and Regional Conferences

Students at SUBR's Urban Forestry program have attended conferences at local, regional, and national levels: International Society of Arboriculture (ISA), Minorities in Agriculture, Natural Resources and Related Sciences (MANNRS), National Urban Forestry Conferences, Society of America Foresters Conference, and the U.S. Forest Service Forest Products Laboratory.

Student Activities

A major student activity organization at the Southern University campus is the Urban Forestry Club. The club offers students opportunities to participate in urban reforestation, promotion of global relief projects, environmental health initiatives, as well as fund raising and recruitment. The urban forestry club was founded officially in the spring semester of 1993. The club has carried out fund-raising activities such as the sale of vegetables and raffles and participated in tree planting activities of various local communities and organizations. Funds have been obtained for students to attend various conferences, workshops, and symposia. The program has an active International Society of Arboriculture Student Chapter and a Society of American Foresters student chapter.

Summer Programs

BAYOU Program—The Beginning Agriculture Youth Opportunities Unlimited is the single most successful recruitment program at CAFCS. This program serves as the primary tool through which faculty and administrators within the college expose students at high school and undergraduate levels to professional career opportunities. Students are brought to campus and exposed to agricultural, fiber, and food sciences through hands-on experiences under the mentorship of professors. The BAYOU program currently consists of 6 phases although expansion is underway. Phases 1 and 6 specifically target high school students. This program has been highly successful in recruiting students nationwide. Applying the BAYOU model with modifications could record even greater success. Introduction of the student-teacher-counselor interphase in this program has greatly enhanced the success of this program. Advantages of interphasing with the BAYOU program include:

- Increased chance of success

- Readily available and accessible audience

- Possibilities of expansion to include more innovative features

- Reduced costs

A BAYOU participant, Dr. Andre Johnson, went on to get a Ph.D. at Pennsylvania State University and has joined Southern University's Urban Forestry faculty. Another, Dudley Bernard has successfully completed his Masters degree in Urban Forestry and is progressing to a Ph.D. program.

Urban Forestry Summer Institute

The Urban Forestry Summer Institute continues to bring in a steady stream of recruits to the Urban Forestry program. Sponsored by the U.S. Forest Service, it is similar to BAYOU except that it targets potential recruits for Urban Forestry.

Milestones in Recruitment Strategies

Recruitment has resulted in systematic growth from 1992 to 2002. From about 10 students in a year, the program has phenomenally grown to 80 students within 6 years. Eight years after the inception of the program, 61 degrees have been awarded. Approximately 34 percent of the graduates were pursuing graduate studies at major U.S. institutions, and 100 were pursuing degrees in Urban Forestry at SUBR.

CONCLUSIONS

Recruitment strategies of minority FNRC professionals at SUBR have been successful. The success can be attributed to a multi-prong approach that involves (a) providing a conducive nurturing environment for minorities training (b) aggressive recruiting strategies, (c) available funding opportunities, (d) exciting learning and research programs, (e) providing excellent internship opportunities, and (f) providing stimulating student activities. Retention strategies have helped maintain a high graduation rate among the students. Internship and placement opportunities have made the recruitment exercise meaningful and boosted retention. The result of this effort is the impact on a diverse workforce in the U.S. Forest Service.

ACKNOWLEDGMENTS

The authors express their gratefulness to Dr. Oghenekome Onokpise of Florida A&M University and the Ford Foundation.

REFERENCES

Abdollahi, K.K. 2001. International Society of Arboriculture, Southern Chapter Publication.

Phills, B.R. 1992. Proc. Soc. Am for Natl. Conv. Bethesda, MD: The Society, 1985-1992. 488-493.

Ricard, R.M. 1997, How important are minorities to tree programs? Urban and Community Forestry . West Hartford Extension Center Publication. West Hartford, CT http://www.canr.uconn.edu/ces/forest/fact10.htm.

Schmitt, E. 2001. Minorities becoming majorities in cities. New York Times, April 30, 2001.

Schultheis, M.B. 2000. New report details substantial civil rights progress at USDA. USDA Government Publication. Washington, DC. http://www.usda.gov/news/releases/2000/05/0151.

Sullivan, W.C.; Kuo F.E. 1996. Do trees strengthen urban communities, reduce domestic violence? Forestry Report R8-FR 56 - Human-Environment Research Laboratory Department of Natural Resources and Environmental, Urbana-Champaign. IL.

REVITALIZING AGRONOMIC AND NATURAL RESOURCES EDUCATION AT FLORIDA A&M UNIVERSITY

Oghenekome U. Onokpise, Robert B. Bradford, Cassel Gardner, S. Reed, and Odemari S. Mbuya[1]

Abstract—In spite of the significance of Agronomy and Natural Resources (ANR) to the Nation's economy, minorities are grossly underrepresented in professions such as soil conservation, crop protection, water quality, plant breeding, seed science and technology, among others. In June 1992, a grant was awarded to Florida A&M University (FAMU) for the "Development of Human Capital in Agronomy and Related Sciences" by the U.S. Department of Agriculture-Cooperative State Research, Extension and Education Services (USDA-CSREES) under a Capacity Building Grants (CBG) Program and matched by the State of Florida. This grant was implemented in October 1992, with an overall objective of educating and training blacks and other minorities including women with strong scientific and technical skills, by re-establishing and building upon the past (1950s and 1960s) of FAMU in the Agronomy discipline. Initial revitalization started with the recruitment of two students with Associate of Arts (AA) degrees from two junior colleges. Soon, more students were recruited into the freshman class. Since 1995, when the first student graduated, there have been a total of 16 graduates in a unique discipline where there are a few minorities. In spite of the fact that the grant expired in 1996, over 50 percent of these graduates had proceeded to graduate school. In fact, all the students who graduated since 2000 are presently in graduate school at different universities. We consider this a very significant accomplishment, given the apathy associated with the ANR professions among minorities and the fact that for almost 20 years no graduates with Agronomy degrees were produced by FAMU. These successes notwithstanding, we are still faced with critical problems of low enrollment in ANR perhaps due to the continued apathy for ANR among minorities.

INTRODUCTION

As with many areas of applied sciences, there are limited numbers of minorities in ANR and related sciences. Agronomy has been directly or indirectly responsible for the unparalleled productivity of the American farmer and the entire agribusiness industry. In the 1980s, Rhodes (1983) indicated that agribusiness contributed about 20 percent of the Gross National Product (GNP), while providing employment for nearly 23 percent of the Nation's labor force. While there may be only 2 percent of the population actually farming today, the Nation's GNP is still more than 20 percent dependent on the agribusiness industry. Breakthroughs in agronomic research were responsible, to a large extent, for tremendous increases in crop production realized between 1950 and 1988 (Brown 1989). This era was characterized by the "green revolution" which saw three-fold increases in wheat yields, due in part, to new and improved varieties. A significant honor bestowed on agronomists deriving from this era, was the award of a Nobel Peace Prize in 1970, to Dr. Norman Borlaug, an agronomist/plant breeder, for his immense contributions. Therefore, to continue this tradition of excellence and provision of food, feed, and fiber for an ever-increasing world population (Falcon 1990, Hilderband 1990), it is important that capacities in agronomic and related natural resource sciences education be continually built and strengthened.

Recent issues and concerns on the decline of blacks and other minority farmers calls for the production of minority graduates that are knowledgeable in the agricultural systems of the United States in this new millennium. Other concerns of environmental quality and justice would suggest that there is a great need for minority graduates who are capable of managing our natural resources and the environment. Yet, minorities are grossly underrepresented in the ANR professions like soil conservation, water quality, crop protection, plant breeding and genetics, seed science and technology, soil survey, and environmental quality. The lack of interest or apathy in agronomy, natural resources, and related sciences has kept the enrollments of minorities for degree programs in these disciplines at extremely low levels. Recruiting and retaining minorities in ANR has always been very difficult (Anderson and others 1996, Ehrenreich 1996, Mobley 1996, Heard 1995, Onokpise and others 1997, Zink 1998).

Due to FAMU's excellence in the recruitment, retention, training, and graduation of minorities; it is uniquely qualified to produce minority ANR specialists. However, inadequate financial resources made it impossible for FAMU to train or graduate any agronomists between 1978 and 1996. To address this problem, a proposal titled "Developing Human Capital in Agronomy and Related Sciences" was submitted to the USDA-CSREES under its competitive Capacity Building Grant (CBG) program. This proposal was successful and funded in August 1992 for 3 years. The grant's goal was to educate and train blacks and other minorities in the agronomic and natural resource professions and subsequently restore agronomy to FAMU. The main objective of this paper is to report on the successful revitalization of the ANR program at FAMU. A second objective is to show the progression of minority graduates into the professions and graduate schools, following graduation from the FAMU ANR program.

RECRUITMENT, RETENTION, AND ENROLLMENT STATUS

Initial Approaches

The success of an undergraduate program over the long term depends on sustaining a high level of recruitment and retention of students at all levels (Zink 1998, Lineham and others 2000). Therefore, the initial effort for utilizing the

[1] Oghenekome U. Onokpise, Professor, Robert B. Bradford, Professor, Cassel Gardner, Associate Professor, S. Reed, Assistant Professor, and Odemari S. Mbuya, Assistant Professor; Division of Agricultural Sciences, College of Engineering Sciences, Technology and Agriculture (CESTA), Florida A&M University, Tallahassee, FL.

approved grant was to set up machinery for recruitment and retention. A part-time secretary was hired to assist the principal investigator to plan and assist with these efforts. Additionally, an excellent partnership was established with the on-campus U.S. Department of Agriculture Natural Resource Conservation Service (USDA-NRCS) to help with retention. With this team in place, our initial emphasis was placed on recruiting graduates from junior and community colleges in order to accomplish workforce diversity objectives of the grant in the shortest time possible. Thus, our first two students were admitted into the junior year of our ANR program. To facilitate this recruitment effort, a fellowship and scholarship awards program was established with awards ranging from $750 to $1,250 per semester regardless of whether students were in-state or out-of-state fee payers. The students recruited for the 1992–93 academic year received $1,250 and $1,000 per semester, respectively. These students became known as U.S. Department of Agriculture Capacity Building Grants (USDA-CBG) fellows and scholars as long as they kept their awards by maintaining a GPA of 3.0 or better.

Other initial approaches taken towards the revitalization of the ANR included (1) joint faculty appointments; (2) purchase of non-expendable laboratory equipment and audio-visual equipment; (3) corporate membership in professional societies like the American Society of Agronomy (ASA); (4) review of curriculum resulting in the production of new brochures. The curriculum review took into account the limitations imposed on the Agricultural Sciences program by the then Board of Regents; (5) the renovation of a room in the building housing Agricultural Programs, into an up-to-date well-equipped laboratory to facilitate experiential learning for ANR students; (6) work study for students who could not qualify for the USDA-CBG fellowships or scholarships. These students worked in the renovated lab and on field research projects. These work studies enabled us to increase enrollment rapidly during the first 2 years of ANR revitalization. Furthermore, specific research projects conducted led to scientific paper presentations, thus providing an intangible outcome of professional development (Kaul and Wetson 1998, Lineham and others 2000).

Internships and Cooperative Education Programs

For retention purposes, it was essential to expose the students to professional experiences in the workplace outside the university environment. Therefore, we aggressively sought partnerships with public and private agencies to place our students for internships and cooperative education programs. The presence of the USDA-NRCS liaison officer within the college became an impetus for accomplishing this objective. Our first set of students interned with the USDA-NRCS in Bismark, ND, and USDA-NRCS, Plant Materials Center (USDA-NRCS-PMC) in Brooksville, FL. These internships were converted to cooperative education programs at their midway points, thereby allowing for 6 months of continued practical experience for students. Over the next 7 years, our students were able to intern at other public agencies, private companies and universities (table 1).

Table 1—Examples of summer internships undertaken by FAMU ANR majors in the past 7 years

Name	Sponsor(s)	Location
Cunningham, Saudia	USDA APHIS	Philadelphia, PA
Gordon, Gary[a]	Pioneer Hybrid International	Dekalb, IL
Harris, Moise	USDA Forest Service	Wakulla, FL
Holmes, Kenneth	USDA NRCS[b]	Bismark, ND
McBride, Da'Amu[c]	USDA Forest Service	Wenatchee NF, WA
Meme, Artanase	Iowa State University	Ames, IA
Menelas, Blutcher	Iowa State University	Ames, IA
Moore, Allen	USDA NRCS-PMC[b]	Brooksville, FL
Noel, Vogel	Florida A&M University	Tallahassee, FL
Pinder, Audric	Tyson Foods, Inc.	Tifton, GA
Williams, Zakiya	USDA NRCS	Philadelphia, PA

[a] Also interned with USDA-NRCS, Columbia, SC, and U.S. Forest Service, Juneau, AL.
[b] Six months internship.
[c] Interned with U.S. Forest Service, Tallahassee, FL, and the Florida Division of Forestry, Tallahassee, FL.

By participating in these internship programs, students developed a "feel" for the profession and a sense of what areas of the discipline they may want to specialize if they decided to go on to graduate school upon graduation. It also enabled them to become ambassadors for a program under revitalization and serve as recruiters as well, under what is often referred to as "Students Recruiting Students" (Ifju 1996, Zink 1998). Regardless of the number of months spent on the internship, students returned to campus for the completion of their baccalaureate degrees. The additional motivation for graduation was given when students realized that they could become potential employees of these agencies after graduation. Thus, our enrollment increased significantly between 1995 to 1997 from a low of 5 students to a high of 20 students.

Graduation and Post-Graduate Activities

In 1995, our efforts were rewarded when one of the two students recruited in 1992 graduated and was hired by USDA-NRCS. Although our grant officially expired in 1996, the program was fully revitalized and in a span of 7 years, 16 graduates have been produced in a unique discipline where there are very few minorities. These are the first graduates in Agronomy to be produced by FAMU in 20 years. Over 50 percent of the graduates have proceeded to graduate schools at different universities while others are working in the public and private sectors (table 2). Since a good number of these graduates are continuing their graduate program at FAMU, they are also helping to strengthen the FAMU graduate education program. We consider all of these very significant accomplishments given the apathy associated with the ANR professions among minorities and the fact that for 20 years no ANR graduates were produced by FAMU.

PROBLEMS ENCOUNTERED

The successes accomplished notwithstanding, we are still faced with critical problems of low enrollment in ANR (table 3). Perhaps the apathy for the ANR professions is still very high among minorities. Therefore, a major means of recruiting, retaining, and graduating young minority males and females will be through continued funding at whatever level possible. We found that providing funds to cover only books was enough to keep a dedicated out-of-state student

Table 2—Examples of post-graduate activities

Name	Year of graduation	Placement
Bournes, Julian	S/2001	Graduate School, Plant Science, FAMU
Bundy, Michael	SS/1995	Leon County Tax Office, Tallahassee, FL
Carey, Chrystal[a]	S/1997	Graduate School, Agribusiness, University of Florida
Cunningham, Saudia	F/1997	USDA APHIS, Plant Quarantine Unit, JFK International Airport, New York
Elvis, Clarke	SS/1999	Graduate School, Plant Science, FAMU
Gordon, Gary	SS/2000	Graduate School, Soil Science, Auburn University
Holmes, Kenneth[a]	S/1998	Director, Americorps, Gainesville, FL
Jno-Baptiste, Jeff	SS/1998	Graduate School, Environmental Science, FAMU
Meme, Artanase	F/1999	Graduate School, Plant Science, Florida A&M University
Menelas, Blutcher	SS/2000	Graduate School, Plant Science, Iowa State University
Moody, Joyet	SS/2000	Graduate School, Soil Science, FAMU
Moore, Allen	S/1995	High School, Agricultural Science Teacher, Jacksonville, FL
Noel, Vogel	SS/1997	Florida Department of Environmental Protection (DEP), Tampa, FL
Pinder, Audric	S/1998	Tyson Foods, Tifton, GA
Stanhope, Andrine	S/1998	Graduate School, Environmental Science, FAMU
Williams, Zakiya	F/1997	Graduate School, Music, Pennsylvania State University

S = Spring semester; SS = summer session; F = fall semester.
[a] Initially worked for the Florida Southwest Water Management District.

Table 3—Number of students enrolled in the Agronomy and Natural Resources Program [ANR]; 1994/1995 – 2000/2001 classification

Year	Freshmen	Sophomore	Junior	Senior
1994–1995	8	5	2	0
1995–1996	10	6	3	2
1996–1997	2	3	7	3
1997–1998	—[a]	3	2	7
1998–1999	—	2	3	4
1999–2000	—	—	3	3
2000–2001	1	—	1	2

[a] First academic year following the expiration of the USDA Cooperative State Research, Education and Extension Service (CSREES)/State of Florida grant.

in the program, when he would otherwise, have withdrawn from the university. We have experienced a severe decline in enrollment (table 3) since the expiration of the capacity building grant. Adequate funding for student recruiting and teaching research in many agricultural sciences has been a problem for a very long time (Childers 1998). It may be necessary to have targeted public and private industry funding for the production of minority graduates in the ANR professions in view of the continued and/or perceived apathy for ANR.

CONCLUSION AND RECOMMENDATIONS

Although a large number of graduates have yet to be produced, the revitalization of the ANR at FAMU is a significant first step towards accomplishing that goal. Many of the graduates are helping to enhance workforce diversity goals in the public and private sectors with regards to the ANR professions. Yet more needs to be done. There is an urgent need for new scholarships, fellowships, and grants-in-aid for program sustainability. Similarly, summer programs at targeted locations will provide hands-on experiences for the students, while exposing them to their future potential workplaces. On-campus work study will also provide experiential learning for the students.

ACKNOWLEDGMENTS

The authors thank the USDA-CSREES for funds provided through the Capacity Building Grant for 1890 Universities and Colleges under grant No. 92-38820-7499. Thanks are also extended to the State of Florida for the corresponding matching funds to complement the USDA-CSREES grant. We are grateful to all the students and officials at FAMU who assisted us in the revitalization of the program at FAMU.

REFERENCES

Anderson, S.; Daley-Laursen, D.; Stocker, L. 1996. Improving natural resources decision making. Journal of Forestry 94 (11): 14-19.

Brown, L. 1989. Re-examining the world food prospect. In: State of the World. W.W. Norton and Company, New York, NY: 41-48.

Childers, N.F. 1998. Accumulated philosophy on student recruiting, teaching, research and funding. Proc. Florida State Horticultural Society. 101: 238-241.

Ehrenreich, D. 1996. Documenting progress: the women in natural resources journal. Journal of Forestry. 94(11): 8-12.

Falcon, W.P. 1990. Future links between U.S. Agriculture and the World Economy. Journal of Prod. Agriculture 3: 269-273.

Heard, M.S. 1995. A plan for improving cultural diversity in the workforce: chainlinks for successful and effective diversity and inclusion. In: S.H. Kolison, Jr., Hill, W.A.; Yancey, J., eds. Embracing diversity in the Natural Resources workforce: A blueprint for success. Tuskegee University: 7-19.

Hildebrand, P.E. 1990. Agronomy's role in sustainable agriculture: Integrated farming systems. Journal of Prod. Agriculture 3 :261-264.

Ifju, G. 1996. To secure the future of the wood science and technology profession. Wood and Fiber Science. 28(2): 145.

Kaul, K.; Wetson, P.A. 1998. Undergraduate research in the biological sciences at Kentucky State University. Journal of Kentucky Academic Science. 59(1): 29-32.

Lineham, P.E.; Miller, D.L.; Jose, S. 2000. Developing an off-campus natural resources conservation program. Journal of Forestry. 98(4): 24-29.

Mobley, S.M. 1996. Barriers to my participation in SAF. Journal of Forestry. 94(11): 16.

Onokpise, O.U.; Rockwood, D.; Willis, T. 1997. Graduating blacks: some joint programs show early success. Women in Natural Resources. 19 (1): 28-31.

Rhodes, V.J. 1983. The Agricultural Marketing System. John Wiley & Sons. 3rd edition, New York, NY.

Zink, A.G. 1998. Elements of a successful undergraduate recruiting program. Women in Natural Resources. 19(3): 9-11.

SESSION III

Women in Natural Resources

Presiding Moderator:

Jane Luzar
University Of Florida

YOU DON'T HAVE TO SPIT AND CHEW

Denise McCaig[1]

Abstract—In the past, public land management agency leaders fit a certain mold. For example, Forest Service District Rangers were tall, loud, and chewed tobacco. Ms. McCaig didn't fit that mold and initially she thought she needed to act like a Ranger in order to be one. Fortunately for her, she discovered that leadership is found in many shapes and sizes. That diversity brings unique strengths to the resource management profession—strengths such as relationship building, conflict resolution, and community building.

INTRODUCTION

As a young professional in the Forest Service, I aspired to be a District Ranger. The Ranger manages a large area of the national forest, supervises many people, and when the buck stops, it stops on his desk. I say "his" desk because all but one of the rangers I knew at that time were men. I believed that I needed to walk, talk, spit, and chew tobacco like the stereotypical ranger to be one. This was a problem because at the time rangers were tall, loud, and chewed tobacco. I was short and soft-spoken. One time I tried chewing tobacco—my legs felt like jello and I started to drool. I never mastered the spitting action. When I expressed my ranger-job interest to others, I was told I wasn't seasoned enough. I still don't know what that means, but a long-time friend still calls me "tough meat."

So what's a woman to do? I went to Washington, DC, where I met diverse professionals who had been successful rangers. I really didn't want to spend all my energy acting like a ranger. I decided I would do the job with my unique strengths and experience.

To my amazement, I eventually became a ranger. Sitting in my office one day I overheard an irate visitor tell the receptionist that he wanted to talk to the man in charge. When the receptionist said, "That would be Denise," the visitor re-emphasized that he wanted to talk to the man in charge. At that point I walked out, smiled, introduced myself and rescued the receptionist.

In addition to a good sense of humor, women and minorities bring valuable skills to the job. Our skills include relationship building, conflict resolution, and community building.

RELATIONSHIP BUILDING

It's all about developing, maintaining, and nurturing relationships. An example of this is the Jemez Pueblo Indians. The Jemez Pueblo Indians were here centuries before I got to the district, and they have a connection to the land that I may never comprehend. Working with them required a relationship of mutual trust. When I was invited to their annual feast days, I was quick to accept. This is a unique experience with traditional dances, singing, and lots of eating. I was invited to a tribal member's home and treated to a table loaded with all types of delicious traditional foods. I ate until I thought I would explode. Then when I tried to walk it off, I was invited to another home and ate again. After the fifth home, I realized I needed to show restraint or find a larger pair of pants.

After going into their homes, eating their food, and joining in their celebrations, I earned their trust and friendship. We worked well together as long as I didn't betray their trust, and we maintained our relationship.

CONFLICT RESOLUTION

We facilitate resolution among various interests. Public land management is conflict management. Controversy is what we do. Rather than becoming the target for various interests' outrage, we can facilitate resolution. The Gallinas watershed plan was the perfect opportunity for me to try out this theory. Several state and federal agencies were developing a plan in a watershed containing multiple land ownerships. When some homeowners objected to our proposed activities, we held several public meetings. I didn't stand in the front of the room alone however. Other state and federal agency representatives stood next to me and described what we were proposing and why. We also listened to the landowners' concerns and incorporated several of their suggestions into our proposal. After this process, the very same people who were ready to remove me from my job, now invited me to stop by their homes for coffee.

COMMUNITY BUILDING

We are part of the communities we serve. We build communities by including all interests and giving them a voice. My best example is the Baca Ranch purchase. Federal and tribal lands surrounded this 95,000-acre private ranch. There were many divergent views about its purchase and management. Congress was interested in the purchase only if there was overwhelming public support. I discussed the purchase with federal agencies, interests groups, state and local governments, the media, and tribal leaders. We facilitated discussions between Washington, DC, administration representatives and local groups. As a result, the environmental coalition and the local cattle growers jointly signed a letter encouraging the purchase. The state legislature, affected counties and several tribes passed resolutions of support for the purchase. Local consensus was so persuasive that Congress passed legislation authorizing and funding the ranch purchase.

We build community every day by including all the interests in a discussion. We should constantly ask, "Who isn't here that should be included in this discussion?"

It doesn't matter how pretty, heavy or scientific a plan is, if the people affected by the decision do not understand and support it, the plan will not succeed.

[1]Denise McCaig, Congressionally Designated Areas Program Manager, U.S. Forest Service, Southwestern Region, Albuquerque, NM.

CONCLUSION

We all bring our unique strengths to the workplace. When her two children are fighting over a toy, a mother knows how to resolve the dispute without escalating the conflict. This is a valuable skill to use with employees, your boss, and Congress. When a forest fire threatened a small New Mexico community, the Hispanic Forest Supervisor addressed his neighbors in Spanish, which the people understood and appreciated. We are the diverse people we serve. We understand the interests of the people we serve and we can enlist their help to solve increasingly contentious issues.

WE NEED WOMEN OF COLOR TO SAVE THE PLANET

Louise Fortmann and Dreamal Worthen[1]

Abstract—Saving the planet involves both serious attention to maintaining ecological functions and services, which in turn has implications for biodiversity and ecosystem health and serious attention to social, political, and economic systems. Because their names are a bit odd, juxtaposing two ideas of "planet saving", "Women Warriors Saving the Planet" and "Saving the Planet from Space Aliens", provides a chance for reflection on just what it might take to save the planet. This article uses two arenas—daily practice and political activism—to explore structures and processes that may impede or facilitate women warriors saving our planet. All of this has implications for our own practice of both biophysical and social sciences. Only one is addressed here—the need for democratization in the academy. This includes recognizing the expertise of nonprofessionals. It involves opening up scales, including our professional meetings and lecture halls, where people speak for themselves in their own vibrant words, rather than having us speak for them with algorithms. Thus, we as scholars have a role in saving the planet. But the bigger role is that of ordinary people performing ordinary acts that have an extraordinary cumulative effect. To do this, these ordinary people must have the persistence, bravery, and fierce spirit of the "women warrior".

INTRODUCTION

Saving the planet involves both serious attention to maintaining ecological functions and services, which in turn has implications for biodiversity and ecosystem health and serious attention to social, political, and economic systems. This afternoon I want to talk about women's roles, especially women of color, in saving the planet. This holiday card from an international research institute is an indication of why I have to talk about this. The really interesting thing about this picture is what it does not show. The back of the card showed the entire drawing from which the card illustration was taken. Here it is, what do you notice? For many of you this will be no surprise. All too often women, and especially black women, are missing from images and imaginings of environmental and natural resource management. For example, according to the National Science Foundation only 1.2 percent of all scientists and engineers (which includes the people we need to save the planet) are black women. Additionally, only 1 percent of the natural resources faculty at 4-year colleges is black—since they don't even bother to provide data on black women—you can imagine how few these are.

Let me shift gears for a minute. You may have seen this cartoon in which a fat American, in an enormous car belching exhaust fumes, exhorted a small poorly dressed man with a machete with "Yo Amigo! We need that tree to fight global warming". For many people in the United States, saving the planet involves persuading or (more often) forcing people in poor countries to change their behavior (be it growing food, having children, hunting wild animals, or gathering medicinal plants) so that we can continue doing whatever we please. This is particularly clear in the enthusiasm for setting up protected areas, which exclude (in the tradition of no good deed goes unpunished) the very people who have protected local biodiversity (in part because their livelihood strategies use far fewer resources than ours).

This viewpoint often goes hand-in-hand with the assumption that someone (scientists, politicians, national or international bureaucrats) has both correctly defined the problem and knows THE answer and that implementing that answer requires extraordinary means, including placing control in the hands of those with THE answer. It is worth noting that relatively few of those with THE answer are women. Under this approach, saving the planet is for a few—it reflects the vision of a few.

In contrast, a feminist approach is based on trying to ensure that the planet is livable for everyone (including plants and other animals) over time. It assumes that there are many problems and many answers operating simultaneously at many different scales and that both the problems and the answers will change over time. While the feminist approach utilizes the knowledge of scientists, it also relies heavily on the ordinary acts of ordinary people to achieve extraordinary results.

Ordinary people, of course, include both women and men and ordinary acts include the ordinary acts of women as well as the ordinary acts of men. But, not only are women's actions erased from the environmental imagination, as we saw at the beginning of this talk, there also may be structures and processes which prevent or discourage them from acting as ecological stewards. Thus, the struggle to save the planet is often inextricably bound up with women's struggles and the struggle for women's rights. One of these rights is the right to property. It may not be intuitively obvious but when women don't have property rights, it can have adverse ecological consequences.

For example, in a study of 27 percent of the households in two villages in central Zimbabwe, 56 percent of the respondents had planted at least one tree in the homestead. But only 44 percent of the women planted trees in their homestead, in contrast to 83 percent of the men. To analyze homestead tree planting, logit models were used. The analysis showed that women, regardless of class, are significantly less likely to plant trees in the homestead than men.

Why might gender adversely affect tree planting? It is clearly not physical strength as anyone, who has planted groundnuts, hauled water, collected firewood, or made groundnut butter (smooth, not chunky!) with a grinding stone (all women's work), knows. It is not knowledge about or need for trees and tree products. In the study area for all but two categories of use, women knew far more tree species

[1] Louise Fortmann, Rudy Grah Professor in Forestry and Sustainable Development, University of California at Berkeley, Department of Environmental Science, Policy and Management, Berkeley, CA; and Dreamal Worthen, Assistant Professor, Florida A&M University, College of Engineering Sciences, Technology, and Agriculture, Tallahassee, FL.

than did men. Neither age nor education had any statistical significance. Tree planting is neither culturally prescribed for women nor prescribed for men in the study area. This leaves insecurity of land and tree tenure as the most persuasive explanation.

This explanation is made even more persuasive by two additional pieces of data. First, divorcees in the village (all of whom who had lost all rights to the trees they had planted and tended during their marriage even when they stayed in the village) were emphatic that they would not plant trees in a new marital compound least they once again be discarded and once again lose everything. Second, gender did not affect tree planting in the community woodlot where women retained their rights after a divorce as long as they continued to reside in the village.

While we must be cautious in coming to sweeping conclusions from a single study, these data certainly suggest that to the extent that the ecological stability and health of a society and its production systems, depends on women's willingness to invest their labor in tree planting, terracing, or property and tenure systems that discriminate against women will have negative societal consequences. Since in many parts of Africa the productive rural population is still disproportionately comprised of women, this finding should give considerable pause to those concerned with maintaining or improving ecological conditions that will continue to sustain agricultural livelihoods. Clearly, we must ensure that local systems of property rights enable women to be ecological stewards.

Here's another example of women's importance to saving the planet—one that concerns democracy. One of the key features of democracy is that it involves the willingness to accept uncertainty in outcomes—that is, to put it bluntly, you may lose. While large national environmental organizations (at least in the United States) are still generally headed by white men, the day-to-day highly local environmental and environmental justice battles are often begun, carried out and sustained by women who found their health, the health of their families, or the health of a local ecosystem threatened. These women, often women of color, have been the primary forces mobilizing friends and neighbors and forcing public officials into action. Women all over the world, including women with no previous political experience, have organized against unsafe nuclear facilities, multiple forms of pollution and hazardous waste, deforestation, and many other forms of environmental degradation.

While women's environmental activism has been important in terms of each individual victory, it may be even more important for its contribution to the growth of democracy. It has been crucial in democratizing the environmental arena by subjecting traditionally powerful interests (timber companies, mining companies, polluting industries) to scrutiny.

CONCLUSION

All of this has implications for our own practice of both biophysical and social sciences. Only one is addressed here—the need for democratization in the university. This includes recognizing the expertise of nonprofessionals. It involves opening up spaces, including our professional meetings and lecture halls, so people can speak for themselves in their own vibrant words, rather than having us speak for them with our algorithms.

Thus, we as scholars have a role in saving the planet. But the bigger role is that of ordinary people performing ordinary acts that have an extraordinary cumulative effect. We need to get ordinary women of color back into the picture in order for this to happen. As academicians it is important that we become inclusive. We have to learn tolerance because that implies that we are tolerating someone. We have to recognize that all people, regardless of ethnicity, income, or physical status have something to contribute. We also have to respect diverse research methods.

SESSION IV

Title VI and Delivery System

Presiding Moderator:

Gloria Manning
U.S. Forest Service
Washington, DC

THE FUTURE STARTS NOW!

Eurial Turner[1]

Good evening. Thank you for inviting me to Tallahassee to be a part of this program. It is indeed a pleasure to join such a large group of distinguished professionals dedicated to educate and prepare future leaders in the natural resource profession. The talent in this room will be extremely valuable as we move further into a new millennium of natural resource management. In a world of uncertainty, there is at least one constant and that is change. Because change is continually happening and we often are slow to respond appropriately to it, it is essential to develop the capacity to forecast change and provide opportunity to adapt to it through proactive measures. This is the best strategy, but it will only be successful if accompanied by courageous leadership willing to respond before a crisis is created.

This century brings with it many new environmental opportunities and challenges for present and future leaders. But it's going to take people with a passion, not just education and technical skills to make a difference.

The environmental issues are complex and often controversial. Solutions don't neatly organize themselves into 30-second sound bites. Most folks don't have the science background, rural connection, passion, or patience to fully appreciate the intricate connections between actions taken or not taken on the ground and long-term consequences. That's where you come in. As educators and industry leaders, you are going to be a critical resource to help find solutions to challenges.

Let's talk about some of the complex issues that educators, managers, and overseers of our natural resources will need to address. As an avid outdoor lover, I was troubled the other day when I read an article in the Sports section of USA Today. The headline read "Surviving the generation gap: Outdoors Industry scrambles to reach an indifferent youth market." The writer focused on a growing trend in America, asserting that America's great outdoors were becoming America's gray outdoors: The ranks of anglers, hikers, bikers, paddlers and climbers are made, mostly of middle-aged white people—baby boomers.

Only 9.5 percent of the goods sold in the outdoor sports industry are sold to people ages 18 to 34, the article said. That number's even smaller in ethnic minority circles. Team sports and video game technology have grabbed the interest of America's young much more than nature. That was sort of a wake up call for me. While it will probably take years for the reality of this phenomenon to manifest itself on forest recreation visitor numbers—mainly because of baby boomers—it's another telltale sign that many of the future generations and differing ethnicities which dwell in urban communities are losing touch with their natural environment, forests, and the land.

The shrewd marketers' answer to the problem is to design snazzy, hip-hop sportswear that shows off youthful physiques, hoping clothes will suddenly lure people to the outdoors. I won't hedge any bets, but high fashion probably isn't the answer to this complicated dilemma.

The problem goes a little deeper than just getting folks to play in the outdoors. It points to a growing disconnect between people and the forests that sustain their livelihoods. People's innate respect for nature is becoming less and less. Researchers say there's a growing concern that people are treating nature as if it's a foreign object. Anything outside the confines of their air-conditioned homes and cars is treated like an enemy. Yet, it's those natural systems that are sustaining us. This disconnect presents a major problem for social and natural scientists alike, since the future of the life-giving ecosystems depends on people living up to their responsibility to maintain them.

The problem this phenomenon presents is compounded by the projections for population growth in this country. There's a real danger that these burgeoning populations will be demanding much more from natural systems with no clue about natural processes or limits. In your career, you have been and will continue to deal with hordes of people who do not fully understand the tie between their basic human needs and a healthy, sustainable environment.

Already, a lot of Americans, especially the 80 percent growing up in concrete environments don't realize that:

1. U.S. forests provide the country's sustainable wood supplies that support the suburban development that is rapidly occurring across the country.

2. Forests offset the carbon dioxide emissions that energy companies emit into the air to fuel homes and autos. That's a growing concern with evidence of the Green House effect.

3. Energy and mineral companies get supplies for some natural gas and coal from the forest.

4. Forests are the infrastructure, foundational base for the economic sustainability of small, rural communities of this country.

5. National forests supply the cleanest water in this country.

6. Sixty million people get their drinking water from watersheds that originate from the national forests.

7. Forests provide for numerous wildlife species, fish habitat to maintain the biological diversity and health we all need and enjoy.

8. Forests supply the recreation and outdoor opportunities so many people demand.

---

[1]Deputy Regional Forester, U.S. Forest Service, Atlanta, GA.

All the products and services that forests provide are interconnected. As you shift emphasis and benefits in any one direction, there will be consequences on all the others—in very complex ways.

Clashes between residents, users of forests, and industry are inevitable. We're already seeing it. We find ourselves refereeing between citizens who use forests and/or live near forests: Industries who supply urbanites needs for housing and fuel are in conflict with preservationists who do not want to see the forest managed. Bikers brawl with hikers and horseback riders for trail access; solitude seekers collide with OHV riders; hunters take on birdwatchers; water-enthusiasts conflict with water supply needs for cities and municipalities. Land developers are encroaching on naturalists to convert green space to subdivisions. All are increasing pressures on forests that are shrinking.

Vacation homes, suburban residences, and industry land are all cropping up as neighbors to forest boundaries. Some residents, landowners and overseers alike have little knowledge about how actions on their property could have residual impacts on surrounding forests. They don't understand how forest ecosystems work nor are they able to cope with the natural processes that come with their environment.

Apart from that, massive urbanization and changes in the diversity of the population comes into play. The need for suburban housing to support more people is in direct conflict with the need to conserve green space. In Atlanta, for example, land with heavy tree cover was nearly reduced to half, going from 47 percent to 27 percent between 1974 and 1996—a little more than two decades. As a result, we're seeing more and more green ordinances cropping up in municipal land management.

Landowners who once held many of the rural values that typify management of forested land bases and are accustomed of management activities are on a decline. And it's difficult to reach out to new nontraditional landowners to offer assistance for caring for their land for the future. It's a great challenge to appeal to their core values so we can work together, be good neighbors, and compliment each other's uses of the land.

I'd be remiss if I didn't mention that one of the greatest hurdles we must clear is the politicalization of what we do. The role of how our natural resources should be managed in this country is hotly debated and getting hotter everyday. We're seeing more and more candidates outlining their platforms with specific promises on how they'd manage forested lands, public and private. These political postures lead to further polarization of people, who want to couch their specific need or interest. It's a difficult task for a forest manager who is trying to get people to the table to work out differences and make decisions about the destiny of their forests and natural environment. It will become a bigger challenge with folks who are largely detached from their natural environment.

Some of you may be asking, "How does this relate to minorities in forestry and natural resources?"

There is a significant shift in demographics taking place in this country.

1. Americans are moving from the North and East to the South and West—where most of the forests and grasslands are located. In a sense, the cities are coming to the forest.

2. Americans are growing older. In 1900, only 4 percent of the U.S. population was over 65; in 1984, the proportion was 11 percent; by 2020, it will be 21 percent.

3. Our workforce in natural resource management does not fully reflect the American public.

4. Over the next 5 years, the U.S. Forest Service alone will hire more than 4,000 new employees from outside the agency. We have a golden opportunity to make significant gains within the civilian workforce!

5. In the next 15 years, minority students will account for 80 percent of the growth in college enrollment. We must position ourselves now to recruit them!

6. Americans are growing more racially and ethnically diverse everyday. Eighty-six percent of immigration in this country is now nonEuropean. Over the next 50 years, 90 percent of our population growth will come from racial and ethnic minorities.

So what does a changing public mean for the natural resource managers and educators?

Here is the challenge: How can we do a better job of attracting employees from underserved groups, especially in areas where they are historically underrepresented and critically needed? How can we better serve our fast growing underserved urban and minority communities?

The successful forest manager of the future is one who will be able to work effectively with people—people who use national forests, those who are adjacent landowners, nontraditional landowners, and differing ethnicities.

That means conservation and environmental education are critical to the future of forests. Future leaders must be able to connect with urban populations and diverse ethnicities. We must ensure that people know that the energy supplying their house with cool air is emitting CO_2 into an atmosphere and it's only offset with planting more trees. Conservation education is a must for any future land manager. We will likely look more to social scientists to help us engage and interact with these groups who are going to be the future constituents, supporters, and advocates for forests.

Outreach to nontraditional landowners is another area for future leaders. We must act as a conduit to those who own land but are uncertain of the best way to be good stewards. We must provide landowners assistance, giving them the tools they need to make the most of their investment for themselves and future generations.

Future Natural resource leaders must be skilled in convening and facilitating joint decisionmaking. People more than ever, are demanding to be a part of the decision-making process that determines the destiny of their forests.

Finally, new leaders must demonstrate excellence and innovation in forest management for the Nation and world to see. Our forests will continue to provide the multiple benefits people have become accustomed to, but we must continue to look for ways to do things better, offering the best science, technology resource and information, and maintaining a strong passion.

Although leadership entails a great deal of responsibility, accountability and work, the end product is the enjoyment of seeing people work toward common goals fulfilling their mission and vision. Future natural resource leaders will continually face the challenge of finding that delicate balance between meeting the public demand and doing what is right for the resource that they have been entrusted to manage.

As the baby boomers such as myself, quickly reach retirement age, the demand for natural resource leaders will increase in all areas within the public and private sector. It has been said that it is better to be prepared with no opportunity than to have an opportunity come along and not be prepared. We should be making the final preparation for our future leaders to enter the workplace, regardless of whether it is in the public or private sector, viewing this as not just a job, but as an opportunity to make a difference.

SESSION V

Graduates of the FAMU 2 + 2
Joint Degree Program

Presiding Moderator:

Terrence Campbell
Centers for Disease Control
Atlanta, GA

FAMU/UF JOINT DEGREE PROGRAM GRADUATES: WHERE WE'VE BEEN AND WHERE WE ARE NOW

Marcus Warwell, Stephanie Steele, and Terrence Campbell[1]

Abstract—The FAMU/UF 2+2 Joint Degree Program in Forestry and Natural Resources Conservation was established to increase the number of minority professionals trained in forestry and related fields. The degree program graduated 8 students between 1996 and 2002. Their experiences in the program were unique and diverse and are reflective of their current career paths. The program was assessed by three of its graduates. Student financial assistance, work and travel experience, opportunity for future employment, and the personal support of the program advisors were identified as positive strengths in the program. Communication between organizations and students, transition between universities and the U.S. Department of Agriculture Forest Service (USFS), and disbursement of funds were identified as areas for improvement.

INTRODUCTION

In 1992, the FAMU/UF 2+2 Joint Degree Program in Forest and Natural Resources Conservation was established. The program's objective is to increase the number of minority professionals trained in forestry and related fields.

The purpose of this paper is to summarize experiences of the FAMU/UF 2+2 Joint Degree Program's graduates. In addition, it highlights the program's positive aspect and provides suggestions for further improvements from the perspective of its authors.

Program Structure

The FAMU/UF Program identifies and recruits minority students with strong scholastic skills and an interest in natural resources. These students are provided with support by the Forest Service via scholarships that adequately cover in-state tuition, fees, books, and some living expenses. Students begin the program at Florida A&M University (FAMU) in the College of Engineering Sciences, Technology, and Agriculture (CESTA). While in CESTA, students enroll in a wide variety of general education and pre-professional courses during their freshmen and sophomore years to earn an Associate of Arts degree in General Studies. Students then transfer to the School of Forest Resources and Conservation (SFRC) at the University of Florida (UF) to complete upper division degree requirements during their junior and senior years. Prior to graduation, students are required to work a minimum of 640 hours in a U.S. Forest Service cooperative internship. These internships are coordinated by the USFS and provide students with an opportunity to work in one of the USFS's three branches; the National Forest System, Research and Development, or the State and Private Forestry program.

Once at UF, students have the option to major in Forest Resources and Conservation (FRC) or Natural Resources Conservation (NRC). Students majoring in FRC study coursework related to forest resource management. This major meets the accreditation standards of the Society of American Foresters and qualifies graduates to meet the federal classification of a forester. The NRC major requires completion of core courses related to natural resource management, while allowing greater flexibility to structure studies towards specific career objectives. Course selection in the NRC program can be tailored to meet federal standards for Forester, Hydrologist, Ecologist, Botanist, Fishery Biologist or other classifications. Upon completing degree requirements, graduates receive a Bachelor of Science degree in Forest Resources and Conservation from UF and a Bachelor of Science degree in Agricultural Sciences from FAMU.

JOINT DEGREE PROGRAM GRADUATES

The FAMU/UF 2+2 Joint Degree Program graduated eight students between 1996 and 2002. The graduates were Maurice Evans, Terrence Campbell, Marcus Warwell, Hector Socias, Stephanie Steele, Orville Fitz-Henley, TiAnna Robinson, and Carlos Barhona. Summaries of the experiences of the first five of these graduates are listed below.

Maurice Evans, the first student to successfully complete the joint-degree program, interned during the summers of 1992 and 1993 on Apalachicola National Forest in Bristol, FL. There, he assisted field crews with wildlife habitat-improvement projects, prescribed burning, and the layout of timber sales. In 1995, he completed an internship at the Deschutes National Forest Silvicultural Lab in Bend, OR. His duties included botanical surveys and installing transects for frequency, cover, and stream profiles. After graduating from FAMU and UF in 1996, Maurice began work as an Assistant Fire Management Officer for Fuels Planning for the Bend/Fort Rock Ranger District on the Deschutes National Forest. He was responsible for inventories and evaluations of on-the-ground conditions to determine quantities and types of fuels. He evaluated data concerning the history of fires in forested areas, including causes, frequency, damages incurred, and benefits gained. He also studied the interrelationship of various facets of the fire management activity with functional resource plans. Currently Maurice is working for the U.S. Forest Service as a Fuels Management Specialist.

Terrence Campbell, the first student to matriculate fully from post-secondary recruitment to program completion, interned at the Mi-wuk Ranger District on the Stanislaus National Forest in Mi-wuk California during the summer of 1993. His responsibilities encompassed assisting

[1]Marcus Warwell, Geneticist, U.S. Forest Service, Rocky Mountain Research Station, Forest Sciences Laboratory, Moscow, ID; Stephanie Steele, Wildlife Biologist, U.S. Forest Service, Holly Springs Ranger District, Oxford, MS; and Terrence Campbell, Health Communications Specialist, USDHHS Centers for Disease Control and Prevention, Atlanta, GA.

with various silvicultural projects including reforestation, stand regeneration monitoring, and post-fire harvesting and cleanup. In addition, he also obtained experience in archaeological site reconnaissance and protection, as well as endangered wildlife monitoring projects, which focused on the Spotted Owl and the Yellow Legged Foothill Frog. During the summers of 1994 and 1996, Terrence decided to pursue his interests in urban forestry and interned with the North Central Forest Experiment Station in Evanston, IL. Working with the Urban Forestry Program Officer for the north-central states, he gained experience in federal grant evaluation and technical assistance to grantees through the Urban Resource Partnership. He also participated in State urban forestry reviews, and administered public use surveys of city parks and green spaces. After graduating from FAMU and UF in 1997, he was hired by the U.S. Forest Service as a Technology Transfer Specialist to work with the Southern Research Station in Athens, GA and Region 8 State and Private Forestry in Atlanta, GA. Between these two offices he worked mainly on urban forestry information technology and communication projects until 2002 when he left the U.S. Forest Service, accepting a position with the Centers for Disease Control and Prevention as a Health Communications Specialist in Atlanta, GA.

Marcus Warwell interned with the Rocky Mountain Research Station (formerly Intermountain Research Station), Moscow Forestry Science Laboratory in Moscow, ID during the summers of 1993, 1994 and 1997. He assisted field crews with installment, maintenance, and sample collection of silviculture, soils, mensuration, and genetics field studies. After graduating from FAMU and UF in 1997, Marcus continued his education at the UF, receiving a Master of Science degree in 2002. Prior to the completion of the degree, he began full time employment with the Moscow Forestry Science Laboratory, where he presently works as a Geneticist. His work involves the investigation of problems related to ecological genetics of conifers in the Rocky Mountains and genetic resistance to white pine blister-rust disease in western white pine and whitebark pine. His activities include design, implementation and interpretation of field, nursery, and laboratory studies as well as the conveyance of the results.

Hector Socias interned with the Allegheny National Forest in Pennsylvania during the summers of 1995 and 1997. He assisted field crews with timber management, archaeological surveys, hawk and owl surveys, recreation management, road engineering surveys, and search and rescue. After graduating from FAMU and UF in 1998, Hector returned to the Allegheny National Forest, where he became a member of the NEPA Plan and Design Team assisting in the development of environmental assessments (EA) and environmental impact statements (EIS). In 1999 and 2000, he was detailed as a Natural Resource Specialist on the Caribbean National Forest in Puerto Rico. In 2001, he accepted a position as a Natural Resource Specialist at the same forest. His responsibility was to implement a natural resource management plan at a National Guard military installation. He is currently working as a Silviculturist on the Ouachita National Forest in Arkansas.

Stephanie Steele interned on the Gila National Forest in New Mexico during the summer of 1999. She worked as a Forestry Aide, and her duties included trail maintenance and construction. In 2001, she interned as a wildlife biology co-op student on the Ocala National Forest. Her responsibilities included surveying birds, collecting alligator egg nests, installing kestrel boxes, and writing biological evaluations. Upon receiving her degrees from FAMU and UF in 2002, she became the first female to graduate the Joint-Degree program. After graduation, she was hired as a Wildlife Biologist Trainee for the U.S. Forest Service serving at the Seminole Ranger District on the Ocala National Forest in Umatilla, FL. Her duties include conducting surveys of various wildlife and their habitats, repairing and installing drift fences, assisting biologists with bear trapping (cooperative with the Florida Fish and Wildlife Conservation Commission), assisting crew members on prescribed fires, and developing management plans. In June of 2004 she was reassigned to the Holly Springs National Forest in Oxford, MS where she is currently working as the District Wildlife Biologist.

POSITIVE ASPECTS

Financial assistance, work and travel experience, opportunity for future employment, and the personal support of the program advisors were identified as positive strengths that contributed to recruitment and retention of the graduates.

Financial Assistance

Meeting financial demands for obtaining higher education represented a significant obstacle for the graduates. Naturally, the program's funding acted as a strong incentive that contributed significantly to their recruitment and retention. Scholarships helped pay for tuition, books, and housing. The program also provided financial assistance for travel to student and professional meetings and symposia. In addition, paid internships provided a means of income during summer months. Also, over the course of their studies, the graduates were provided the opportunity to work as Research Assistants with the program's advisors while attending classes.

Work and Travel Experience

The graduates valued their work and travel experiences while interning with the U.S. Forest Service. These work experiences provided hands-on opportunities to explore work preferences and broaden familiarity in various natural resource professions. Most internships required substantial travel to new and unique areas. For some internships, work and leisure travel provided opportunities to experience urban and rural settings across several states. For example, one summer internship required work in Montana, Idaho and Washington. This provided the graduate with an opportunity to visit Yellowstone and Glacier National Parks, as well as a variety of national forests and northwestern cities.

Opportunity for Future Employment—The favorable likelihood of future employment with the Forest Service reduced graduates' anxiety and provided a positive incentive for success while in school. Although the program did not guarantee employment upon graduation, graduates were given some assurances. For example, students were made aware of USDA and Forest Service initiatives that valued increased work force diversity. In addition, the U.S. Forest

Service invested considerable resources into the professional development of the students and showed willingness to address student needs. The program supported student participation in symposia hosted by Minorities in Forestry and Related Science (MINFORS) and Minorities in Agricultural, Natural Resources and Related Sciences (MANRRS). Attending these symposia gave students the opportunity to realize their employment potential through networking with professionals from a variety of agencies, businesses, and organizations.

Program Advisors' Personal Support

The personal care provided by the program's advisors, Dr. Kome Onokipise at Florida A&M and Dr. Donald Rockwood at the University of Florida contributed significantly to the enhancement of success for some of the graduates. Their personable and family-oriented style of advisement compensated for many of the disorders attributable to the program's first years. The advisors were also extremely accessible, and at times acted as professor and/or research supervisors for the graduates.

Attending Two Universities

Graduates valued the enriching experience of earning dual degrees while attending both FAMU and the UF. FAMU is a historically black university (HBCU) located in the state capital, Tallahassee, FL. Approximately 13,000 students attend FAMU. The University provides a unique learning environment oriented towards African-American culture. In contrast, UF located in Gainesville, FL is a much larger institution with approximately 46,000 students enrolled. The university offers an extensive variety of resources to broaden student academic and social experiences.

SUGGESTIONS FOR PROGRAM IMPROVEMENT

The graduates proposed suggestions for improvement in three areas of the program based on difficulties they encountered while students: communication between organization and students, transition between organizations, and the disbursement of funds.

Communication between Organization and Students

Written guidelines—Graduate's experienced bouts of uncertainty and confusion that resulted from an inability to access critical information from either the universities and or the U.S. Forest Service. The assignment of a full-time U.S. Forest Service liaison officer, Mr. Ted Willis, and the inclusion of students in annual meetings improved communications between the organizations and students. However, students in the program need written guidelines for reference. These guidelines should include specific information on the student's obligations, benefits, and projected status in a timeline format.

Recommended additional courses related to communication—Graduate success in the program requires effective communication across a diversity of cultural and professional settings. A course or workshop that introduces students to formal concepts related to intercultural communications is recommended. AEE 3073 Intercultural Communications taught by Dr. Marta Hartmann in the College of Agriculture and Life Sciences at UF is an excellent example. Also recommended is a professional development course or workshop. Information should be provided on the professional work environment and ethics complete with

case studies similar to the curriculum in the FAMU-School of Business and Industry.

Internship assignment—Matching an internship with the interests of the interning student is essential. The graduates' internship experiences strongly influenced the direction of their careers and where they now live. Some of the graduates' former FAMU/UF program classmates cited incompatibility with their initial internship as a major reason for leaving the program. Program administrators should seek to increase student involvement in the internship assignment process to reduce the likelihood of a student having a negative internship experience. Increased involvement would also provide students with a greater sense of responsibility, control and direction. The U.S. Forest Service should also take steps to promote student and graduate success by ensuring that personnel are ready and willing to receive and encourage the students' professional development. Understandably, however, ideal internship matches are not always possible. Ultimately, it is the students' responsibility to exercise patience while developing specific expertise, experience, and networking to attain a desired position.

UF and FAMU bookstores—During some semesters students experienced significant delays in receiving scholarship funds to purchase text books and study materials. A relationship should be established between the UF and FAMU bookstores and the U.S. Forest Service so that students can get their supplies when needed.

Transitioning between Organizations

Transitioning between two distinctly different universities and going from college to a professional career with the U.S. Forest Service can be challenging. To reduce the demands associated with these periods, program administrators should seek to better prepare students by giving them more information during orientations. For example, orientations should include a financial planning session to introduce students to the financial considerations associated with each transition. In addition, students should be exposed to a general U.S. Forest Service employee orientation early in the program to familiarize them with the organization.

Summer transfer to UF—In preparation for transitioning from FAMU to UF, students should be provided with a packet or Web site addresses containing information about UF parking, critical phone numbers, maps, on and off campus housing, and financial aid. This information should be distributed to FAMU students at the beginning of their sophomore year. This way the students will be more prepared to address challenges associated with summer transfer. As indicated by Onokpise and others (1997), students would be better prepared to meet the demands of the UF School of Forest Resources and Conservation's (SFRC) rigorous summer Dendrology course if they took a "PreDendrology" course. In the absence of a full course, a section could be taught in the Forest Rural and Urban Environment by Dr. Kome Onokpise at FAMU. To be effective, the course or section should closely follow specifics of the UF SFRC's Dendrology course format.

Internship Orientation—In preparation for U.S. Forest Service internships, students should be encouraged to get involved with campus organizations that participate in outdoor activities such as hiking and camping. If possible, students should be encouraged to attend a weekend training session focusing on hiking, camping, and safety outdoors. This training session could be set up through the USFS or an outdoors store.

CONCLUSION

Program administrators should continue to recruit students who, (1) convey a love and respect for nature, (2) demonstrate the discipline to acquire professional expertise through academic pursuit, (3) maintain a commitment to both personal and professional growth, and (4) display a heightened awareness of and respect for other cultures.

Underrepresentation of minority groups in natural resources limits the potential of the natural resource profession to meet many social and natural resource challenges. Programs such as FAMU/UF joint-degree program address this issue by producing well-trained minority professionals. The FAMU UF 2+2 Joint Degree Program and programs like it are valuable public assets that should continue to be supported and improved.

ACKNOWLEDGMENTS

The authors would like to thank the U.S. Forest Service (USFS), Florida Agricultural and Mechanical University (FAMU), and the University of Florida (UF) for their financial and administrative contributions toward the establishment and continuation of FAMU/UF 2+2 Joint Degree Program. Special thanks are extended to Dr. Oghenekome Onokpise and Donald L. Rockwood, and Mr. Ted Willis for their continued commitment to the success of the program and its graduates.

REFERENCES

Onokpise, O.U.; Rockwood, D.L.; Willis, T. 1997. Graduating blacks: some joint programs show early success. Women in Natural Resources. 19: 28-31.

REVIEW OF ECOLOGICAL ADAPTATION IN TEMPERATE AND BOREAL FOREST TREE SPECIES

Marcus Warwell[1]

Abstract—Most temperate and boreal forest tree species in the northern hemisphere exhibit characteristic patterns of adaptation to cope with varying environmental pressures existing across their geographic distribution. The study of ecological adaptation of plants provides a means to estimate distributional patterns of adaptation and predict plant growth and survival on new sites. These relationships are used to guide forest managers in gene conservation, reforestation, and afforestation. This paper briefly summarizes basic principles associated with intraspecific ecological adaptation and highlights the significance of its continued study in relation to climate change.

INTRODUCTION

Concepts discussed in this paper are based upon evolutionary theory which has been applied to understand many processes outside of biology. It is likely that our appreciation for diversity in fields such as Forestry and Natural Resources Conservation is influenced by fundamental concepts contained within evolutionary theory where increased diversity often relates to improved productivity and sustainability across a greater range of environmental change.

The objective of this paper is to (1) provide a brief review of basic concepts associated with the study of ecological adaptation in forest trees and (2) convey the significance of continued study of ecological adaptation in relation to global climate change.

Effective long-term management of forest ecosystems for sustainability through gene conservation, reforestation or afforestation requires an understanding of the structure and dynamics of ecological adaptation for forest tree species (Kogan 1975). Ecological adaptations are inherent variations among biological organisms which arise from a necessity to cope with environmental change. These adaptations are expressed by forest trees in characteristics such as growth potential, growth rhythm, cold hardiness, pest resistance, and structural physiology (e.g., tolerance to heavy snow load). Failure to understand and manage for intraspecific (within species) adaptation can lead to maladaptation and associated reductions in forest genetic diversity, growth, yield, and health (Bennet 1964, Rice and Emery 2003).

HISTORIC PERSPECTIVE

It is likely that early civilizations applied concepts related to species ecological adaptation in the cultivation of agricultural crops. European and Asian naturalists and biologists began developing concepts of intraspecies ecological adaptation more than two centuries ago. Early accounts include those of C. Linnaeus, who, in 1739, noted variations among maturing tobacco plants that were collected from different origins and grown together (Langlet 1971). De Vilmorin was among the first pioneers to document performance of seed sources on a common site (Callaham 1964). His work, which began in 1823, distinguished patterns of variation among 30 sources of Scots pine (Pinus sylvestris L.) (Langlet 1971). The biologists who followed conducted studies with increasing sophistication and broadened the scope of research in this area.

Contemporary thinking regarding the ecological basis of adaptive genetics in forest tree species has benefited from two pioneering studies. The first was provided by Langlet (1936), who demonstrated continuous adaptive variation (clinal variation) along a latitudinal gradient in Scots pine. Numerous studies that followed demonstrated clinal variation and collectively established clines as the predominant pattern of variation among most widely distributed forest trees. Subsequent work by Campbell (1979) used physiographic and geographic variables, such as elevation, and aspect to describe and predict adaptive variation in growth and survival traits in Douglas-fir [Pseudotsuga menziesii var. menziesii (Mirb.)]. This work established the use of quantitative methodology to estimate seedling adaptability using ecological factors at the location of the seed source as descriptors. Contemporary studies have since further refined and expounded on these methodologies and findings. More comprehensive historical summaries are provided by Heslop-Harrison (1964) and Morgenstern (1996).

STUDY AND APPLICATION OF ADAPTATION

Common Garden Test

At present, ecological adaptation in forest tree species is discerned through common-garden testing. A common garden provides a uniform environment in which differences between individuals within a species can be compared to detect genetic variation. Kleb's concept is the logical basis of this test (Kozlowski and Pallard 1997). It states that a phenotype, the physical manifestation of an individual tree, is the result of its genetic constitution or genotype, the effect of its environment, and the interaction between its genotype and environment. This statement is represented mathematically as:

$$P=G+E+G*E$$

Where:

P is the phenotype; G is the genotype; E is the environment and G*E is the interaction of genotype and environment.

In these common-garden tests, seed or cuttings from individuals within a species are collected from their native locale and grown together in a common environment. In a uniform environment, the E effect in the model is held "relatively" constant. Hence, all phenotypic variation is attributable to genotypic expression relative to the common-test environment (G*E).

---

[1]Geneticist, U.S. Forest Service, Rocky Mountain Research Station, Forest Sciences Laboratory, Moscow, ID.

Provenance Tests

A provenance test is a common-garden test that tests seeds according to their specific site of native origin. In this paper, a provenance is defined as a specific geographic location that corresponds with a naturally occurring population. Variations in trait expression between populations in provenance tests are analyzed to detect significant differences. If significant differences are detected, regression analysis can be used to assess relationships between seedling trait expression and ecological factors associated with the seedling origin. If significant relationships are identified, these data can be used to develop models to predict and describe the distribution of adaptation across geographic space.

The ecological range of provenances sampled, test environment and duration of provenance test influences the usefulness of provenance test results. Provenance tests require the sampled populations to be both geographically and ecologically representative of a species in the region of study (Campbell 1986). The interpretation of data from a provenance test are limited to the range of environmental variation sampled across in the species distribution. In addition, provenance tests require the individuals from the sampled population to be subjected to conditions that force expression of adaptive differences (Campbell 1986). Trait expression is often specific to seedling age, environmental conditions or their combination. Hence, a provenance test results' applicability is often dependent on its duration of study.

For the purpose of assessing adaptive differences within a conifer species in relation to climate, data from 2- to 4-year-old provenance tests have been shown to be effective (Rehfeldt and others 2004).

Intraspecific Ecological Adaptation Models

The data obtained from common-garden tests are used to develop models that estimate the geographic distribution of ecological adaptation within a species and predict forest tree growth and survival on foreign sites. This information is used to establish seed zones, which are essential in guiding forest managers in the selection of seed source for reforestation. Contemporary models are based on geographic features, such as elevation, which are assumed to act as surrogates for climate variables (Rehfeldt 1995). These models are theoretically limited in usefulness to the regions from which populations were tested and lose validity when the climate of the tested provenances changes. Methods described by Rehfeldt and others (2004) use techniques developed by Hutchinson (1984) to estimate climate across vast regions that enable the direct use of climate variables to develop models capable of predicting the performance of populations on foreign sites (Booth and others 1989, Rehfeldt 1995). These climate-based seed-transfer models are more accurate and are less limited in geographic range when compared with models based on geographic features. In addition, these models provide a means to identify the effects of present climate on adaptedness and predict the effects of future climate change on performance and distribution of forest tree species.

PATTERNS OF ADAPTIVE STRUCTURE

Most forest tree species that are native to temperate and boreal zones in the Northern Hemisphere exhibit characteristic patterns of genetic variation. These patterns arise from changing environmental pressures that occur across species' distribution over time and geographic space.

Physiological Plasticity and Adaptation

Over time, evolutionary processes shape a balance between physiological plasticity and adaptation. Physiological plasticity controls the finite range of ability of an individual to adjust to changing factors in its environment. If changing environmental factors exceed the limitations of an individual's physiological plasticity, subsequent generations may persist through adaptation. Adaptation results from the evolutionary process of selection, which is the survival and perpetuation of offspring that have inherited the most suitable genes from generation to generation to cope with specific environmental pressures. Natural selection is the principal factor among evolutionary processes, which include migration (i.e., seed and pollen gene flow), mutation, and non-random mating that determines where combinations of adaptive genes occur within a species distribution (Morgenstern 1996).

A simplistic illustration of the expression of physiological plasticity and adaptation in forest trees is provided in figure 1. It depicts height growth in a low-elevation provenance test for trees collected as seed from two species occupying an elevational gradient. Trait expression, which is shown to correlate with environmental variation, provides indirect evidence of ecological adaptation (Rehfeldt 1987). Hence, a general comparison of the elevation origins and growth performances in the provenance test of species A provides indirect evidence of physiological plasticity, while species B exhibits indirect evidence of ecological adaptation.

Forest tree species are unique in their balance between physiological plasticity and adaptation and can respond differently to changing conditions, despite occupying the same range and sharing similar ecological requirements (Brubaker 1988, Betancourt and others 1990, Huntley 1991). The extent to which a species is oriented toward either of these two modes influences the breadth of its realized niche (Levins 1968). Coniferous species' distributions in western North America are exemplary of this pattern (Burns and Honkala 1990). Douglas-fir and lodgepole pine (Pinus contorta) are specialists. Their orientation between physiological plasticity and adaptation is balanced more toward adaptation and their ecological distribution is characteristically broad. In contrast, western white pine (Pinus monticola Dougl.) and western larch (Larix occidentalis Nutt.) are generalists, relying more on

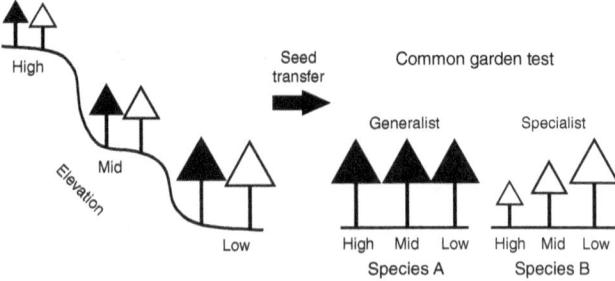

Figure 1—Hypothetical growth performance of seedlings collected from two forest tree species occupying an elevation gradient and placed in a low elevation, common garden. The growth performance of species A is indicative of a generalist that conveys adjustment through physiological plasticity, while species B is a specialist that conveys adaptation.

physiological plasticity. Their ecological distribution is, characteristically, relatively small. Ponderosa pine (Pinus ponderosa Dougl.) is considered intermediate, because it exhibits a relative balance between physiological plasticity and genetic adaptation (Refeldt 1994).

CLIMATE'S ROLE IN FOREST TREE ECOLOGICAL ADAPTATION

Climate factors are the principal environmental selection pressure that act on most temperate and boreal forest tree species in the northern hemisphere (Rehfeldt 2000, Woodward 1987). An analysis of ecological adaptive variation within most forest tree species will reveal evidence that supports a general pattern of populations that have become attuned to different climatic optima along an environmental gradient (Rehfeldt 2000). Figure 2 provides an example of this pattern where elevation acts as a surrogate for climate factors. It depicts elevational clines among populations of lodgepole pine. Each point represents the mean performance in height growth or freezing injury of seedlings planted in a common environment, which originated from populations at elevations indicated along the x-axis. Figure 2 also reveals a common negative correlation among many forest tree species, where growth potential decreases as cold hardiness increases. This relationship results from adaptations in which cold-climate populations have an intercorrelated network of traits adapted to a short-duration growing season; whereas, warm-weather populations have adapted to long duration growing seasons (Rehfeldt 1987). Figure 3 provides a second example of an adaptive pattern in relation to climate using a direct climate measure. It depicts a climatic cline among populations of spruce (Picea engelmannii Carr.). Each point represents the mean timing of cessation of shoot elongation (indicated along the y-axis) for seedlings planted in a common environment in relation to the predicted 30 year mean degree-days < 0°, which is a measure of winter coldness at the site of the populations geographic origin (indicated along the x-axis). This illustration shows that spruce seedlings originating from colder provenances tend to cease growth early, while spruce seedlings originating from warmer climates tend to cease growth later even when grown in the same common growing environment.

Although populations that constitute most forest tree species are attuned to different climatic optima, the majority do not appear to actually occupy sites where their optimal climate occurs. These patterns appear to result from competition between populations, brought about by density-dependent

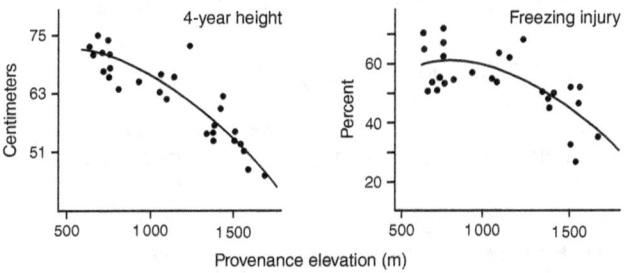

Figure 2—Clines in genetic variation among populations of lodgepole pine illustrating negative relationships between (left) growth potential and (right) freezing damage and provenance elevation. Growth potential of native populations decrease and cold hardiness increases as elevation increases and associated climate becomes colder (Rehfelt 2000).

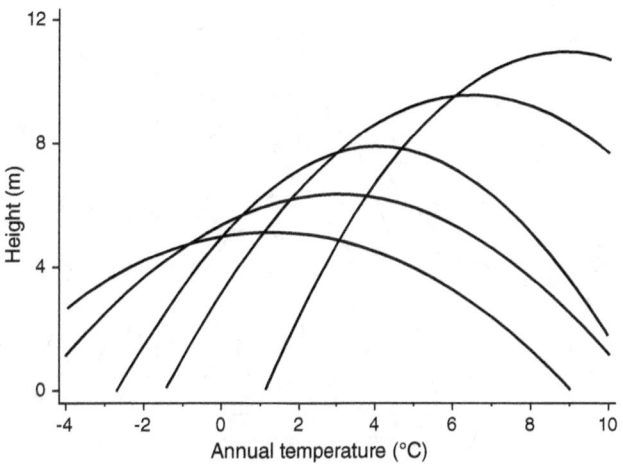

Figure 3—Response functions driven by mean annual temperature that predict 20-year height for five lodgepole pine populations illustrating (1) genetic variation in growth potential, (2) genetic differences in cold hardiness, and (3) a negative relationship potential and cold hardiness (Rehfeldt and others 1999).

selection and selection by the physical environment (Rehfeldt and others 2002). This relationship has been demonstrated in both lodgepole pine (Rehfeldt and others 1999) and Scots pine (Rehfeldt and others 2002).

Climate Change and Forest Tree Adaptation

Global climates are rapidly changing (IPCC 2001). Historical evidence from the Pliestocene epoch indicate that some plant species adapted well to past climate change. Adaptation of contemporary forest tree species will vary greatly depending on degree and rate of climate change and species genetic structure (Rehfeldt 2000). An inability of a population to respond to rapid climate change through adaptation or migration will result in its extinction. Projected change in global climate could impact annual temperatures up to 5°C, while rising precipitation up to 100 mm in (IPCC 1996). Because forest trees have long generation times and forest tree populations tend to migrate very slowly, a climate change of this magnitude would likely have major impacts on contemporary forests. Spruce is predicted to experience a reduction of approximately 89 percent of its present climatic habitat in the Western United States by the decade of 2090 based on an average of Hadley and CCMA GCM scenarios of 1 percent per year increase GGa (Rehfelt and others 2004). Those species with populations adapted to climate that occupy sub-optimal climates will have complex and nonuniform responses. Response models with increased annual temperatures for lodgepole pine (fig. 4) (Rehfeldt and others 1999) and Scots pine (Rehfelt and others 2002) predict reduced productivity for populations that presently occupy a climate warmer than their optima, and increased productivity for those populations that occupy a climate colder than their optima. Over the long term, a shift in climate would likely force geographic and genetic redistribution through evolutionary processes among those forest tree species that are adapted to different climates. Lodgepole pine may still require as many as 12 generations to stabilize (Rehfeldt and others 1999). These estimates are based on the assumption that climate change will stabilize (IPCC 1996). More recently this assumption has been brought into question (IPCC 2001), thereby asserting the possibility

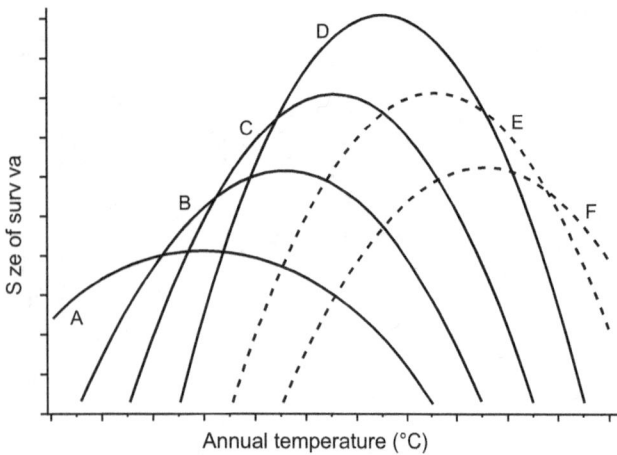

Figure 4—Diagrammatical representation of the response of lodgepole pine populations to gradients in the mean annual temperature (Rehfeldt and others 1999).

of forest tree species being caught in a perpetual lag in adaptation and ultimately jeopardizing the sustainability of forest health and productivity in contemporary temperate and boreal forests.

Under some scenarios, maintenance of near optimum forest health and productivity with global climate change may require an improvement of adaptation within populations by transferring seed of contemporary populations to anticipated future climatic zones. This process could help reduce multi-generational lag in ecological adaptation. However, greater understanding of processes related to long-distance seed transfer, including its interactions with secondary ecological factors of adaptation should be better understood before seed transfer is recommended.

SUMMARY

1. The study and management of ecological adaptation in forest tree species have been conducted for over two centuries.
2. Presently, the study of ecological adaptation in forest tree species remains dependent upon classic methodology of common-garden testing.
3. Climate is a primary factor controlling the distribution of temperate and boreal forest tree species. Most forest tree species exhibit a characteristic pattern of response to environmental variation that represents a unique balance between physiological plasticity and adaptation.
4. Present models for predicting ecological adaptation in forest tree species are based on geographic variables that act as surrogates for climate. These models are limited in geographic range of application, predict adaptive clines with less accuracy in comparison to climate based models, and cannot account for changing climate. The development of models based directly on climate variables is required.
5. Projected global warming trends will likely disrupt the genetic structure of forest tree species in the northern hemisphere, resulting in complex, range-wide responses. The resulting transitional period will likely require multiple

generations to naturally stabilize tree populations. During this transition period, losses in forest productivity and health may be addressed through seed transfer of contemporary genotypes to anticipated future climatic types.

REFERENCES

Bennett, E. 1964. Historical perspectives in genecology. Scottish Plant Breeding. Station Record: 49-115.

Betancourt, J.L.; Van Devender, T.R.; Martin, P.S. 1990. Synthesis and prospectus. In: Betancourt, T.R.; Van Devender, T.R.; Martin, P.S., eds. Packrat middens, the last 40,000 years of biotic change. Tucson, AZ: University of Arizona Press: 435-437.

Booth, T.H.; Suzette, D.; Searle, S.D.; Boland, D.J. 1989. Bioclimatic analysis to assist provenance selection for trials. New Forest. 3: 225-234.

Brubaker, L.B. 1988. Vegetation history and anticipating future vegetation change. In: Agee, J.K.; Johnson, D.R., eds. Ecosystem management for parks and wilderness. Seattle: University of Washington Press: 41-61.

Burns, M.B.; Honkala, B.H., tech coords. 1990. Silvics of North America: volume 1, conifers. Washington, DC: U.S. Dept. of Agriculture, Forest Service. 675 p.

Callaham, R.Z. 1964. Provenance research: Investigation of genetic diversity associated with geography. Unasylva- Nol 73-74 -FAO/IUFRO meeting on forest genetics. Vol. 18(2-3).

Campbell, R.K. 1974. A provenance-transfer model for boreal regions. Norsk Institutt for Skogforskning 31(10): 544-546.

Campbell, R.K. 1979. Genecology of Douglas-fir in a watershed in the Oregon Cascades. Ecology 60: 1036-1050.

Campbell, R.K. 1986. Mapped genetic variation of Douglas-fir to guide seed transfer in southwest Oregon. Silvae Geneica. 35:85-96.

Heslop-Harrison, J. 1964. Forty years of genecology. New York, NY: Academic Press. 2:159-247.

Hutchinson, M.F. 1984. A summary of some surface-fitting and contouring programs for noisy data. Canberra, Consult. Rep. ACT: CSIRO Division of Mathematics and Statistics/ Division of Water and Land Resources. 24 p.

Hutley, B. 1991. How plants respond to climate change: migration rates, individualism and the consequences for plant communities. Annals of Botany 67(Supplement 1):15-22.

IPCC 1996. Climate change 1995: the science of climate change contributions of working group 1 to the second assessment report of the intergovernmental panel on climate change. Cambridge, U.K.: Cambridge University Press.

IPCC 2001. Climate change 2001: the scientific basis. In: Houghton D.Y J.T.; Griggs D.J. and others, eds. Contributions of working group 1 to the second assessment report of IPCC. Cambridge, U.K.: Cambridge University Press.

Kogan, M. 1975. Plant resistance in pest management. New York: John Wiley and Sons: 103-146.

Kozlowski, T.T.; Pallard S.G. 1997. Physiology of woody plants. New York: Academics. 411 p.

Langlet, O. 1936. Studier över tallens fysiologiska variabilitet och dess samband med klimatet. Medl. Statens Skogsförsöksanstalt. 29:1-188.

Langlet, O. 1971. Two hundred years genecology. Taxon 20: 653-722.

Levins, R. 1968. Evolution in changing environments. Princeton, NJ: Princeton University Press. 120 p.

Mauseth, J.D. 1995. Botany: an introduction to plant biology. Saunders College Publishing. 499 p.

Millar, C.I.; Libby, W.J. 1989. Disneyland or native ecosystem: genetics and the restorationist. Restoration and Management Notes. 7(1): 18-24.

Morgenstern, E.K. 1996. Geographic variation in forest trees. Vancouver, BC: UBC Press.

Rehfeldt, G.E. 1987. Components of adaptive variation in Pinus contorta from the Inland Northwest. Research Paper INT-375. 11 p.

Rehfeldt, G.E. 1994. Evolutionary genetics, the biological species, and the ecology of the interior cedar-hemlock forest. In: Symposium proceedings of Interior Cedar-Hemlock-White Pine Forests: Ecology an Management. DNRS, WSU, Pullman, WA.

Rehfeldt, G.E. 1995. Genetic variation, climate models and the ecological genetics of Larix occidentalis. Forest Ecology and Management. 78:21-37.

Rehfeldt, G.E. 2000. Genes, climate and wood. In: The Leslie L. Schaffer lectureship in forest science. Vancouver, B.C. Can. 15 p.

Rehfeldt, G.E. 2004. Inter- and intra-specific variation in Picea engelmannii and its congeneric cohorts: biosystematics, genecology and climate-change. USDA, Forest Service, Rocky Mount. Experiment Station, Ft. Collins, CO.

Rehfeldt, G.E.; Tchebakova, N.M.; Parfenova, E.I. 2004. Genetic responses to climate and climate-change in conifers of the temperate and boreal forests. Recent Res. Devel. Genet. Breeding, 1(2004): 113-130.

Rehfeldt, G.E.; Tchebakova, N.M.; Parfenova, Y.I. [and others]. 2002. Intraspecific responses to climate in Pinus sylvestris. Global Change Biology. 8: 912-929.

Rehfeldt, G.E.; Ying, C.C.; Spittlehouse, D.L.; Hamilton, D.A. 1999. Genetic responses to climate in Pinus contorta: niche breadth, climate change and reforestation. Ecological Monographs. 69: 375-407.

Rice, K.J.; Emery, N.C. 2003, Managing microevolution: restoration in the face of global change. Fort Ecol Environ. 2003;1(9): 469-478.

Woodward, F.I. 1987. Climate and plant distribution. Cambridge University Press. London.

SESSION VI

Fire in the Urban/Wildland Interface

Presiding Moderator:

Marsha Kearney
U.S. Forest Service
Tallahassee, FL

FLORIDA'S WILDLAND FIRE RISK ASSESSMENT ANALYSIS

Jim Brenner, Jim Karels, Sue McLellan, Kass Green, and Julie Coen[1]

Abstract—The Florida Division of Forestry has recently embarked on the development of a statewide fire risk assessment system using the latest in remote sensing data and GIS technologies. The core component of the system is a GIS-based Fire Risk Assessment application using ArcInfo integrated with the FLAMMAP fire risk model. This system will assist fire managers with the mitigation of the harmful effects of wildlife and will function as a valuable planning tool for local fuel reduction and fire prevention efforts. GIS layers of wildland fire susceptibility, population density, land value, and fire response accessibility will be weighted, ranked, and combined to develop estimates of "Levels of Concern." The application will be flexible, such that the input values can be easily adjusted and the model re-run to produce new estimates of risk as level of concern change. This paper reviews achievements and issues associated with integrating remote sensing, GIS, and external models for fire risk assessment.

INTRODUCTION

For as long as there has been vegetation growing in Florida's wildlands, there have been periodic wildfires. As a result most of the indigenous species (plant and animal) have evolved with fire over many thousands of years. Wildfire is a natural phenomenon initially finding its origin in lightning but also with anthropogenic roots. Humans have spread fire to virtually every ecosystem on Earth. In addition to using and controlling fire, humans are the primary ignition source vectors for the propagation of fire and modifiers of fuel sources (Pyne 1992).

The role of fire in the wildlands of Florida has sparked a heated controversy that has been going on since the later part of the 19th century. The U.S. Forest Service, in an attempt to determine why Southern land managers continued to use fire as a management tool, contracted with a psychologist to research this behavior. Dr. Shea published an article in American Forests in 1940, titled "Our Pappies Burned the Woods," where he was quoted:

"With the closing in of the agrarian environment, it [burning the woods] has become predominantly a recreational and emotional impulse... the sight and sound and odor of burning woods provide excitement for a people who dwell in an environment of low stimulation and who naturally crave excitement.... Their explanations that wood fires kill off snakes, boll weevil and serve other economic ends are something more than mere ignorance. They are the defensive beliefs of a disadvantaged culture group."

Herbert Stoddard (Tall Timbers Research Station 1961) countered this with "The conditions under which developed the magnificent virgin stands of southeastern pines, having included frequent burning, surely carefully controlled fire for the benefit of animal life adjusted along with the forests to periodical, though uncontrolled, burning through the ages has the merit of following an established and successful procedure. In our opinion, to exclude fire permanently from the park-like pinelands of the Southeast is to jeopardize both the flora and fauna and to contribute to their replacement by other and inferior types of animal life and vegetation. How many who are advocating total fire exclusion in this region have seriously considered the consequences of disturbing this age-old adjustment?" Although the use of prescribed fire by land managers is generally accepted by forestry professionals today, the general public is still frequently confused and even angered by its use.

First among the concerns about wildland fires are the rapidly growing population pressures seen in many rural areas of the country; these same rural population pressures are evident in Florida. This paper defines wildland fires as those fires, which burn vegetative cover: grass, grain, brush, timber, or slash (Garner 1989). In the past, rural typified an agricultural community; today, rural is also characterized as residential. During the early settlement of the country, rural residents reduced forest fuels and fire proofed their properties as part of rural fire protection practices. As the populations moved to urbanized areas, rural fire protection practices became urban fire practices. Today, new rural communities are becoming increasingly popular; however, their behavior patterns have reversed; forest fuel loads are often left undisturbed or even increased because of aesthetic or scenic reasons. In areas of dense rural residential settlement homes can actually add to the fuel load available to a wildfire increasing the size and magnitude of the fire. In short, early settlers relied on fire practices to reduce risk or fire-proof their properties; the new rural settlers rely on urban fire organizations such as the volunteer fire departments for fire protection.

Today, many areas only experience infrequent fires that result from escaped human-caused fires, intentionally set incendiary fires, or from lightning. These fires frequently occur when conditions are so severe that control measures may be ineffective in stopping the fire. As a result, major economic losses are experienced by land managers and homeowners. In addition, there is the very real threat to the lives of the residents in the areas threatened as well as the firefighters attempting to put out fires in areas where the fuels have been left to accumulate over an extended period of time.

At this time it is the intent of the Florida Division of Forestry to conduct a "Risk Assessment Analysis" that will allow agencies and organizations at both the state and local levels to obtain a clear picture of the challenges to wildland fire management in Florida today. This will put the appropriate tools in the hands of land managers, local planners, county administrators, as well as emergency personnel to prioritize their work in mitigating future wildfire hazards in Florida. This paper outlines the scope and objectives of the Florida Fire Risk Assessment project and the methodology employed by Pacific Meridian.

---

[1] Jim Brenner, Jim Karels, and Sue McLellan, Florida Division of Forestry, Forest Protection Bureau of Agriculture and Consumer Services, Tallahassee, FL.; and Kass Green and Julie Coen, Pacific Meridian Resources, Emeryville, CA.

Florida's fire managers face a complex problem that is compounded by increasing fire intensities due to accumulation of vegetative materials, continued residential growth into wildland fire-prone areas, and increasing firefighting costs. Florida has been progressive with respect to total wildland fire management for many years. Advanced spatial technologies are being brought to bear on the issue and will provide a valuable decision-making tool. Florida needs a process to assess fire hazards and risks, and the values to be protected in order to more accurately deal with the threat from wildfire, as well as manage the largest open burning program in the country. This process will provide managers with a strategic view of the state to improve public safety and protect them from property losses like those experienced over the past few decades.

Increasing growth of rural populations, increasing urban sprawl, increasing usage of wildlands for recreation, and increasing forest fuel loads all pose an immediate and direct threat to the contact zone between wildlands and people. This contact zone is termed the Wildland Urban Interface. The Wildland/Urban Interface is defined as the line, area, or zone where structures and other human developments meet or intermingle with undeveloped wildland or vegetative fuels (United States Fire Administration 1990, U.S.D.O.I. 1995). The Wildland/Urban Interface has become the site of a potential major fire problem that will continue to escalate as the nation moves into the 21st century (Davis 1990). When people and wildlands come into contact conflict arises, either directly from the threat of wildfire or from an inadequate emergency service infrastructure necessary to protect the Interface. Florida has several distinct types of urban interface characteristics due to its unique historical development. The 'block' subdivision, for example, has caused a tremendous challenge to mitigation and fuel reduction efforts.

The Florida Division of Forestry supports a wildland fire risk analysis because it would promote efficient, safe management of fire by assisting both private and public organizations to:

- Rapidly identify areas that may require additional tactical planning

- Allow agencies to work together to better define priorities and improve emergency response

- Develop refined analysis of complex landscape and fire situations using GIS

- Increase communication with local residents to address community priorities and needs

- Plan for resource needs

- Identify resource allocation based on potentially severe fire problems

Project Scope

Florida possesses a unique set of characteristics that make much of the state highly susceptible to wildfire:

- The State is blessed with an abundance of wildlands. Unfortunately, the state has also experienced an explosion of new residents into these wildlands, creating a wildland/urban interface problem in a large portion of the State.

- Florida's weather is conducive to starting and spreading numerous and sometimes large wildfires. Florida's rate of lightning strikes is unequaled in the nation. Lightning, coupled with extended periods of drought, set the stage for catastrophic fire episodes. Human-caused fires are ever increasing as the population rises, and account for a major portion of Florida's wildland fires. Table 1 shows the average percentages of fires by cause for the past 10 years in Florida.

- Florida's wildland vegetation evolved with fire. The vegetation is adapted to burn periodically. Fine fuels, which are easily ignited and spread fire rapidly, are abundant throughout Florida. The lack of managed fire in much of the wildlands has promoted an accumulation of these fuels that will burn with such intensity as to hamper suppression efforts

To reduce the loss of life and property due to wildfire, communities and fire management organizations need to actively manage fire risk. However, managing fire risk is extremely difficult because fuel hazard constantly changes across the landscape and through time, and fire behavior is extremely sensitive to changes in land development, fuel hazard, weather conditions, and topography. In addition, many social, technical and institutional barriers exist to proactive fire risk management and planning. Some of the most worrisome problems and needs are:

Problem 1: Currently, fire suppression and mitigation activities are highly dependent upon the knowledge and intuition fire management personnel. While local knowledge is irreplaceable, it can also be limited because of the human mind's inability to simultaneously conceive of all possible fuel conditions and fire paths.

Need: Fire suppression personnel need accurate fire risk assessment tools to simulate future fire events, and to test the sensitivity of the simulations to changes in variables such as fuel, weather, and land use.

Problem 2: The dramatic nature of wildfires focuses public attention on fire suppression and not on prevention. For example, immediately following the Oakland hills fire in 1993, residents called for fuel management and wider streets (to improve emergency response). However, within 1 year of the fire, efforts to widen streets were abandoned because of property owner opposition. Fire risk awareness tends to be highly correlated with elapsed time following a catastrophic fire.

Table 1—Average percentage of the number of fires in Florida 1990–1999 by cause

Lightning	Camp fire	Smoking	Debris	Arson	Equipment	Railroad	Children	Unknown	Misc.
18.9	2.3	1.9	18.5	24.1	5.0	0.9	5.8	14.0	8.6

Need: Fire management agencies need educational tools, including fire risk visualization, that make the threat of fire immediately apparent to property owners.

Problem 3: Funding for fire management is heavily concentrated in fire suppression instead of fire prevention. This concentration is partially a result of the catastrophic nature of fire and partly a necessity—directly attacking a burning fire in a specific location is usually a necessity, while broadly applied preventive measures seem discretionary. However, most fire management professionals agree that funding spent on fire prevention and mitigation has the potential to greatly decrease losses from wildfires.

Need: Fire management agencies need efficient fire planning tools, which allow them to assess and prioritize fire risk mitigation before a fire occurs.

Project Objectives

Discussions concerning wildfire management usually center on estimates of fire hazard and risk. Fire hazard describes the fuel at a particular location as determined by the fuel type, loading, condition, ease of ignition, and difficulty of suppression. For the purpose of this study we will define hazard as: a fuel complex defined by kind, arrangement, volume, condition, and location that forms a special threat of ignition and resistance to control. Fire risk is the likelihood that an ignition will occur and the probable magnitude and consequences of the resulting fire and for the purposes of this study is defined as the chance of a fire starting as determined by the presence or activity of a causative agent. Numerous models for assessing fire risk have been developed throughout the world (Chuvieco and others 1999, Schoning and others 1997). While the earliest models were non-spatial, recent advances in GIS have allowed for the development of spatial fire risk models. Even the simplest fire risk assessments include variables that account for fuel, topography, and weather. More sophisticated models add variables for assets at risk, housing density, and impediments to fire suppression such as the width, curviness and steepness of roads. Ultimately, the risk assessment undertaken in Florida will take into account these variables.

The objective of the project is to develop a Fire Risk Assessment System (FRAS) that:

- Identifies and defines the individual elements that compose wildland fire risk and hazard in the State of Florida

- Maps fuels Statewide

- Models and maps "Levels of Concern" where cooperative efforts between the State, and public and private landowners are needed to focus fuel reduction work

- Allows for analysis of the sensitivity of the location of "Levels of Concern" to changes in model input variables

- Facilitates updating of the model to account for changes in fuels and land use

METHODOLOGY

FRAS will combine several landscape characteristics to create a map of "Levels of Concern" for the State of Florida,

- Wildland fire susceptibility

- Fire effects

- Population density

- Measures of ability to respond to fire occurrences

How the characteristics combined and the relative weight of each characteristic will be determined through interaction with the State of Florida personnel. The following describes the methodology that will be used to develop the above landscape characteristics.

Wildland Fire Susceptibility Index (WFSI)

The WFSI will be a GIS coverage that combines the potential for fire occurrence with a model of fire behavior to spatially represent wildland fire susceptibility for the State of Florida. The methods used to create the index have been developed in conjunction with Don Carlton, Pacific Meridian's fire modeling consultant.

Estimating the Potential for Fire Occurrence (PFO)

PFO is calculated using an estimate of the probability of each acre or cell in the GIS database igniting. To do this, the State of Florida will be stratified into areas with uniform fire occurrence rates called Fire Occurrence Areas (FOA). Fire occurrence information, for both federal and state lands, has been collected. The federal and state data will be combined to create a fire occurrence database for the entire State of Florida that includes at a minimum, fire location, fire size, and fire cause and will be used to develop the FOAs. The time period for the fire occurrence information will be determined through discussion with the State of Florida (most likely a period of 20 years). Once the fire occurrence database has been checked for accuracy, an ignition density value will be assigned to each cell. The cells will be stratified by assigning breaks in the density values (either by percentiles or equidistant breaks) to create discrete FOAs with similar ignition density values. This ordination is done to group cells into a defined number of areas. The final step will be to calculate the probability of an acre igniting for each acre in an FOA. The probability is calculated by dividing the actual number of ignitions in the FOA by the time frame for the ignition data, with the output expressed in fires per 1,000 acres per year.

Modeling Fire Behavior

The FlamMap program will be used to develop a layer of fire behavior for the State of Florida. FlamMap is a computer program that generates fire behavior data for a given set of weather and/or fuel moisture data inputs. The model outputs are based on Dr. Mark Finney's FARSITE (and the Pacific Meridian/Finney FIRE!) fire behavior model. FlamMap outputs are GIS coverages of flame length, fireline intensity, spread rates, etc. The inputs required to run FlamMap include, surface fuels, upper canopy crown closure, slope, aspect, elevation, and potential weather.

The surface fuels layer will be developed through the interpretation of Landsat Thematic Mapper (TM) satellite imagery. Fuels will be mapped to the 13 Fire Behavior Prediction System (FBPS) fuel models described originally by Albini and further described by Anderson(1982). The 13 fuel models fall within basic groups: grass, chaparral and shrub, timber, and slash (table 2). The crown closure layer will also

Table 2—Fuel models for Fire Behavior Prediction System

Fuel model	Typical fuel complex
	Grass dominated
1	Short grass (1 foot)
2	Timber (grass understory)
3	Tall grass (2.5 feet)
	Chaparral and shrub fields
4	Chaparral (6 feet)
5	Brush (2 feet)
6	Dormant brush, hardwood slash
7	Southern rough
	Timber litter
8	Timber litter with normal dead
9	Hardwood litter/open pine with grass
10	Timber litter with heavy dead
	Slash
11	Light logging slash
12	Medium logging slash
13	Heavy logging slash

be developed from the Landsat TM imagery. Slope, aspect, and elevation will be derived from Digital Elevation Models (DEM's) and the potential weather will be gathered from the National Weather Service stations with the cooperation of the State of Florida.

The fire behavior modeling process will begin with the development of Weather Influence Zones for the State. The Weather Influence Zones will be generated using historical weather data for the State of Florida from the National Weather Service and the State. This weather data will be used to develop percentile weather for each Weather Influence Zone. Percentile weather will be developed for four categories including low, moderate, high, and extreme for input into FlamMap. The proportion of fires that occur by percentile weather category will be determined and used to create a fire behavior layer using FlamMap. The FlamMap model will calculate fire behavior for every cell in a raster representation of the landscape described by the input layers. Output values will include flame length, heat per unit area, fireline intensity, and rate of spread. The output values of each cell represent how the present fuels will burn under assumed landscape, weather, and environmental conditions.

Creating a Layer of Wildland Fire Susceptibility Index (WFSI)

Outputs from the FlamMap model will be combined with the layer described above to develop a GIS coverage of Wildfire Susceptibility for the State of Florida. The wildland fire susceptibility analysis integrates the probability of an acre igniting and the wildland fire behavior in terms of an expected fire size. The process combines the data from the FOAs with fire behavior data developed by FlamMap. This analysis calculates a WFSI for each 30x30 meter cell in the study area. The analysis also includes a factor that will limit the size of a fire, because of containment by suppression resources and/or the presence of non-burnable surfaces, such as water or rock.

The factors affecting fire size will be assessed by determining the relationship between rate of spread and expected fire size when the fire is contained by initial attack resources

(contained) and when the fire is not initially contained (escaped). It may also be necessary to calculate a maximum fire size for the area. The expected fire size for contained fires can be calculated using a model that obtains the area burned using inputs of rate of spread, time to the containment of the fire, and mid-flame wind speed. Data from fire planning models can be used to develop a relationship between rate-of-spread and containment time of the fire which can then be used to obtain a relationship between rate of spread and fire size. In the case of escaped fires, past fires can be used to develop the relationship between rate of spread and fire size. This includes the area the fire covers in a defined period of time and rate of spread during the specified period of time. Finally, there may also be a need to establish a maximum fire size. The maximum fire size can be estimated using historical fire information.

Calculating the Wildland Fire Susceptibility Index

The WFSI is calculated as:

WFSI = (Expected acres burned in the FOA) / (Total Burnable Acres in the FOA)

Where:

"Expected acres burned in the FOA" = Final Fire Size (FFS) * Number of Fires per Year in FOA

The "Total Burnable Acres in the FOA" value is determined simply by subtracting the non-burnable acres in the FOA from the total acres in the FOA. To obtain a value for "Expected acres burned in the FOA" the process is slightly more complicated. For each cell in the FOA, a rate of spread is calculated for each percentile weather category using FlamMap. A fire size is calculated for each rate of spread using a formula for either contained fires or escaped fires or by using a maximum fire size. The result is fire size for each rate of spread for the cell. The final fire size is then calculated as a weighted average of the four fire sizes. The weighting factor for each fire size is the percent of fires that occur in each weather class for the FOA. For example, the extreme weather class may have a frequency of occurrence of 3 percent, but 4 percent of wildland fires historically occur in this weather class. Therefore, the weighting factor for the extreme class is 0.04. The output of the weighted average is the final fire size for each cell. The final fire size is multiplied by the number of fires per year in the FOA to obtain a value for "Expected Fire Size". This "Expected Fire Size" is divided by the "Total Burnable Acres in the FOA" to obtain the index value for the cell.

The final fire size is based on the assumption that the wildland fire is burning uniformly and continuously in fuel and topographic situation as is described in the cell. Since there are no contagion effects considered, the calculated value for the WFSI is best viewed as an index that ordinates Wildland Fire Susceptibility based on the probability of wildland fire ignition (FOA) and fire spread potential (FlamMap). If the expected acres burning could be precisely determined, then the WFSI could be viewed as the "probability of an acre burning".

Fire Effects

The fire effects layer is developed using a combination of the following input layer: cultural resource sites, utility corridors (gas pipelines, transmission lines), hazardous waste sites (Superfund, underground/aboveground storage tanks), threatened and endangered species habitat, urban interface, expensive operations (muck/peat bogs, swamps), plantations, and sensitive areas. A combination of these input layers will provide the best representation of actual fire.

Population Density
The Population Density layer is derived from Census Bureau data. The population density layer will aid in determining where the urban interface/intermix areas are located.

Fire Response Accessibility
The fire response accessibility layer includes dead-end roads and the buffered roads, drainage ditches, critical roads, inaccessible areas (based on distance from roads), crew locations/crew numbers at each location, and local fire department locations. As with the fire effects layer, using a combination of input layers will represent fire response/ accessibility and significantly improve the risk assessment model.

Estimating Levels of Concern
The focus of the Risk Assessment is the development of the Fire Risk Assessment Model to estimate "Levels of Concern." GIS layers of Wildland Fire Susceptibility, Fire Effects, Population Density, and Fire Response Access will be combined and ranked to develop Level of Concern estimates. Each layer will be ranked for their relative importance to fire planning and management, weighted relative to each other, and scored to produce a derived "Level of Concern" layer (fig. 1). Ranks and weights will be developed through interaction with the State of Florida personnel and Pacific Meridian's team members. Pacific Meridian will develop an interactive model that allows an open-ended combination of layers to be modeled for "Levels of Concern." Ranking and weighting will be flexible, so those values can be adjusted and the model easily re-run. This will allow for efficient tuning of the model and allow for updates to the input layers.

Application Development
The final task of the Risk Assessment is the development of a software application that allows the State of Florida to easily change input variables to develop new GIS layers of "Level of Concern." To develop a model meaningful to the State of Florida and other users, Pacific Meridian will work in conjunction with key team members in order to establish the needs of the end users.

The FRAS will allow for user input in the form of menus and forms. Forms will be developed that allow the user to rank input layers as well as define entity relationships. Users will be able to interactively rank input layers as well as determine entity relationships. Application development will adhere to strict quality assurance standards to produce an application that is easy to use and effective in its deployment.

CONCLUSION
The advancement of geospatial technologies and capabilities in the last decade has been phenomenal. The use of GIS data and satellite imagery, the integration of advanced environmental models, presented to a manager in a user-friendly interface, while providing decision making capabilities is something we could only dream about just a few years ago. The development of the Florida's Fire Risk Assessment System will play a significant role in the way in which fire managers in this State approach wildfire suppression, mitigation planning and public outreach. This valuable tool will provide the State of Florida with a consistent statewide approach that will be critical for decision-making in the coming years as the socio-environmental dynamics of Florida undergo increasing pressure from competing economic and development forces.

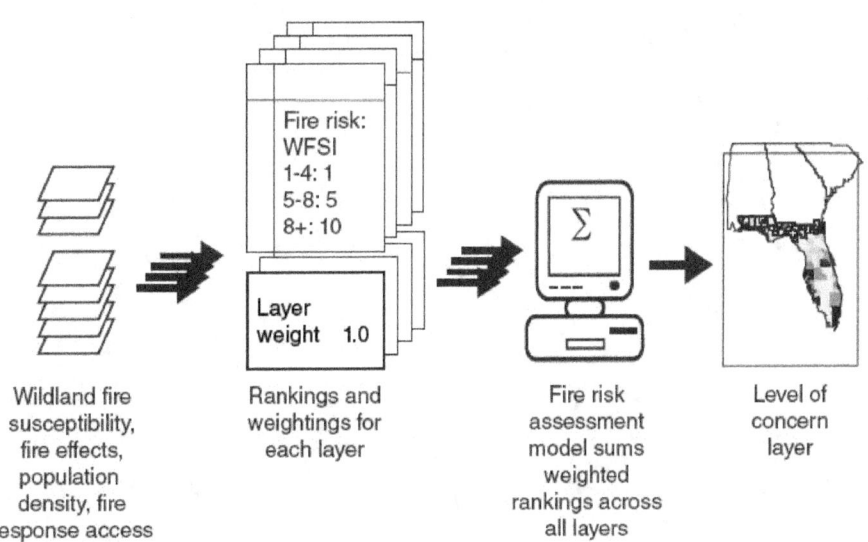

Figure 1—Fire Risk Assessment Model.

REFERENCES

Anderson, H.E. 1982. Aids to determining fuel models for estimating fire behavior. USDA Forest Service. General Technical Report INT-122. Intermountain Forest and Range Experiment Station, Ogden, UT. 22 p.

Chuvieco, E.; Javier Salas, F.; Carvacho, L.; Rodriguez-Silva, F. 1999. Integrated fire risk-mapping. Pages 62-91 in Remote Sensing of Large Wildfires in the European Mediterranean Basin. Springer, Berlin. Emilio Chuvieco ed.

Davis, J. 1990. The wildland-urban interface: Paradise or battleground? Journal of Forestry. 88(1): 26-31.

Garner, M.E. 1989. Risk mitigation of wildfire hazards at the Wildland Urban Interface. Masters Thesis, University of Arkansas, Fayetteville, AR.

Pyne, S.J. 1982. Fire in America, a cultural history of wildland and rural fire. Princeton University Press. 654 p.

Schoning, R.; Bachmann, A.; Allgower, B. 1997. GIS-based framework for wildfire risk assessment. Final Report for MINERVE 2, Zurich, Switzerland.

Tall Timbers Research Station. 1961. The cooperative quail study association. Tall Timbers Plantation, Tallahassee, FL. Misc. Publ. 1.

United States Fire Administration. 1990. Wildland fire management: Federal policies and their implications to local fire departments.

U.S. Department of the Interior. 1995. Federal Wildland Fire Policy, Memorandum. Final Report. Washington, DC.

EXPLORING SOCIAL FOUNDATIONS THAT SUPPORT COMMUNITY PREPAREDNESS FOR WILDFIRE

Shruti Agrawal, Martha C. Monroe, Pamela Jakes, Erika Lang,
Kristen Nelson, Linda Kruger, and Vicky Sturtevant[1]

Abstract—A community's vulnerability to wildfires is a function of social and ecological factors. There are steps that agencies and individuals in a community can take to increase preparedness against wildfires. This paper presents an overview of the model of community preparedness used and tested in the study "Community partnerships: Landscape level strategies to reduce the risk and loss from catastrophic fires." The preliminary results of this study shed light on actions that some communities are taking to be prepared for wildfires and the social foundations that support these actions. The second section of the paper focuses on social capital, one of the social factors that impacts preparedness initiatives.

INTRODUCTION

Since civilization began, fires have been an important part of human life in North America. Ignited either by lightning, or purposefully lit by Native Americans to clear grasslands and forests, fires have resulted in fire-dependent vegetation communities dominated by fire-tolerant pines, shrubs and grasses. Fire brings about change that is biologically essential to maintain a healthy ecosystem (Wade 1989).

In the 20th century, Federal agencies across the United States initiated intensive fire exclusion and prevention efforts. No doubt these efforts helped decrease the incidence of wildfires and the amount of areas burned, but at the same time these led to accumulation of dead and live vegetation in the forests. More people are moving into the wildland/ urban interface, and with the already accumulated loads of vegetation, an occurrence of wildfire is a major threat to homeowners and communities.

With more incidences of wildfires threatening human lives and property, Federal, State and local fire agencies across the United States are taking steps to be more prepared to fight fires and to protect human lives and property. For example, since the 1998 fires in Florida that burned 500,000 acres and damaged or destroyed about 300 structures, the Florida Division of Forestry and other State and local agencies in Florida have added wildfire-fighting equipment, improved communication systems, and provided wildfire training to structural firefighters.

Different communities might respond to a disaster or its threat in different ways. How they act might be a result of their past experience with the disaster, economic condition, cultural orientation, awareness about the issue, and the nature and extent of the threat (Kreps 1984). Disaster responses vary, based on whether the action is taken prior to the disaster or as a protective measure during the disaster. For example, during a wildfire, immediate steps are taken at the local, State, and Federal level to control the fire so there is minimum damage and loss of life—this is good disaster management. However, there are steps that a community can take prior to a disaster to be more prepared and to reduce the threat itself—this is good disaster preparedness. Such steps would involve the cooperation between both the individuals in the community and the agencies responsible for mitigation.

Model for Community Preparedness

"Community preparedness: landscape level strategies to reduce the risk of wildfires" is a national level research study funded by the National Fire Plan through the U.S. Forest Service, North Central Research Station, Minnesota (Jakes and others 2003). This study examines the actions that communities at risk of wildfires are taking to increase wildfire preparedness and the social resources or conditions that are necessary to implement and support these actions. The study focuses on 15 communities, five each in the Southeast, Pacific Northwest and the Northeast, that have a wildfire risk and that are doing things to reduce that risk. The research focuses on two questions:

1. What steps has the community taken to increase wildfire preparedness?

2. What social resources/conditions have been necessary to support these steps?

To find answers to these questions, we developed a model for community preparedness that emphasizes the social and ecological factors that might influence preparedness for wildfires (fig. 1). These factors are affected by decisions made at the individual and the community level. Individuals

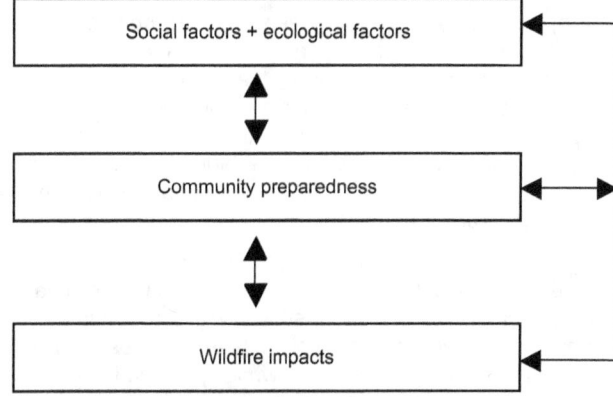

Figure 1—Model for community preparedness.

[1] Shruti Agrawal, Graduate Student, and Martha C. Monroe, Associate Professor, School of Forest Resources and Conservation, Gainesville, FL; Pamela Jakes, Project Leader, North Central Research Station, U.S. Forest Service, St. Paul, MN; Erika Lang, Graduate Student, and Kristen Nelson, Professor, Department of Natural Resources, University of Minnesota, St. Paul, MN; Linda Kruger, Research Social Scientist, Pacific Northwest Research Station, U.S. Forest Service, Seattle, WA; and Vicky Sturtevant, Professor, Department of Sociology and Anthropology, Southern Oregon University, Ashland, OR.

have resources that they can implement to influence wildfire preparedness initiatives. For example, they can reduce their vulnerability to wildfires by their choice of building materials, landscaping, and access. Communities also have resources that influence and are used to implement their decisions relating to zoning, planning, education, and other activities that impact wildfire preparedness. Thus, decisions made at both the individual and community level together result in a set of actions aimed at increasing wildfire preparedness. As a result of these actions, it is assumed that the community will have fewer fires, and if there are fires, the community will minimize its losses and recovery or restoration will be quicker and more effective.

The study focuses primarily on social factors (human capital, natural capital, resource base, resiliency, agency involvement, and social capital) that play a role in a community's vulnerability to wildfires. Our desired outcome is to increase wildfire preparedness by suggesting actions a community can take, given its social and landscape characteristics.

METHODS
We pilot tested the model in three communities—the Gunflint Trail community in northeastern Minnesota; Bend, OR; and Waldo, FL. We selected these communities because we wanted to test this model in communities that represent different ecosystems, different population size, different levels of perceived risk of wildfires, and different levels of ongoing efforts related to wildfire preparedness.

Gunflint Trail—It is in a boreal ecosystem and has a history of fires. This area recently experienced a wind event that resulted in a massive increase in the fuel load. Individuals, the community, and different levels of government in Gunflint Trail are involved in several wildfire preparedness activities.

Bend, Oregon—This is a fairly large community in a high-desert, pine-chaparral ecosystem. It has a frequent and recent fire history. Bend is very representative of communities in high-amenity recreation areas that are experiencing significant population growth. Bend has several ongoing activities related to wildfire preparedness led primarily by government agencies with community buy-in.

Waldo, Florida—The area represents the flatwoods pine ecosystem, which is very common in Florida. Fire occurs frequently in this ecosystem. Unlike the other two pilot communities, industrial plantations surround Waldo, FL. Officials in Waldo, FL have worked with the University of Florida's Conservation Law Clinic to explore the possibility of an ordinance to encourage forest management activities that would help create a "safety belt" for the town.

In each of these communities we used key informant interviews to collect information on steps the community has taken to increase wildfire preparedness and the resources that have been necessary to implement these steps. In each community we interviewed people whose jobs made them responsible, in part, for wildfire preparedness, including the Federal lands fire management officer, the State agency fire management officer, county emergency preparedness official, local fire chief, and sheriff. In addition, we interviewed people whose job responsibilities are tied to wildfire preparedness in the community, including real estate agents, bankers, developers, and contractors. From each of these people,

we obtained names of citizens who are active in wildfire preparedness. We also interviewed these involved citizens. Interviews lasted from one to several hours. On average, we interviewed 15 people in each pilot community.

We expanded our wildfire preparedness model to include the necessary social foundation discussed above: social capital, human capital, cultural capital, agency involvement, and landscape (fig. 2). For example, a resourceful member of the Gunflint Trail Volunteer Fire Department used information provided from government sources to research, adapt and install sprinkler protection systems for structures along the Gunflint Trail; this is as an example of human capital. An example of an agency involvement is the case where Florida Division of Forestry recently hired Wildfire Mitigation Specialists to coordinate public education with regard to wildfire preparedness in areas at risk of wildfire. Five regional mitigation teams are deployed to reduce fuel loads on public and private property, and one has been active in Waldo, FL helping with prescribed fires and maintaining fuel breaks. Realizing the need for better and timely communication of information, town managers in Alachua County set up their own disaster communication system; this is an example of social capital. Under this new system, in the event of a disaster, fire or tornado, a representative from one town takes up a post at the Alachua County Fire Rescue headquarters and passes current information to other town managers.

SOCIAL CAPITAL
The second section of this paper discusses one of the social foundations that may impact community preparedness—social capital. In this section we focus on three communities in the southeast United States—Palm Coast, FL, Bastrop, TX, and communities around the Mississippi Sandhill Crane National Wildlife Refuge, MS.

Social capital helps describe what may make some communities function better than others. Putnam (2000) defines social capital as "features of social organization such as networks, norms, and social trust that facilitate coordination and cooperation for mutual benefit." It helps generate trust, understanding, sense of belonging and the cultural will to solve problems collectively. Social organizations like the church, Parent-Teachers Association, Women's Club and Lion's Club enhance interaction within the community. Putnam (2000) emphasizes that "working together is easier in a community that has large stocks of social capital" and can lead to positive outcomes like less crime and economic development.

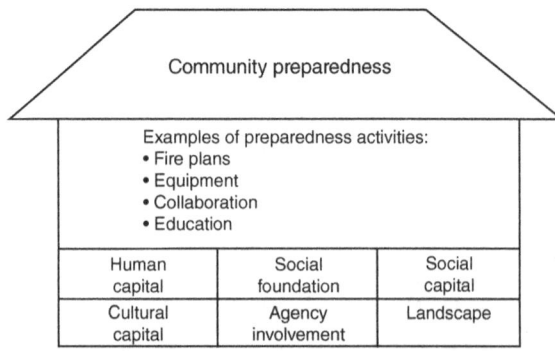

Figure 2—Social foundations for community preparedness.

Several studies have focused attention on the role of social capital in alleviating poverty (Collier 1998), fostering economic growth (Putnam 2000), increasing child academic achievement (Coleman 1988), and attaining jobs (Granovetter 1973). High social capital is associated with cooperative problem solving, effective governance, and rapid economic development (Putnam and others 1993). Social capital plays an important role in fostering social networks that are needed to take collective action (Putnam 2000). Thus, if a community has large stocks of social capital, people in that community should be more willing to participate in community activities and solve problems they face together. For example, residents in a subdivision vulnerable to wildfires may work together to conduct a prescribed fire, install dry hydrants, rent a chipper, or widen an access road.

We are defining social capital as the social characteristics of the community characteristics that facilitate accomplishment of shared goals. Communities with high social capital often have many social networks. Social networks are the structural component of social capital. Measures for networks look at type, size, structure, and relationship of networks. For example, groups such as homeowners' associations are being identified as critical to increasing wildfire preparedness. In addition, people in such communities have shared values, beliefs and norms of trust and reciprocity. Finally, the presence of community leadership rounds out the key components of social capital.

Some of the indicators for social capital used in this study are: long-term residents, social organizations, networks, and leaders in multiple roles. In a community prepared for wildfire, we might expect to see active and motivated residents doing things to protect their property and/or working with their neighbors to reduce their risk, serving on committees, and using good communication networks within agencies and organizations. People who have lived in the area for a long time might have greater affinity for the place and therefore work harder to protect it from fire.

Palm Coast, FL

This is a model community established in the 1970's. The community does not have long-term residents. Most people who came here are retirees from elsewhere, especially Michigan, New York, and New Jersey. Many moved here without knowing the area's vulnerability to wildfires. In Palm Coast, lots were sold with no building deadline, resulting in some streets having a few houses surrounded by vacant lots. Absentee landowners may own these lots across the world, and if the vegetation on these lots is not managed it becomes a wildfire threat to the neighbors. The town has a history of two catastrophic wildfires in 1985 and 1998 (Monroe and others 2003).

During the study, we asked officials and residents to describe what they have done to be prepared for wildfire and looked for the presence of social capital in the community. We asked "How would you rate the level of "civic mindedness" in your community on a scale of 1 to 10 and why?" We also looked for the presence of clubs and other social organizations and membership in these voluntary organizations.

People responsible for fire protection and mitigation are taking appropriate actions. They are also taking steps to educate the community about wildfires. The town has numerous clubs providing abundant opportunities for people to connect and know each other. Palm Coast, FL has good networks and improved emergency communication within State, Federal, and county organizations. For example, in Palm Coast, FL, all county agencies are kept informed through regular conference calls and meetings.

The level of social capital is reflected in the formation of the citizen task force after the 1998 fires and their recommendations for reducing the threat. Palm Coast, FL now has a vegetation reduction ordinance that directs the city code enforcement office to send letters to identified hazard lot owners informing them of their options for mitigation on their property. Though we initially thought that long-term residents might be an important criterion, Palm Coast, FL's retiree population from elsewhere is still able to display high social capital.

Bastrop, TX

The second community is Bastrop, Texas. It is a historic and a fast growing community. Its growth is attributed to its proximity to the capital city of Austin and their attractive 'lost pines.' Development around Bastrop has fueled an Wildland/Urban Interface (WUI) problem and the Tahitian Village sub-division is particularly challenged. In this community, we asked questions about preparedness and social capital.

Bastrop has a history of civic participation. The Ladies Reading Circle in Bastrop active for over 100 years started the public library and organized the historical society that operates the local museum. Leaders in this community play multiple roles, thus increasing connectedness within departments. For example, the head of the Water and Wastewater Department for the city of Bastrop is a member of the Rural Fire Advisory Council set up by the Texas Forest Service and a former chief of the Bastrop Volunteer Fire Department (Monroe and others 2004).

High levels of civic participation are reflected in the neighborhood gatherings held at Tahitian Village, where homeowners assess their own risk. Another example is the overly successful Mulchfest where homeowners dropped off yard waste and took home mulch. An increase in citizen participation in volunteer fire departments indicates increasing citizen involvement. Bastrop County hosts a regional Wildfire Training Academy that provides high quality wildfire fighter training.

Communities near the Mississippi Sandhill Crane National Wildlife Refuge (MSCNWR), Jackson County, MS—one of the three coastal counties in Mississippi that has experienced growth in the past several years. The population in this county has increased by 14 percent in a period of 10 years, from 115,243 in 1990 to 131,420 in 2000. The biggest threat faced by the coastal counties is hurricanes; the most recent one was Hurricane Georges in 1998. Wildfire is probably the second major threat in the region; a major wildfire in MS is about 1,000 to 2,000 acres. Among the three Jackson county communities, Van Cleave is at high-risk for wildfires, whereas Gautier and Ocean Springs are at medium-risk. These three communities border the MSCNWR. In this region, years of fire suppression have resulted in overgrowth of the understory. Officials at the 19,000-acre MSCNWR are playing an active role in reintroducing fire into the ecosystem.

Most people in Jackson County are unaware of the growing WUI problem and the need to take initiatives to improve their preparedness for wildfires. Agencies and local organizations like Mississippi Forestry Commission (MSFC), MSCNWR, U.S. Forest Service, local fire departments, The Nature Conservancy (TNC) and the Cooperative Extension Service realize the risk and are taking steps to reduce their vulnerability to wildfires (Monroe and others 2004).

Agencies and organizations in Jackson County share an excellent working relationship with each other and their partners. For example, the MSCNWR and the MSFC work well with local fire departments and with each other. During a fire, the volunteer fire departments work with the MSFC to fight the fires. The local fire departments are present to assist the MSCNWR or the MSFC during a prescribed burn. There is good communication within fire agencies at the county level through county and state level meetings. Coastal counties have several organizations and networks at the county and local level that foster participation and communication within different sectors of the community.

CONCLUSION

This research will lead to recommendations for actions that other at-risk communities can take based on the ecological and social characteristics of the community. The basic premise of this model of community preparedness is that fires are inevitable. But if a community has taken steps to be prepared for wildfires and they experience a wildfire, they are more likely to sustain minimum losses and recover more quickly than less prepared communities. Thus understanding and identifying factors that contribute to increased risk of wildfire and developing mitigation programs to reduce those risks could be one of the first steps for a community at risk of wildfires.

Not all communities are created equal in terms of available natural, human, physical, and social capital. By focusing on elements of social capital that seem to improve preparedness, this study may be able to recommend strategies to support community development and partnerships. Networks, partnerships, and open communication between agencies and landowners are required for effective wildfire preparedness. Creating wildfire education programs is another way to improve a community's preparedness for wildfires. However we need to realize that not one program fits all communities. Thus, for a wildfire education program to be effective it should be relevant to local residents and empower and motivate them to work together and make their own decisions about preparedness activities.

REFERENCES

Collier, P. 1998. Social capital and poverty. Social Capital Initiative Working Paper No. 4, The World Bank.

Coleman, J.S. 1988. Social capital in the creation of human capital. American Journal of Sociology 94 (Issue supplement: Organizations and institutions: sociological and economic approaches to the analysis of social structure): S95-S120.

Granovetter, M.S. 1973. The strength of weak ties. American Journal of Sociology. 78 (6): 1360-1380.

Jakes, P.J.; Nelson, K.; Lang, E. [and others]. 2003. A model for improving community preparedness for wildfire. In: Homeowners, communities and wildfire: science findings from the National Fire Plan. Proceedings from the Ninth International Symposium on Society and Resource Management. June 2-5, 2002, Bloomington. IN. Gen. Tech. Rep. NC-231. St. Paul, MN: U.S. Department of Agriculture, Forest Service, North Central Research Station.

Kreps, G.A. 1984. Sociological inquiry and disaster research. Annual Review of Sociology. 10: 309-330.

Monroe, M.; Agrawal, S.; Jakes, P. 2003. The Palm Coast community: steps to improve preparedness for wildfire. St. Paul, MN: U.S. Department of Agriculture, Forest Service, North Central Research Station.

Monroe, M.; Agrawal, S.; Jakes, P. 2004. Bastrop, TX: steps to improve preparedness for wildfire. St. Paul, MN: U.S. Department of Agriculture, Forest Service, North Central Research Station.

Monroe, M.C.; Agrawal, S.; Hudson, R. 2004. Communities near the Sandhill Crane National Wildlife Refuge: steps to improve community preparedness for wildfire. St. Paul, MN: U.S. Department of Agriculture, Forest Service, North Central Research Station.

Putnam, R.D. 2000. Bowling alone: the collapse and revival of American community. NY: Simon & Schuster.

Putnam, R.D.; Leonardi, R.; Nanetti, R.Y. 1993. Making democracy work: civic traditions in Modern Italy. Princeton: Princeton University Press.

Wade, D.D. 1989. A guide for prescribed fire in southern forests. Technical Publication R8-TP 11: National Wildfire Coordinating group.

SESSION VII

Forest Products/Forest Extension/Forest Economics

Presiding Moderator:

Alfred Lorenzo
Florida A&M University

HIGHLIGHTS OF WOOD PRODUCTS RESEARCH ACTIVITIES AT USDA FOREST PRODUCTS LABORATORY

Irene Durbak[1]

Abstract—This paper provides a brief overview of the research mission of the Forest Product Laboratory, highlighting some of the many diverse groups and activities that make the Forest Products Laboratory a unique and valuable institution for wood research innovation, information, and conservation. Research in the areas of economics, mycology, biopulping, wood preservation, transfer efforts, and research.

INTRODUCTION

It was an honor and a pleasure to participate in the Symposium "Celebrating Minority Professionals in Forestry and Natural Resources." Likewise, it was an honor to represent the Forest Products Laboratory (FPL) of the U.S. Forest Service, where I have been privileged to work for more than 20 years. My field is economics research related to national resource assessments.

In June 1910, the FPL opened its doors as a Federal research facility, within the U.S. Department of Agriculture (USDA) and the Forest Service, in Madison, WI. Since its inception, FPL has been a national center for public research in wood science, wood product utilization, and resource sustainability. It is recognized both nationally and internationally as an unbiased technical authority on wood science and wood use.

The mission of FPL is to conduct innovative wood and fiber utilization research that contributes to conservation and productivity of the forest resource. All research units participate in a collaborative team effort focused on contributing toward the FPL mission.

RESEARCH AREAS

From the beginning, FPL has taken an interdisciplinary approach to research, concentrating a variety of research disciplines and groups in one location. The current staff consists of 284 employees, which include 64 scientists in the following fields:

- Plant Pathology
- Forest Products Technology
- Wood Science
- Soil science
- General and Chemical Engineering
- Chemistry
- Microbiology
- Economics and Statistics

The FPL staff also includes about 50 other research support professionals. These include a patent attorney who helps obtain patents for innovations developed at FPL and throughout the Forest Service.

In addition to the permanent research scientists and research support staff at FPL, there are usually visiting scientists from various countries and other research collaborators, who come for extended periods to work on particular studies. FPL is also fortunate to have many student employees and volunteers, who contribute greatly to research studies and various support tasks.

ECONOMICS RESEARCH

My research group includes research foresters and economists. We study issues related to timber demand and technology assessment. For many years, we have participated in the RPA Timber Assessment, a nationwide Forest Service effort to develop national assessments and long-term outlooks for timber resource supply and demand in the United States. Results of the most recent Timber Assessment are in the March 2002 issue of the Journal of Forestry.

Many of our studies provide trend analyses, projections, and other information about solid wood and paper product markets. We compile historical statistics and develop economic models for assessing the resource. We assess the impact of changes in technology and economic markets on wood and fiber utilization. We also study national demand for fuelwood, carbon storage, and the influence of these on climate change and as socioeconomic measures of forest sustainability.

I am involved in studies related to market trends, fiber use, and competitiveness in the pulp and paper industry. We have developed an economic model that covers North America and that simulates and projects regional capacity growth, product demand and supply, fiber use, and product shipments, including international trade. We have used this model to develop long-run projections for pulp and paper and for raw fiber materials (pulpwood and recovered paper).

OTHER RESEARCH AREAS

Mycology

The Center for Forest Mycology Research includes botanists, plant pathologists, microbiologists, biological science technicians, and a curator. Its mission is to obtain, describe, identify, and preserve specimens of wood fungi. Researchers develop new or improved methods for classifying and preserving wood fungi, study the role of fungi in decomposing wood, and explore potential applications for wood decay fungi.

[1] Economist, U.S. Forest Service, Forest Products Laboratory, One Gifford Pinchot Drive, Madison, WI.

The FPL collection of wood-inhabiting fungi is the largest in the world, containing 15,000 living specimens and 75,000 dried specimens. Researchers often travel throughout the United States and the world to collect and identify wood fungi. One researcher who studies tropical wood fungi is stationed in Puerto Rico.

Fungi that inhabit wood can be both harmful and beneficial. They are harmful when they stain or otherwise degrade the appearance, strength, or other physical property of wood products. But fungi can also be beneficial, as when used instead of chemicals to process wood chips into pulp fiber.

Biopulping

Biopulping is a major research area in the Institute for Microbial and Biochemical Technology at FPL. In biopulping, special fungi are used to help remove the lignin that binds wood fibers, thus "softening" the wood chips before pulping. This process saves energy and improves the quality of the material produced. Two 50-ton biopulping trials were recently conducted at FPL as part of an effort to scale-up biolpulping for industrial use. A mobile biopulping unit is taken to paper mills throughout Wisconsin to demonstrate the potential application of biopulping in papermaking.

Wood Preservation

The objectives of the Wood Preservation Research Unit are to find new and better ways to prevent the degradation and decay of wood in use and to improve the environmental performance of treated wood. The microbiologists, forest products technologists, and physical science technicians in this group study the effectiveness and environmental impact of new and improved wood preservative treatments. With the phase-out of chromated copper arsenate (CCA) for some applications, FPL researchers are studying alternative preservatives and their effects on the environment, particularly in sensitive areas such as wetlands.

One major research objective of the Wood Preservation Unit is to develop effective preservatives and treatment methods that would prevent decay and destruction by termites and other organisms in a wide range of wood species, nationally and internationally. In recent research, a particular naphthalenic compound was found that not only prevents wood decay but also kills native termite colonies. An effective and environmentally benign termicide developed in collaboration with entomologists at the Agricultural Research Service (ARS) station in New Orleans is now available for licensing: http://www.ars.usda.gov/is/pr.

Wood Adhesives

Taking treated wood one step further, researchers in the Wood Adhesives Research Unit address the issue of bonding of treated wood. The chemists, chemical engineers, and physical science technician in this unit develop improved, environmentally friendly adhesives. Research topics include volatile organic emissions in wood products containing adhesives and the mechanism of adhesive failure. The Wood Adhesives Unit is exploring new primers that enhance adhesion of material that does not bond easily, such as wood treated with preservatives and wood composite products.

Engineered Wood Products and Structures

In the final step, treated and untreated wood and wood components are used in a wide range of structural and nonstructural products. This is the focus of the Engineered Wood Products and Structures Research Unit. Researchers include physicists, forest products technologists and general engineers. Their mission is to extend the wood resource through engineering technology. They aim to improve the design and use of wood-based materials in different structures, from residential homes to nonresidential buildings and timber bridge systems. Research studies address issues such as indoor moisture, material durability, component connections, and structural resistance to high winds. One current area of research is the reuse of wood components recovered during demolition of old building structures.

RESEARCH TECHNOLOGY TRANSFER

A major function at the FPL, as in other research organizations, is technology transfer—getting research results into useful applications "on the ground." Researchers provide information about their study results and conclusions through publications and presentations at technical meetings and workshops. Technology transfer can also involve marketing activities aimed at promoting and facilitating the successful adoption and wide use of new technologies. The Technology Marketing Unit at FPL is charged with this mission. This diverse group of professionals includes a chemical engineer, marketing specialist, forest products technologists, and communication and visual information specialists.

The Technology Marketing Unit works in collaboration with various organizations and interest groups, which include economic development groups, forest products industries and associations, small businesses, universities, extension specialists, the National Association of Counties, and the National Forest System staff. Technology transfer activities include:

- Identifying customer research needs

- Interfacing between customers and researchers

- Developing and distributing user-friendly publications

- Conducting demonstration and pilot projects

RESEARCH DEMONSTRATION PROJECTS

Small-Diameter Round Timbers

One major focus area for the Technology Marketing Unit is promoting small-diameter round timbers (SDRT) for various applications. Efforts to thin overstocked forest areas to minimize future fire hazards will undoubtedly produce large volumes of small-diameter logs. Developing markets for this timber will become increasingly important.

Research at FPL is addressing technical issues in using SDRT. For example, researchers are studying new drying methods, developing special connections for round components, and addressing challenges posed by juvenile wood properties. Small-diameter logs have been found to have the required strength for use in structural building components.

To showcase a variety of connections that can be used in roundwood construction, a small-diameter demonstration structure (an octagonal park shelter) was designed and built by employees on FPL grounds. SDRT was also used for the vertical structural members in another type of small demonstration structure sponsored by FPL—two hexagonal information kiosks for the 2002 Winter Olympics in Salt Lake City, UT.

Research Demonstration House

Our newest structure at FPL is the Research Demonstration House, which serves as both an ongoing research laboratory and a showcase for innovative building materials. The Research Demonstration House was built in 2001 in partnership with the Southern Pine Council, APA—The Engineered Wood Association, the Advanced Housing Research Center at FPL, and Windsor Homes builders. This demonstration project is part of a national initiative, the Partnership for Advancing Technology in Housing (PATH), which was launched cooperatively by Federal agencies and the private sector in 1998. Partners include the National Association of Home Builders, product manufacturers, consumer groups, universities, and Federal, State, and local agencies.

The goals of the PATH initiative and the FPL Research Demonstration House are to:

- Illustrate proper design and construction practices for wood-framed house construction

- Serve as an ongoing field laboratory for research studies and design improvements

- Provide training material through video recordings of the construction process

- Showcase new building technologies and materials

One of the new building materials used in the Demonstration House is the composite roof shingle made from industrial waste wood and recycled milk jugs. These shingles are designed to have a service life of 50 years. The house also features wood flooring made from small-diameter Douglas-fir.

Water Filtration Systems

This brief overview of research activities at FPL concludes by highlighting wood fiber filters for removing water contaminants. Pilot projects demonstrate and monitor the effectiveness and cost of these filters in different applications. On the Wayne National Forest, wood fiber filters are being used to remove acidic heavy metals from acid mine drainage. In other demonstration projects, wood fiber filters are being used to remove nutrients and pesticides from agricultural runoff and oil from highway and parking lot runoff.

CONCLUSION

For more than 90 years, researchers at the Forest Products Laboratory have been studying ways to better utilize and conserve the forest resource. Major strides in technological knowledge and innovation have been achieved through a continued, steady research effort; through teamwork, partnership, and collaboration with researchers and support staff at universities and other organizations; and through communication and partnership with communities, both nationally and internationally.

ACKNOWLEDGMENTS

Information in this paper is based on material provided by staff of the Office of Communications and by many researchers at the Forest Products Laboratory.

CELEBRATING MINORITY INVOLVEMENT IN EXTENSION FORESTRY OPPORTUNITIES

William G. Hubbard and Ben D. Jackson[1]

Abstract—The Cooperative Extension System, consisting of federal, state and local partners assists local citizenry with educational solutions to problems and issues relating to forestry, agriculture, family and consumer sciences, youth and 4-H and other areas. This citizenry consists of persons of many colors and backgrounds. Increasingly the Extension Service, through the county Extension delivery system is working with nontraditional landowners. These are minorities such as African-, Hispanic- and Native- Americans and citizens with limited resources. Because of this, more minorities are needed in Extension to reach these "nontraditional and underserved" clientele groups. These groups may consist of forest landowners, urban residents, youth, policymakers and others. This paper reviews the Forestry and Natural Resources Extension infrastructure in the southern United States and discusses how minorities might get involved from the teaching and educational perspective.

INTRODUCTION

The Extension System within the United States of America consists of federal, state and local partners. The U.S. Department of Agriculture Cooperative States Research, Education and Extension Service (CSREES), state land-grant institutions and county governments make up this unique partnership. Their mission is to bring research and other knowledge to the people of the United States so as to improve their current economic, social, or environmental situations. Each partner brings something of importance to the table. U.S. Department of Agriculture CSREES provides federal oversight and directs resources approved by the federal legislatures through Congress for targeted programs. The state land-grant institutions including the 1862, 1890 and 1994 universities provide much of the research and knowledge generation and develop many of the technology transfer products. Finally the county Extension system utilizes grassroots approaches to deliver the information to the people. This same county-based system performs an equally important task in that the information needs of the citizens are delivered to the land-grant university and the federal partner to develop new research programs and the resources to deliver technology transfer back through the System.

Needs and opportunities for minorities and other nontraditional players abound within this system. First and foremost, there is a drastic need to more fully address the needs of the minority citizen. In forestry, thousands of African-Americans for example own forest land. They need assistance on how to manage and sell forest products, how to handle estate and heir situations and a host of other issues. Providing environmental education to minority youth is another example of a huge need within the Extension forestry arena. Too often, these young people live in urban environments with little or no connection to the environment. Studies have found that involving these youths in environmental education efforts has a tremendous impact on their self-esteem and confidence (Green 2000).

The workforce of the Extension Service will also need to be more diverse than it is today to handle the needs of addressing minority and underserved landowners. The 1862, 1890, and 1994 institutions need to work more closely together to develop joint programs that address the needs of the various forestry and natural resource clientele. Traditionally, these strengths have resided at the 1862 universities. Many of these institutions have formal, accredited forestry/natural resource programs. In 2002, Alabama A&M University, an 1890 institution located in Huntsville, AL became the first forestry school to earn its accreditation from the Society of American Foresters, which is the national forestry accrediting body. Other 1890 universities also have forestry and natural resource programs including Florida A&M University and Southern University in Louisiana. Efforts to provide employment opportunities for graduates of these programs will need to be stepped up within the Extension System if we are to have an impact on addressing the countless issues faced by minority and underserved audiences. As of 2003 only one 1890 institution had an Extension Forester (Tennessee State University) although others teaching and research faculty with outreach and service interests in forestry and natural resources exist.

This paper provides a summary of Extension forestry in the South along with notes on other needs and opportunities relating to minority hiring and programming within the Extension System.

A DYNAMIC HISTORY

The concept of Extension actually took root in the South. Dr. Booker T. Washington from Tuskegee University developed a specialized wagon that was used for demonstrations and farm and city visits. Here he and Dr. George Washington Carver highlighted results of research being conducted at Tuskegee and elsewhere. He and his colleagues showed both black and white farmers and sharecroppers how to be better farmers and businessmen. They and others also showed new improvements in the home economics (now referred to as family and consumer sciences) arena. Because of the success of their programs and the need to deliver more, the USDA and Tuskegee hired the first county agent of a Cooperative Extension Program in 1906 (Cooper 1976). It is interesting to note also that on that same day, the first county Extension agent to work in a county was hired in Texas. These modest beginnings have resulted in a nationwide system of county agents, state specialists and national program leaders who together comprise the Cooperative Extension System. Some estimates put the number of Extension Service employees at over 20,000 individuals with at least that many volunteering their time in Extension related activities. The System has an office or presence in just about every county in the country.

[1] William G. Hubbard, Southern Regional Extension Forester, and Ben D. Jackson, Extension Timber Harvesting Specialist, The University of Georgia, Athens, GA.

While agriculture, youth, and home economics dominated the scene for about the first 80 years of Extension's existence, forestry, natural resources and the environment are beginning to garner more interest and support. In 1978 Congress passed the Renewable Resources Extension Act with an authorized level of 15 million dollars to be doled out to the 1862 universities. The actual appropriated levels have fallen far short and have averaged around 3 million until recently when supporters were successful in raising this level to over 4 million dollars per year. Along with this raise in funds was the first ever across-the-board provision of funds to the 1890 institutions. Each 1890 institution received $10,000 in 2002 and $12,500 in 2003. The Act requires the resources be used for expanded Extension activities on private forest and rangelands including wildlife and fisheries management, youth/environmental education, forest management, urban forestry and wood products development (aquaculture, a strong focus at many 1890 universities is not included as a fundable RREA Extension option).

With state budgets declining in the late 1990's and early 2000's, the work of Extension foresters and natural resource professionals has taken on an added purpose. No longer can these professionals work in a vacuum. They are beginning to work more closely together across state lines with their colleagues. They are also realizing that many agencies are interested in education and have the capacity to provide these services to the same clientele that Extension has traditionally served. In light of this, Extension has had to reinvent itself as a collaborative player in the education game, not the sole provider. As a result, programs have become more robust and are beginning to reach more audiences with cutting-edge information.

Putting Extension Forestry Knowledge to Work in the 21st Century

Citizens, especially forest landowners, youth and policy makers have little knowledge or understanding of Extension forestry and natural resources. This is unfortunate since the educational assistance that is provided by these professionals can have a significant impact on the 10 million people in our country who own close to 400 million acres of forest land. These private forests help provide hundreds of thousands of jobs and billions of dollars to our economy. They also provide clean air and water, habitat for numerous wildlife species, and recreational opportunities from hunting to hiking to bird watching. There is also a tremendous need to educate new landowners as it is estimated that thousands of tracts of land are sold and subdivided each year. In addition the educational needs of our youth can be addressed through programs involving 4-H, Project Learning Tree and others. Finally, our public officials and policymakers need natural resource information to make informed decisions relating to the use of the land and the products it produces.

There are many different types of Extension forestry programs in the South and nationwide, ranging from traditional rural to progressive urban, and from pine silviculture management to hardwood multiple-use management. In the 90 years or so the Cooperative Extension System has been in existence, forestry, wildlife, and other natural resource specialists have helped citizens by "putting knowledge to work."

In the South over 140 forestry and natural resource specialists employed by universities and Cooperative Extension Services assist with educational programs like income and estate tax preparation, reforestation, timber and wildlife management, natural fisheries management, youth programs, urban forestry programs, forest products utilization, and a host of other natural resource-related programs. It has been a unique and highly successful relationship, albeit one whose effectiveness, might not be able to be evaluated for many years to come. Program planning is done to gather input and feedback from current and potential clientele, develop educational objectives, design effective programs and evaluate the impact.

Today's Extension forest resources specialists often work within the university environment. Some have "split" appointments combining their official Extension duties with those of teaching and/or research. Aside from university committees and responsibilities, these foresters must also devote time to developing a specialty area. In many cases they are granted promotion and tenure based on successful publishing and mastery in a specialty area. Combine this with the duty of responding to questions and developing programs and materials for forest landowners, farmers, youth, urbanites, decision and policymakers, and the general public, and Extension becomes one of the most fascinating but overwhelming natural resource professions today.

The actual number of Extension foresters, their responsibilities and the specific structure of Extension forestry vary tremendously by state and even by year within a state. Some states have numerous forestry and natural resource specialists at the state or regional level where others have only one or two (table 1). Understanding the university system also helps to understanding an Extension forester's duties and responsibilities. In some states, the specialist is a "100-percent" college of agriculture Extension employee while in other states they may receive some of their funding from the Extension System, forestry school or department itself. In most states, Extension foresters are located on campus, while in some instances state and regional specialists are located off campus in strategic locations close to key partners, the clientele base or for other geographical purposes.

Table 1—Extension forestry and natural resource personnel by appointment in the Southern United States (2003)

State	State specialists	Professional non-faculty	Area agents	County agents	Total
AL	7	1	0	0	8
AR	13.7	1	0	0	14.7
FL	3.6	1.5	0	2	7.1
GA	7	2.5	0	0	9.5
KY	6.5	1	0	0	7.5
LA	3.3	0	5	0	8.3
MS	11.3	9	1	2.1	23.4
NC	10.75	1	0	0	11.75
OK	3.25	1	0	0	4.25
SC	7.62	3	2	3.66	16.28
TN	5.93	1.4	0	0	7.33
TX	6.5	0	0	0	6.5
VA	8.91	4	3	0	15.91
Total FTE's	95.36	26.4	11	7.76	140.52
Average	7.34	2.03	2.03	0.85	0.60

FTE's = full time equivalents.

Regardless of where the forester is physically located, he or she works closely with the county Extension delivery system to provide programs to landowners and other audiences. He or she also works with state forestry and natural resource agencies in either a continuing education capacity or assisting county foresters, wildlife specialists and others with education and technology transfer to landowners and other forestry professionals. In the South for example, state forestry agencies employ somewhere in the neighborhood of 1,300 professional foresters. These individuals benefit from their association with the university and Extension. They utilize materials developed at the state level in their outreach programs to meet the educational needs of their clients. They also provide the Extension forester with valuable input regarding local interests and needs. Federal programs such as the Forest Stewardship Program (FSP), Forest Land Enhancement Program (FLEP), Conservation Reserve Program (CRP), and Urban and Community Forestry Program (UCF) have all provided opportunities for Extension and state forestry agencies to work closely together on educational activities. These relationships at the county level are important and necessary due to the lack of foresters and natural resource specialists in Extension at the county level. By some estimates, these specialists comprise less than 5 percent of all Extension employees.

EXTENSION IN ACTION

Due to the variety of Extension forest resource professionals employed in the South, programs are necessarily unique by state (table 2). One state may employ an urban forester to develop natural resource educational programs for city residents while another may have an individual interested in wildland-urban interface issues. Because of this, programs are often shared and duplicated regionally to the extent possible. Mississippi, for example has one of the few federal income tax specialists employed by Extension in the South.

Because of this sharing, Extension has developed a regional and national reputation in numerous areas. These include projects such as the Master Tree Farmer and Master Wildlifer satellite video conferences (cosponsored by Southern Regional Extension Forester, the U.S. Forest Service, Clemson University and others), the Urban Forestry Institute

(a continuing education course managed by the University of Florida, and the U.S. Forest Service for foresters, arborists and others working in cities and communities across the country and internationally), and the Southern Hardwood Management Manual (a Forest Service publication with numerous authors, including those with Extension appointments).

Extension accomplishes its mission through a variety of means, including traditional one-on-one conversations with foresters, forest landowners, teachers, etc., video and slide show productions, workshops, television and radio programs, newspaper articles and electronic media, including the Internet. This latter form deserves elaboration as it already provides great service for Extension because it stores, organizes, synthesizes, and transmits valuable forestry information to the many audiences served.

Access to the web now enables Extension to do things that even a few years ago were thought to be impossible. Imagine sitting down at a computer, much like you would in front of a television, and rather than flipping channels hoping to find something educational, you are able to locate the information you desire, view it on screen or print it out on your printer— perhaps it is information on new EPA regulations relating to harvesting in wetlands or the new tax code regulations that explain the capital gains treatment. Even better yet, streaming video is becoming more accessible so you can watch programs like the Master Tree Farmer and Master Wildlifer programs.

The Cooperative Extension System has taken a lead role in assisting their many audiences with the information explosion resulting from these new technologies. These technologies will allow the forest landowner to access forestry libraries, experts and a whole host of information through his or her computer. An insect or diseased plant can be imaged at the local county Extension office, transmitted via the phone line or cable to a state forest health Extension specialist and at the speed of light, an answer and recommendations can be sent back. Information that was just last year inaccessible to remote parts of the South will eventually come alive on the computer monitor.

Table 2—Extension forestry and natural resource full time equivalents (FTE's) by discipline in the Southern United States (2003)

State	Forestry	Continuing education	Urban forestry	Environmental education	Wood products	Wildlife	Total
AL	4.6	0	0.9	0	1	1.5	8
AR	4.4	1	0	6	0	3.3	14.7
FL	3.9	0.5	0	0.7	0	2	7.1
GA	5.25	0.5	1	2	0	0.75	9.5
KY	4.5	0	0	0	2	1	7.5
LA	6.4	0.5	0	0	0.4	1	8.3
MS	18.4	1	0	0	0	4	23.4
NC	5	1	0	1	3	1.75	11.75
OK	2	0	0	1	0.25	1	4.25
SC	11.67	1	0.79	1	0	1.82	16.28
TN	4.33	0	0	0	1	2	7.33
TX	2	0	1	0	0	3.5	6.5
VA	11.06	1	0	0	2.35	1.5	15.91
Total	83.51	6.5	3.69	11.7	10	25.12	140.5
Average	6.42	0.50	0.28	0.90	0.77	1.93	10.81

A listing of publications for 13 of the southern states and links to a variety of educational resources and related Web sites can be found at www.soforext.net and www.forestryindex.net.

EXTENSION FORESTRY IN THE FUTURE

High technology or not, forestry Extension specialists have a responsibility to provide factual information. Today's environmentally sensitive climate illustrates the unique role university Extension foresters play in disseminating information. Agencies such as the United States Department of Interior's Fish and Wildlife Service (USDI-FWS), and the Environmental Protection Agency, for example, have been given regulatory powers over certain forest management practices. In recent years, these issues have become very contentious and resulted in many public debates regarding private property rights and sustainable forestry. Cooperative Extension in many southern states has acted, through their forest management and related resource specialists as a moderating and facilitating force in these battles. Although everyone has an opinion, and there is no such thing as an unbiased viewpoint, Extension foresters hold the unique position of assisting in conflict resolution and consensus building in a neutral arena by virtue of their employment as a public education provider. These are relatively new areas for many Extension foresters, who for most of their careers, have focused on providing educational services relating to the biological and managerial aspects of tending forests.

Developments in the past few years in the forest industry have also demonstrated the importance of university-based educational assistance. Through the Sustainable Forestry Initiative®, for example, the American Forest and Paper Association has embarked on an intensive campaign to assist their members (forest products companies of varying sizes), those who harvest timber from company and private nonindustrial lands and others in the practice of sustainable forestry. Two components of this initiative are reforestation information for non-industrial landowners and logger education. Extension is assisting with these efforts in most of the southern states. The results have been that we have a better educated logging industry that provides more economical and environmentally sound service to the private landowners, and a better educated private landowner with regards to reforestation opportunities, best management practices, wildlife management, etc. These new programs add to an already comprehensive relationship between the forestry and forest products industries and the university Extension specialists.

CONCLUSION

As the Southern forestry community prepares for the new century, its key players of landowners, industry, environmental groups, non-governmental organizations, government and university will need to work together on various educational fronts to include reaching out to more potential underserved employees and clients. First of all, in an increasingly urbanized society, the forestry community needs to develop an educational strategy for both youth and adults that centers around sustainable forest management. People of all backgrounds and cultures need to understand that to continue to use wood and paper products like they do will require the harvest of trees, and that these trees, regardless of which region or even country they come from need to be managed in a sustainable fashion. Extension foresters will continue leadership roles in this educational arena; however, all members of the forestry community will need to participate in the process. On the other educational fronts, emphasis will continue to be needed in providing quality information to private landowners, the natural resource professionals, and the forest industry professionals. Bringing more minority professionals on board will assist with many of these efforts.

REFERENCES

Cooper, J.F. 1976. Dimensions in history. Tallahassee, FL.

Green, G.T. 2000. The effect of an outdoor recreation program on the resilience of low income, minority youth. Thesis (Ed.D.). University of Georgia. Athens, GA.

Hubbard, B.; Jackson, B. 2001. Extension forestry: knowledge at work in the twenty-first century. Forest Landowner. Vol (60) No. 3: 5-10.

THE ROLE OF NAFTA IN INTERNATIONAL TRADE OF FOREST PRODUCTS

Zacch Olorunnipa[1]

Abstract—The role of NAFTA in international trade of forest products was examined in this paper. It was shown that the gradual removal of tariffs and other trade barriers has led to substantial expansion of trade in forest products and other products. It was also shown that, NAFTA countries (Canada and the United States in particular) were the most dominant exporters and importers of all wood products traded in the world between the years of 2000 and 2004. The paper also offers some suggestions for increasing the participation of minority professionals in international trade of forest products.

INTRODUCTION

The acronym NAFTA stands for North American Free Trade Agreement—a tri-country trading block involving the United States, Canada and Mexico. The North American Free Trade Agreement (NAFTA) which became effective in January 1994, was created to achieve the following major objectives: (a) to contribute to the expansion of world trade; (b) to create, expand and secure markets for the goods produced in members' territories; (c) to reduce distortions in trade; (d) to create new employment opportunities; (e) to improve working conditions and living standards in member's territories; and (f) to address related environmental and conservation issues.

Operationally, NAFTA specifically calls for the gradual removal of tariffs and other trade barriers on most goods (including forest products) produced in North America. Kouparitsas (1997) has observed that, in addition to tariff reform, there are three broad agreements on non-tariff barriers (NTBs). First, all countries will eliminate prohibitions and quantitative restrictions applied at the border, such as quotas and import licenses. Second, the three countries

have agreed not to impose new user fees and to phase out existing user fees by June 1999. Third, NAFTA will permit eligible business people to bring in the tools of their trade, such as professional samples and other goods, on a duty free basis. NAFTA also includes investment provisions that reduce the barriers to capital flows between the parties.

It has now been about a decade since NAFTA became effective. To what extent has NAFTA achieved its stated objectives? What economic impacts has NAFTA made in general? More specifically, what contributions has NAFTA made to international trade in forest products? What is the status of minority professionals' participation in global forest product trade? These major issues are addressed in this paper.

The paper is organized into six sections: Section one contains the introduction while section two presents (in tabular form) the historical development of NAFTA. A review of selected literature regarding the impact of NAFTA is provided in section three. Available data with respect to the share of NAFTA in global trade in forest products are

Table 1—Historical development of the North American Free Trade Agreement (NAFTA)

Dates	Major development
October 3, 1987	President Reagan sent notice of intent to sign a trade agreement with Canada to the U.S. Congress to initiate the "fast track" approval process.
January 2, 1988	Free Trade Agreement (FTA) between the United States and Canada was signed by the leaders of the two countries.
January 1, 1989	United States and Canada FTA took effect. It calls for the elimination of all import tariffs over 10 years (by January 1, 1998).
August 21, 1990	The Mexican government sent a formal request to the United States to enter into FTA negotiations.
September 25, 1990	President George H.W. Bush notified the U.S. Congress of his intent to negotiate a FTA with Mexico.
February 5, 1991	United States, Mexico, and Canada announced their intention to pursue a North America Free Trade Agreement.
June 1991	NAFTA talks began. Agenda included market access, trade rules, sciences, investment intellectual property rights, and dispute settlements.
December 17, 1992	United States, Canada, and Mexico signed the NAFTA, which includes the provision to eliminate many of the agriculture trade barriers existing among the three countries.
November 17, 1993	U.S. Congress passed the NAFTA.
January 1, 1994	NAFTA became effective.

[1] Professor, Florida A&M University, Agribusiness Program, Tallahassee, FL.

analyzed and discussed in section four. The focus of section five is on the status of participation of minority professionals in international trade of forest products. Finally, section six concludes the paper.

HISTORICAL DEVELOPMENT OF NAFTA
What initially started as a bilateral trade agreement between two countries (the United States and Canada) was the "embryo" that developed to become NAFTA after about a 6-year period of incubation. It all began in 1987 when the "father" of NAFTA, President Reagan, notified the Congress of his intention to sign a trade agreement with Canada and initiated a "fast track" approval process. By January 2, 1988, a Free Trade Agreement (FTA) was signed by the leaders of the two countries – President Reagan of the United States and Prime Minister Mulroney of Canada. The FTA called for the elimination of all import tariffs over 10 years, by January 1998. This probably motivated the Mexican government who applied and was formally admitted into the FTA in 1991. Other significant stages passed through by NAFTA prior to its inception in 1994 can be seen in table 1.

PREVIOUS STUDIES ON THE IMPACT OF NAFTA
Several reports and studies have evaluated the impact of NAFTA on various sectors of the economies of the countries in NAFTA. The U.S, Department of Commerce, Trade Information Center reports on its Web site that since the implementation of NAFTA in January 1994, trade among its three member countries has increased by more than 200 percent. While discussing the role of NAFTA on U.S. wood exports, Baachelda 1999 opined that "Few would question that U.S. wood product sales to Mexico have benefited from the North American Free Trade Agreement (NAFTA). NAFTA's market access provisions seem to have softened the impact of the peso devaluation on U.S. wood exports by reducing or eliminating tariffs on U.S. forest product exports to Mexico" (p.1). According to the estimates provided by Bolle 2000, employment in Alabama has enjoyed a net gain of 2,000 jobs in 5½ years due to NAFTA.

Using time series analytical procedures, Thompson 2002 estimates that NAFTA has had a net positive impact on forest products. His results show the net effect of NAFTA on Alabama pulpwood production as an average annual increase of 3 percent with softwood production increasing an average of 8 percent, and hardwood production declining an average of 6 percent annually. Prestemon and Buongiorno 1966 employed the partial equilibrium model to predict the effects of NAFTA on Mexico's imports of intermediate wood products, scrap and waste paper, pulp, and newsprint from the United States and Canada. The study showed that the value of Mexican imports of forest products from the United States and Canada would increase by 21 percent to 85 percent. Additionally, Mexican imports of fir lumber, hardwood lumber, softwood plywood, and newsprint from the United States were projected to increase the most, while imports of particleboard, hardwood veneer, scrap and wastepaper, and wood pulp were projected to be the least affected because of lower initial tariffs and inelastic demand.

In a recent review of NAFTA's decade of existence, the Office of the United States Trade Representative (OUSTR) has noted on its Web site that the dismantling of trade barriers and opening of markets have led to economic growth and rising prosperity in the United States, Mexico and Canada.

Furthermore, it is estimated that the total volume of trade among the three NAFTA partners expanded from $289.3 billion in 1993 to $623.1 billion in 2003. According to this report, each day NAFTA countries conduct nearly $1.7 billion in trilateral trade. Finally the report assert that "In the ten years since NAFTA, productivity rose 28 percent in the United States from 1993 to 2003, in Mexico up 55 percent and in Canada up 23 percent" (OUSTR 2004).

NAFTA AND GLOBAL TRADE IN FOREST PRODUCTS
The importance of forest and forest products in the economic development of the NAFTA countries cannot be over emphasized. According to the Food and Agricultural Organization (FAO) data, about 25 percent of the area of NAFTA countries is forest land. Approximately, 15 percent of the world's forest area is located in NAFTA countries. Canada and the United States together produce 40 percent of the world's industrial roundwood and over one-third of all processed wood products, including almost half the world's paper pulp (FAO 2001).

Numerous factors including global population increase, technology, affluence, and trade liberalization have led to noticeable growth in world trade in forest products both in value and volume. Trade in primary forest products such as logs, sawn wood, panels, pulp, and paper reached nearly $273 billion in 1997 (Bourke and Leitch 1998). Using FAO estimates, Bourke and Leitch report that the consumption of roundwood increased by about 40 percent between 1970 and 1996. They noted further that fuelwood consumption expanded more rapidly than industrial roundwood consumption, increasing by 57 percent to 1,864 million in 1996.

The international trade in forest products is highly concentrated geographically, with developed countries accounting for most of the international trade in forest products. According to the FAO report, only plywood exports are dominated by developing countries, with Indonesia alone accounting for 41 percent, and Malaysia accounting for an additional 20 percent (FAO 2001).

The global trade status of all wood products from 2000 to 2004 can be seen in figures 1 and 2. These figures indicate that two of the countries in NAFTA, Canada, and the United States were respectively the most dominant exporter and importer of wood products. Among the 10 major exporters and importers of all wood products reported in figures 1 and 2, NAFTA countries (excluding Mexico) contributed about 49 percent of total export and 37 percent of total imports in 2000. By 2004, NAFTA's contribution to the global all wood products export had declined slightly to 41 percent while its contribution to global all wood products import had increased considerably to 51 percent.

Canada and the United States are consistently the first and third largest exporters of wood products each year from 2000 to 2004. These same countries also rank first (U.S.) and fourth (Canada) as importers of wood products during the same period (2000 to 2004). The value of Canadian export of wood products increased from about $13.8 billion in 2000 to about $17.0 billion in 2004. The value of U.S. imports of all wood products grew substantially from about $15.5 billion in 2000 to about $23 billion in 2004.

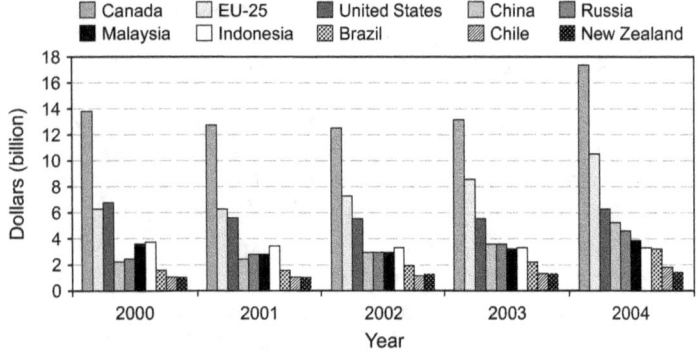

Figure 1—Global exports—all wood products.

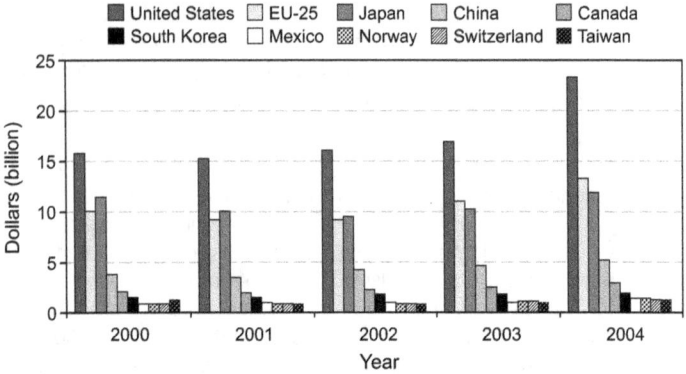

Figure 2—Global imports—all wood products.

PARTICIPATION OF MINORITY PROFESSIONALS IN INTERNATIONAL TRADE IN FOREST PRODUCTS

Data is hard to come by regarding the current level of participation of minorities in international trade of forest products in the NAFTA countries. However, all indications suggest that this participation is at best very low. This assertion is based on the findings of previous related studies. For example, Kuhns and others (2002) reported that women and minorities are under-represented in the urban forestry/ arboriculture profession in the United States. This trend of under-representation is likely to spill over to trade in forest products.

One of the major objectives of NAFTA is to improve working conditions and living standards in members' territories. Without any doubt, the economic well-being of the minority communities in NAFTA countries is inextricably linked to their involvement in business activities. Therefore, to increase the level of participation of minorities in international trade of forest products, each country should consider the following suggestions:

- Create incentives to attract more minorities to train and pursue careers in forestry and related fields

- Disseminate information on business opportunities on forest products to minorities

- Organize training for minorities on export and import procedures and requirements

- Establish and update data banks on minorities in forest products business in each country

- Operate International Trade Loan (ITL) to provide short-term and long-term loans to small businesses involved in export/import of forest products

- Organize international trade fairs to specifically feature forest products and provide incentives for minorities to participate

CONCLUSION

This paper has examined the role of NAFTA in international trade of forest products. A historical development of NAFTA was presented. It was evident that, after a decade of existence, NAFTA had made significant contributions to the economic development of its member countries. The gradual removal of tariffs and other trade barriers has led to substantial expansion of trade in forest products and other products. It was also shown that NAFTA countries (Canada and the United States in particular) were the most dominant exporters and importers of all wood products. However, it was noted that the participation of minorities in international trade of forest products was dismally low. Suggestions were offered for remedying this situation.

REFERENCES

Baachelda, C.1999. "As its economy improves, Mexico buys more U.S. forest products." AgExporter, July, 1999.

Bolle, M. 2000. NAFTA: Estimated US job "gains" and "losses" by State over 5 ½ years, Congressional Research Report. Washington DC.

Bourke, I.J.; Leitch, J. 1998. "Trade Restrictions and their Impact on International Trade in Forest Products." FAO, Rome, 1998.

Food and Agricultural Organization (FAO). 2001. State of the World's forests. Rome. Italy, 2001.

Kouparitsas, M. 1997. A dynamic macroeconomic analysis of NAFTA in economic perspective. www.questia.com/Index.jsp?CRID=nafta&OFFID=se1&KEY=nafta.

Kuhns, M.R.; Bragg, H.A.; Blahna, D.J. 2002. Involvement of women and minorities in the urban forestry profession. J. Arboric. 28(1): 27-34.

Office of United States Trade Representative (OUSTR). 2004. NAFTA: A decade of success. http://www.ustr.gov/Document_Library/Fact_Sheets/2004/NAFTAA_Decade_of_Success.html.

Prestemon, J.P.; Buongiorno, J. 1996. The impacts of NAFTA on U.S. and Canadian forest product exports to Mexico. Canadian Journal of Forest Research. 26: 794-809.

Thompson, H. 2002. "A Time Series Analysis of the Impact of NAFTA on Alabama Pulpwood Production." International Studies Program Working Paper Series, at AYSPS, GSU paper0206, International Studies Program, Andrew Young School of Policy Studies, Georgia State University).

U.S. Department of Commerce, Trade Information Center. North American Free Trade Agreement, how can U.S. companies benefit. http://www.ita.doc.gov/td/tic/fta/NAFTA/.

MINORITIES, AN UNDER-REALIZED MARKET SEGMENT IN NATURAL RESOURCE-BASED RECREATION: POTENTIAL ECONOMIC RETURNS TO DIRECTED MARKETING

Michael Thomas[1]

Abstract—A review of several recent studies of recreational value (consumer surplus) and economic expenditures generated by resource-based recreational activities shows disproportionately low participation rates by minorities for many of these activities. For example, in Florida, demographic minorities (e.g., African-American, Hispanic and Asian) seldom participate in activities such as beach visits, biking, boating, and hunting. Using estimates of value generated to the majority market segment (European-Americans) and assuming comparable participation rates, it becomes possible to estimate the potential economic impact of directed marketing efforts toward minority segments.

INTRODUCTION

Public agencies charged with managing natural resources for recreational activities are required to be responsive to the public by providing recreational opportunities for all. For many agencies such as the U.S. Forest Service, National Park Service and many State wildlife and park agencies, this has meant providing a variety of recreational facilities for the public at-large. These often include things such as campgrounds, picnic areas, beach access/frontage, boat ramps, and piers—almost anything that complements the native natural resource.

Yet, simply providing facilities for the public may not be enough. These agencies must also be sensitive to the wide variety in public opinions and make an effort to accommodate their multiplicity of preferences. For example, if efforts by the U.S. Forest Service were to focus exclusively on camping to the exclusion of other opportunities, unless camping is enjoyed broadly by society, the agency may fail to equitably address the desires of other societal segments.

Improving participation among underrepresented groups should not be simply a question of equity but also a degree of efficiency. The possibility exists of generating additional value to the public (classically termed consumer surplus in economics texts) by more effectively employing an underutilized resource. The better marginal use of these public resources may pay large dividends to society. If a particular market segment is not utilizing a public good because of poor information, large transactions costs or other barriers, there should be no appreciable cost burden to existing users caused by adding new and differently-valued uses. The exceptions to this are congestible goods, where additional use can add a burden to all current users. However, before overcrowding becomes an issue, additional public use of these resources should not be viewed as a zero sum game until the point where congestion (overcrowding) is realized. Previously, the restricted use of certain public resources may result in a limited choice of activities. For example, tradition or historic precedent may deter "nontraditional" forms of recreation from being added to the array of "traditional" campground activities.

Reviewing the results of several recent recreational studies in Florida, it is possible to determine if a select group of traditional forms of recreational activity enjoy a wide degree of support across racial and ethnic segments. If some forms of these traditional forms of recreation have a strong, but narrow, degree of support, public agencies may want to consider how to increase market share among these underrepresented groups.

STUDY OBJECTIVES AND METHODOLOGY

Using recent demographic data from four recreational surveys in Florida, this study will determine if minorities participate in significantly lower proportions than their composition in the local communities for several traditional resource-based recreational activities. When this condition exists, an estimate of potential value (consumer surplus) will be made by projecting on minorities, visitation rates comparable to the majority users, and calculating the potential consumer surplus by using generic estimates for the value of these recreational activities.

To document the phenomena of disproportional use and potential consumer surplus, four recent studies (within the past six years) of recreational activities will be reviewed. These studies include a wide variety of outdoor natural resource-based recreational activities including pier use (fishing and sight seeing), boating, saltwater beach use and biking/skating.

For each case, the actual participation rates are compared to the study area's demographic composition to determine the level of underrepresentation, if any. The estimate of potential visits is then calculated by assuming the underrepresented group could participate at the same level as the principal group. This potential rate is then multiplied by the minority's demographic composition in the region or state, and the total number of visits for the activity in question to produce the potential number of visits. Visits are either taken directly from the case study or gleaned from the Florida Statewide Comprehensive Outdoor Recreation Plan (SCORP) (Florida Department of Environmental Protection 1994). To estimate the potential consumer surplus or value, the potential visits are multiplied by an estimate of the per user benefit for activity participates as reported by Rosenberger and Loomis (2001).

[1] Program Leader and Associate Professor, Agribusiness Program, College of Engineering Sciences, Technology and Agriculture, Florida A&M University, Tallahassee, FL.

RESULTS

Case 1—Florida pier use (fishing and related activities)

The first case is based on the results of a statewide survey of public pier users in Florida (Thomas and Stratis 2001). Conducted in 2000 by the Florida Fish and Wildlife Conservation Commission, this study was an effort to document the economic impact of expenditures related to the use of public piers and boat ramps. The survey considered questions such as primary activity while visiting the pier, reasons for the visit, ideal features desired by the visitor and their basic demographics, including gender and race. Table 1 shows the participation rates by race and ethnicity compared to their statewide composition based upon the 2000 U.S. census.

Note that white nonHispanics and blacks participate at higher rates than their demographic composition (72.5 percent vs. 65 percent and 20.1 percent vs. 14.6 percent, respectively) and that other race/ethnicity groups participate at lower rates. The participation rates and demographic proportions are all significantly different at the 95 percent level or better. Using the SCORP visitation data and Rosenberger and Loomis (2001) estimates of activity value ($31.88 value per trip), the potential statewide annual gain for the underrepresented groups of Hispanics and Asians is in excess of $10 million and $2 million, respectively (table 1).

Case 2—Tallahassee, Florida biking and skating trail

A study by Lorenzo (2002) in Tallahassee, FL to determine attitudes and demands for a rail-to-trail park revealed a slightly different outcome. During his survey of 209 users of the St. Marks Bike Trail during the summer of 2002, he found white nonHispanics comprise a disproportionately large part of the users with all minorities underrepresented. Table 2 displays the biking and skating participation rates by race and ethnicity compared to their Leon County composition based upon the 2000 U.S. census.

White nonHispanics, Asians and other minority groups participate at higher rates than their demographic composition in the Tallahassee and Leon County area (82.1 percent vs. 66.4 percent, 2.5 percent vs. 1.9 percent and 6.2 percent vs. 1.5 percent, respectively) and that Hispanics and blacks participate at rates lower than their composition proportions. All participation rates differ significantly from their demographic representation at the 90 percent level or better.

Combining the SCORP statewide visit data and the Rosenberger and Loomis (2001) estimates of value derived from biking ($10.51 value per trip), the potential economic value for underrepresented groups in Florida is in excess of $130 million statewide, annually (table 2).

Case 3—Brevard County, Florida boating study (fishing excluded)

During the spring of 2001, Thomas (2001) conducted a survey of 636 people who recreationally engage in boating activities. The participants were divided into groups that primarily fished while in their boat (fishing-from-boat), and those who simply boated (recreational boating). White nonHispanics and Asians recreationally boated in disproportionately larger proportions than their county-wide makeup (92.8 percent vs. 83.7 percent and 2.3 percent vs. 1.5 percent, respectively), with blacks, Hispanics and other minorities underrepresented in the activity. Table 3 presents the recreational boating participation rates by race and ethnicity compared to their Brevard County composition based upon the 2000 U.S. census. All participation rates differ significantly from their county level demographic representation at the 95 percent level or better.

Turning to the SCORP report for statewide visit data and the Rosenberger and Loomis (2001) estimates of value for boating ($24.82 value per trip), the potential value summed across minorities is nearly $5 million annually (table 3).

Case 4—Brevard County, Florida boating study (fishing only)

Turning next to those Brevard County boating participants primarily fishing from their boat, Thomas (2001) found that white nonHispanics and Asians participated disproportionately more often than their county-wide makeup (92.8 percent vs. 83.7 percent and 2.3 percent vs. 1.5 percent, respectively), with blacks, Hispanics and other minorities underrepresented in the activity. Table 4 presents the fishing-from-boat participation rates by race and ethnicity compared to their Brevard County composition based upon the 2000 U.S. census. All participation rates differ significantly from their demographic representation at the 95 percent level or better.

Combining the SCORP report for statewide visit data and the Rosenberger and Loomis (2001) estimates of value derived from recreational saltwater fishing ($31.88 value per trip), the potential value to underrepresented groups is approximately $20 million per year (table 4).

Case 5—Beach Use in Florida

In 1994, Tomasi and Thomas (1997) conducted a statewide telephone survey of 2,020 people who had visited a Florida beach over the past 12 months. They found that white nonHispanics use the beach in disproportionately larger numbers than their statewide makeup, with blacks, Hispanics, Asians and other minorities underrepresented in the activity (85.6 percent vs. 65 percent, 4.2 percent vs. 16.8 percent, 8.1 percent vs. 14.6 percent and 0.9 percent vs. 2.7 percent for white nonHispanic, Hispanic, black and Asian, respectively). Table 5 presents the beach participation rates by race and ethnicity compared to their statewide composition based upon the 2000 U.S. census. All race and ethnicity groups participate at rates significantly different than their proportions in Florida at the 95 percent level or better.

Using the SCORP report for statewide visit-occasion data and the Rosenberger and Loomis (2001) estimates of value derived from recreational saltwater beach visits ($30.00 value per trip), the cumulative potential gain in total value to underrepresented minorities is nearly $200 million annually (table 5).

DISCUSSION AND CONCLUSION

There is the potential for substantial economic return from improved marketing to underrepresented groups. Looking at only five select "traditional" forms of natural resource dependent recreational activities, there is at least $300 million in lost potential value. Additionally, this is an annual loss and only represents a few forms of recreation in Florida.

The five cases presented demonstrate a wide variation in the use of natural resource-based services by race and ethnicity. While some may argue this validates a form of de facto discrimination, another, market/economic based

Table 1—Participation rates, value, and potential economic gains by race and ethnicity for pier use in Florida

Race/ethnicity	Census proportions	Participation rate	Two standard errors of mean	Visits	Value dollars	Potential gain in value dollars
White (non-hispanic)	.650	.725	.0137	1,918,592	61,164,702	NA
Hispanic	.168	.044	.0028	116,439	3,712,065	10,461,000
Black	.146	.201	.0111	531,913	16,957,386	NA
Asian	.027	.002	.0011	5,293	168,730	2,109,128
Other	.009	.002	.0011	5,293	168,730	590,000

Table 2—Participation rates, value, and potential economic gains by race and ethnicity for bicycling and skating in Florida

Race/ethnicity	Census proportions	Participation rate	Two standard errors of mean	Visits	Value dollars	Potential gain in value dollars
White (non-hispanic)	.664	.821	.0200	43,486,000	457,045,000	NA
Hispanic	.035	.012	.0016	635,000	6,680,000	12,803,000
Black	.291	.080	.0102	4,237,000	44,535,000	117,462,366
Asian	.019	.025	.0034	1,324,000	13,917,000	NA
Other	.015	.062	.0041	3,284,000	34,515,000	NA

Table 3—Participation rates, value, and potential economic gains by race and ethnicity for recreational boating in Florida

Race/ethnicity	Census proportions	Participation rate	Two standard errors of mean	Visits	Value dollars	Potential gain in value dollars
White (non-hispanic)	.837	.928	.0054	1,781,000	44,207,000	NA
Hispanic	.046	.003	.00002	5,000	142,000	2,048,000
Black	.084	.031	.0024	59,000	1,476,000	2,524,000
Asian	.015	.023	.0068	44,000	1,095,000	NA
Other	.018	.015	.0011	28,000	714,000	143,000

Table 4—Participation rates, value, and potential economic gains by race and ethnicity for recreational fishing-from-boats in Florida

Race/ethnicity	Census proportions	Participation rate	Two standard errors of mean	Visits	Value dollars	Potential gain in value dollars
White (non-hispanic)	.837	.928	.0054	6,085,000	194,016,000	NA
Hispanic	.046	.003	.00002	19,000	627,000	8,989,000
Black	.084	.031	.0024	203,000	6,481,000	11,080,000
Asian	.015	.023	.0068	150,000	4,808,000	NA
Other	.018	.015	.0011	98,000	3,136,000	627,000

Table 5—Participation rates, value, and potential economic gains by race and ethnicity for recreational saltwater beach use in Florida

Race/ethnicity	Census proportions	Participation rate	Two standard errors of mean	Visits	Value dollars	Potential gain in value dollars
White (non-hispanic)	.650	.856	.0051	26,118,000	783,540,000	NA
Hispanic	.168	.042	.0022	1,281,000	38,430,000	115,323,000
Black	.146	.081	.0031	2,471,000	74,130,000	59,496,000
Asian	.027	.009	.0004	274,000	8,220,000	16,476,000
Other	.009	.003	.0001	91,500	2,730,000	5,492,000

and proactive viewpoint would consider this information as motivation for better marketing and preference research. Essentially there are two approaches policymakers may take to improve conditions for these underrepresented groups: improve the marketing of existing recreational services and/or discover and invest in new recreational services.

Better promotion of existing services would mean reaching and educating underrepresented groups as to the current forms of recreation and the potential benefits they provide users. For example, one approach might be a campaign promoting beach related activities via minority targeted media. If the preferences of minorities are similar to those of the majority, a targeted effort will likely be successful. However, if minority preferences are significantly different or if they face significant financial or social constraints limiting their access, these efforts will likely fail.

An alternative approach would involve learning more about minority preferences for resource based recreational services. This may involve extensive marketing research and gaining a more thorough understanding of alternative recreational activities. Using a traditional activity as an example, if African-Americans regard fishing as a highly desired activity involving natural resources, policy makers may want to take this into consideration when allocating funds between boat ramp and pier construction. If a policy maker desires to redirect funds that were originally designated for, say boating, to this underrepresented group, they may want to select facilities that permit improved fishing from the shore at the expense of more boat ramps.

To acquire these potential benefits for an economy, a better understanding of minority tastes and preferences is essential and may return large benefits to both the minority segments and the economy as a whole. Assuming that public managers of natural resources are to serve the entire market, it becomes increasingly important to first recognize these large discrepancies in market participation and second to close the gap, generating increased economic value and efficiency. To better gage the gambit of potentially new activities and/or how an agency might reach minority market segments, it is reasonable to increase the involvement of the same minorities within agencies responsible for providing resource-based activities.

REFERENCES

Florida Department of Environmental Protection. 1994. Florida's Statewide Comprehensive Outdoor Recreation Plan. Division of Recreation and Parks, Office of Park Planning. Tallahassee, Florida.

Lorenzo, A. 2002. Unpublished report on the use of the St. Marks bike trail. College of Engineering Sciences, Technology and Agriculture, Florida A&M University, Tallahassee, Florida.

Rosenberger, R.; Loomis, J. 2001. Benefit transfer of outdoor recreation use value. U.S. Dept. of Agriculture, Forest Service. General Technical Report RMRS-GIR-72.

Thomas, M. 2001. Schedule of estimated regulatory cost to amend the Brevard county manatee protection rule (68C-22.006, FAC). A supporting survey use to determine the economic impact of amending the existing rule. Tallahassee, FL: Florida Fish and Wildlife Conservation Commission.

Thomas, M.; Stratis, N. 2001. Assessing the economic impact and value of Florida's public piers and boat ramps: A final companion report to the executive document of March 2001. Tallahassee, FL: Florida Fish and Wildlife Conservation Commission.

Tomasi, T.; Thomas, M. 1997. Natural resource damage assessment for the Tampa Bay oil spill: recreational use losses for Florida residents. Unpublished report to the Florida Department of Environmental Protection submitted by the Environmental Economics Research Group, Lansing Michigan.

SESSION VIII

Urban and Community Forestry

Presiding Moderator:

Vernise Travis Miller
Ford Foundation

EDUCATIONAL OPPORTUNITIES IN THE APPLICATION OF GEOGRAPHIC INFORMATION SYSTEMS IN URBAN AND COMMUNITY FORESTRY

Tommy L. Coleman, Wubishet Tadesse, and Teferi D. Tsegaye[1]

Abstract—As we continue to move forward into this millennium, humanity is becoming more vigilant in improving the appearance of its urban cities and communities. The primary focus of these initiatives is the establishment and/or improvement of forests in urban cities and communities. On the surface, this may appear to be a simple task; however, the establishment and maintenance of trees in urban areas are met with several infrastructural and environmental pollution problems that encompass all parts of the forest environment, namely the soil, water, and air of our urban area. Trees are constantly bombarded with toxic air created by the release of oxides of sulfur, nitrogen, and carbon from our factories and automobiles. These sources also release small minute particulate matter into the atmosphere known as PM10 and PM2.5 that affect the respiratory process of plants. Also, trees are affected by water pollution that occurs as atmospheric oxides of nitrogen and sulfur are absorbed by rain droplets and by runoff water from city streets and exposed areas of bare soil.

The infusion of Geographic Information Systems (GIS) technology into educational programs involving urban and community forestry is one means of examining the effects of pollutants on urban and community forest species. It is essential that city planners and decisionmakers have access to the most modern technology possible as they expand and redesign our urban areas. Improvements in GIS technology have made it possible for planners to have access to comprehensive systems comprised of digital data layers of their city's land area, transportation network, surface hydrology, utilities, recreational, housing, and industrial areas on a desktop computer. A working knowledge of GIS tools will afford planners an opportunity to assess the impact of their plans on communities and urban areas before actual implementation of the plans. This paper addresses the GIS education program at Alabama Agricultural and Mechanical University (AAMU) and its application in training students in several degree programs.

INTRODUCTION

The AAMU Department of Plant and Soil Sciences (SPS) has been involved in the training of minorities in the application of remote sensing (RS) and GIS technology for over 20 years. In the early years, training was limited to a few undergraduates involved in work study programs and graduate students pursuing a Master of Science (M.S.) degree in soil science, environmental science, plant science, and forest operations management. Today, both undergraduate and graduate students have an opportunity to pursue a degree with a minor in RS/GIS technology whose academic degrees are from the departments of Plant and Soil Sciences, Community Planning and Urban Studies, Computer Sciences, Civil Engineering, and Electrical Engineering.

This paper addresses the infusion of GIS technology into educational programs involving urban and community forestry. Urban forestry is the management of publicly and privately owned lands, in and adjacent to urban areas. More specifically, urban forests include many different environments such as green belts, parks, street rights-of-way, residential areas, reserved lands, industrial and commercial parks, underdeveloped and speculative land, flood plains, parking lots, adjacent agricultural lands, and rivers and watersheds (Wenger 1984). It is essential that city planners and decisionmakers have access to the most modern technology possible as they expand and re-design urban areas. Improvements in GIS technology have made it possible for students and professional planners to have access to comprehensive systems comprised of digital data layers of their city's land area, transportation network, surface hydrology, utilities, recreational, housing, and industrial areas on a desktop computer. At Oregon State University, students evaluate alternative treatments for a research and teaching forest using a stand development model that incorporates crown and wood quality attributes (Marshall and others 1997). A working knowledge of GIS tools will afford planners an opportunity to assess the impact of their plans on communities and urban areas before actual implementation of the plans.

The succeeding paragraphs describe the GIS program and training opportunities at AAMU's Center for Hydrology, Soil Climatology, and Remote Sensing (HSCaRS) laboratory. The course requirements for a minor in RS/GIS, for undergraduate and graduate students and short courses (certificate) available for current professionals are presented.

DISCUSSION

Course Requirements

The Department of Plant and Soil Science offers degree programs in Forestry, Environmental Science, and Plant Science. Students who choose to major in Plant Science may specialize in either Horticulture or Crop Science and minor in RS/GIS. In the Environmental Science degree program, students can specialize in Soil Science or Environmental Science with a minor in RS/GIS. Students who choose a degree in Forestry have the option to specialize in Forest Management or Forest Science with a minor in RS/GIS. Further specialization or emphasis area within these programs may be selected, with the help of a departmental advisor (Alabama A&M University 2001).

The minor in RS/GIS supports AAMU's National Aeronautics and Space Administration (NASA) University Research Center in HSCaRS. It fulfills a major Center objective, namely, increasing the number of underrepresented minorities in NASA-related scientific fields. The list of courses and credits available for students to select in order to qualify for the RS/GIS minor is provided in table 1.

[1]Tommy L. Coleman, Professor, Wubishet Tadesse, Assistant Professor, and Teferi D. Tsegaye, Associate Professor, Center for Hydrology, Soil Climatology, and Remote Sensing (HSCaRS), Department of Plant and Soil Sciences, Alabama A&M University, Normal, AL.

Table 1—List of courses available for remote sensing/geographic information system minor

Prefix	No.	Course title and credits
		Undergraduate
SPS	365	Introduction to Geographic Information Systems and spatial analysis—3 credits
SPS	366	Climate and global change—4 credits
SPS	465	Applications in geostatistics—3 credits
SPS	471	Use and interpretation of aerial photography—3 credits
SPS	474	Remote sensing of the environment I—4 credits
SPS	481	Hydrology and watershed management—3 credits
EE	303	Electromagnetic field theory—3 credits
EE	304	Numerical methods & digital computations—3 credits
EE	410	Microwave engineering—3 credits
CMP	204	Visual programming—3 credits
MTH	383	(CMP 305) Numerical analysis—3 credits
CMP	409	Computer graphics—3 credits
		Graduate
SPS	565	Applications in geostatistics—3 credits
SPS	571	Use and interpretation of aerial photography —3 credits
SPS	574	Remote sensing of the environment I—4 credits
SPS	576	Quantitative approaches in remote sensing—3 credits
SPS	581	Hydrology and watershed management—3 credits
SPS	775	Advanced principles of Geographical Information Systems—4 credits
SPS	776	Quantitative approaches in remote sensing—3 credits
SPS	778	Remote sensing of the environment II—3 credits
SPS	779	Advanced environmental geostatistics—3 credits
CMP	501	Organization of digital computers—3 credits
CMP	503	Unix and C programming—3 credits
CMP	515	Numerical analysis—3 credits

SPS = plant and soil sciences; EE = electrical engineering; CMP = computer science; and MTH = mathematics.

Students at the undergraduate level must select a combination of courses that equals 18 credit hours and must include SPS 365, 465, and 474. If the courses are included in their major degree area, they can select others from the list to fulfill the 18 credit hour requirement. Graduate students must also complete 18 credit hours at the graduate level with the inclusion of SPS 565, 574, 576/776, 775 and 778. The courses identified at the 500-level series are for M.S. students and the 700-level series are for Doctoral students. Also, if the courses are currently listed in the student's major degree area, another course from the list must be selected to complete the 18-credit hour requirement.

To support the course instruction activities for the RS/GIS minor is the extensive HSCaRS research program that provides unique opportunities for undergraduates and graduate students to gain valuable experience in their chosen field of study. HSCaRS has three state-of-the-art fully equipped laboratories dedicated to remote sensing and GIS instruction and research. They include two indoor laboratories for data entry, analysis, visualization and display (figs. 1A and 1B), and an outdoor laboratory for data gathering and monitoring local conditions (fig. 2A).

The laboratories are equipped with both computer hardware and software used by industry and Federal and State agencies that employ individuals trained in RS and GIS technology.

The outdoor research and teaching laboratory known as the Alabama Mesonet (ALMNet) is comprised of 7 fully equipped weather stations and 21 soil profile stations that continuously record selected meteorological and environmental flux data (fig. 2A). It is located in North Central Alabama covering Madison County and portions of Jackson, Limestone, Marshall, and Morgan Counties encompassing an area of 6300 km2. Seven of the sites [the Winfred Thomas Agricultural Research Station (WTARS), Hytop, Newby Farm, Hartselle USDA, Stanley Farm, and Hodges Farm] are also listed in the Soil Climate Analysis Network (SCAN) sites of the National Water and Climate Center (NWCC) of the U.S. Department of Agriculture (USDA), Natural Resources Conservation Service (NRCS). The complete distribution of the SCAN sites throughout the United States is given in figure 2B. The AAMU HSCaRS Research Center and the NWCC have established a long-term agreement (Agreement No. 68-7482-2-9Y) for the purpose of collecting hydro-meteorological information from northern Alabama and thereby expanding the NRCS SCAN Network. The seven weather stations and soil profile stations located at each SCAN site referenced above are fully automated and provide near real-time observations at five-minute intervals that are averaged and transmitted every 60 minutes to the NWCC and HSCaRS for quality control checking and dissemination. The data collected at each weather station include relative humidity, radiation, rainfall, air and soil temperature, wind speed, and wind direction. The five soil profile stations located at each of the SCAN sites are comprised of soil moisture and soil temperature sensors dispersed within a radius of 10m of each weather station. The soil moisture sensors records soil moisture fluxes at five depth intervals from 5 cm to 102 cm (2 to 40 inches). The soil temperature sensors also record soil heat fluxes at five depth intervals from 5 cm to 102 cm.

These data from the seven SCAN sites are available in near real-time at the following web page address: http://www.wcc.nrcs.usda.gov/scan/Alabama/alabama.html. Additionally, graphical displays of the data from each of the seven ALMNet SCAN sites are available at http://wx.aamu.edu/ALAMNET.html (figs. 3 through 7). Figure 3 is a representation of the

Figure 1—HSCaRS research (A) visualization (B) laboratories.

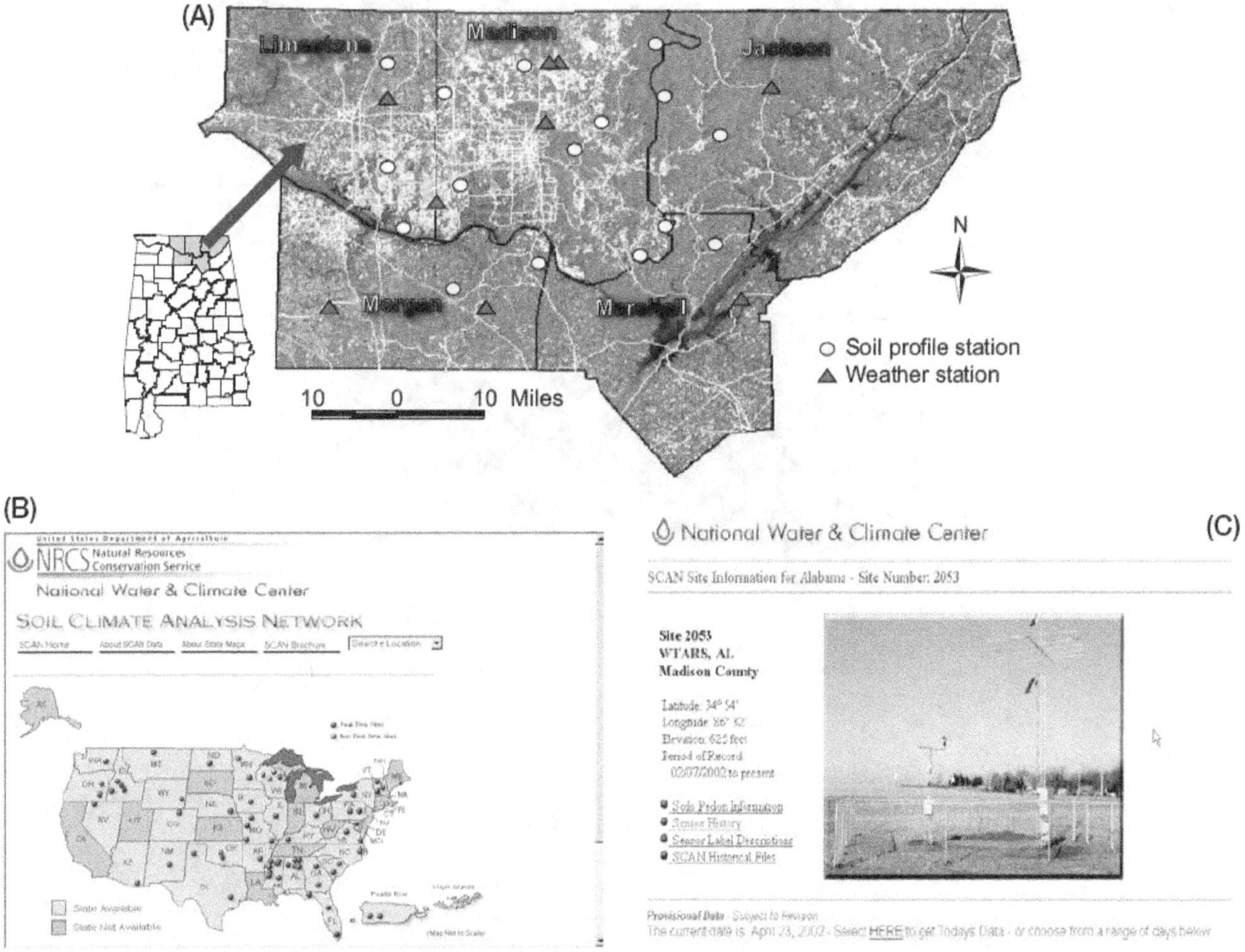

Figure 2—Location of the Alabama Mesonet (ALMNet) - (A) weather stations and soil profile stations, (B) locations of SCAN sites in the United States, and (C) view of instrumentation at the Winfred Thomas Agricultural Research Station SCAN site.

ALMNet web page that shows the location of the weather stations or SCAN sites and soil profile stations on a backdrop of a digital elevation model (DEM) of the area. The seven ALMNet SCAN stations that transmit data back to the NWCC and HSCaRS are shown at the bottom of the web page. Interested parties only need to click on the button to obtain the data recorded at any of the SCAN sites. Figure 4 is a display of the web page for Mr. Thornton Stanley Farm located in Morgan County, AL. Monthly plots of the data recorded at this site can be accessed by clicking on the desired date and data needed. Examples of the type of graphical plots that can be produced from these data are provided in figures 5, 6, and 7. The monthly plot of precipitation during August 2002 at the AAMU campus site is shown in figure 5. Figure 6 is a plot of the volumetric soil moisture at the AAMU campus site during August 2002 at five depths. A plot of the soil temperature at the AAMU site is shown in figure 7.

In addition to these seven sites, there are sixteen other soil profile stations (fig. 2A) dispersed over the 6300km2 area that are equipped with soil moisture and temperature sensors, soil heat flux plates, and a tipping bucket rain gauge. The soil moisture sensors records soil moisture fluxes at five depth intervals from 5cm to 102cm. The soil temperature sensors records soil heat fluxes at three depths 5cm, 10cm, and 20cm. Soil heat flux-plates records the soil heat-flow at 5cm and 10cm in watts/m2. These data are recorded at 15-minute intervals and stored on data loggers. The data are downloaded every 2 weeks and transported to HSCaRS for quality control checking and dissemination. Additionally, laboratory measurements of the thermal conductivity, diffusive and specific heat capacity of the soil at each soil profile station are available.

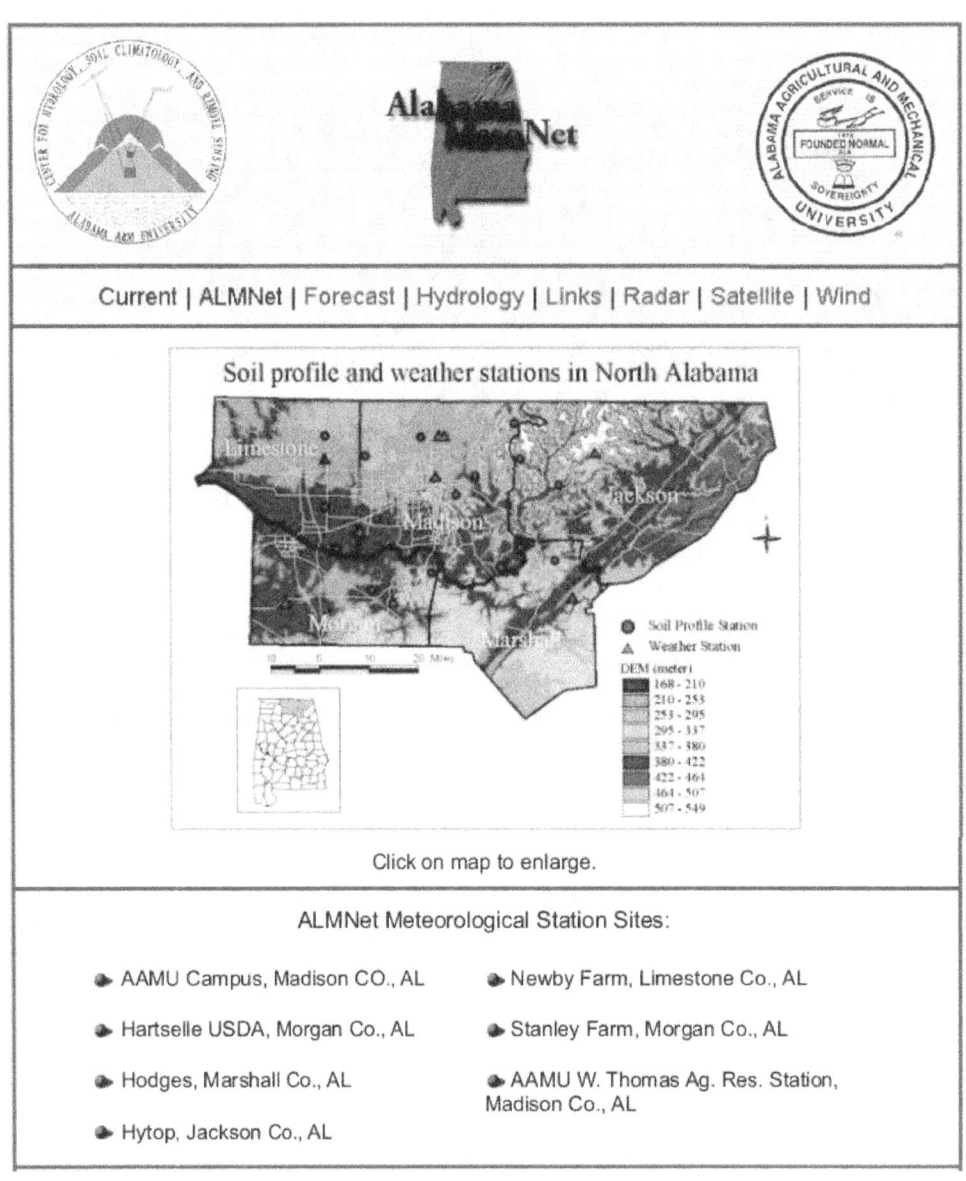

Figure 3—Web page for ALMNet showing the seven SCAN sites in Alabama.

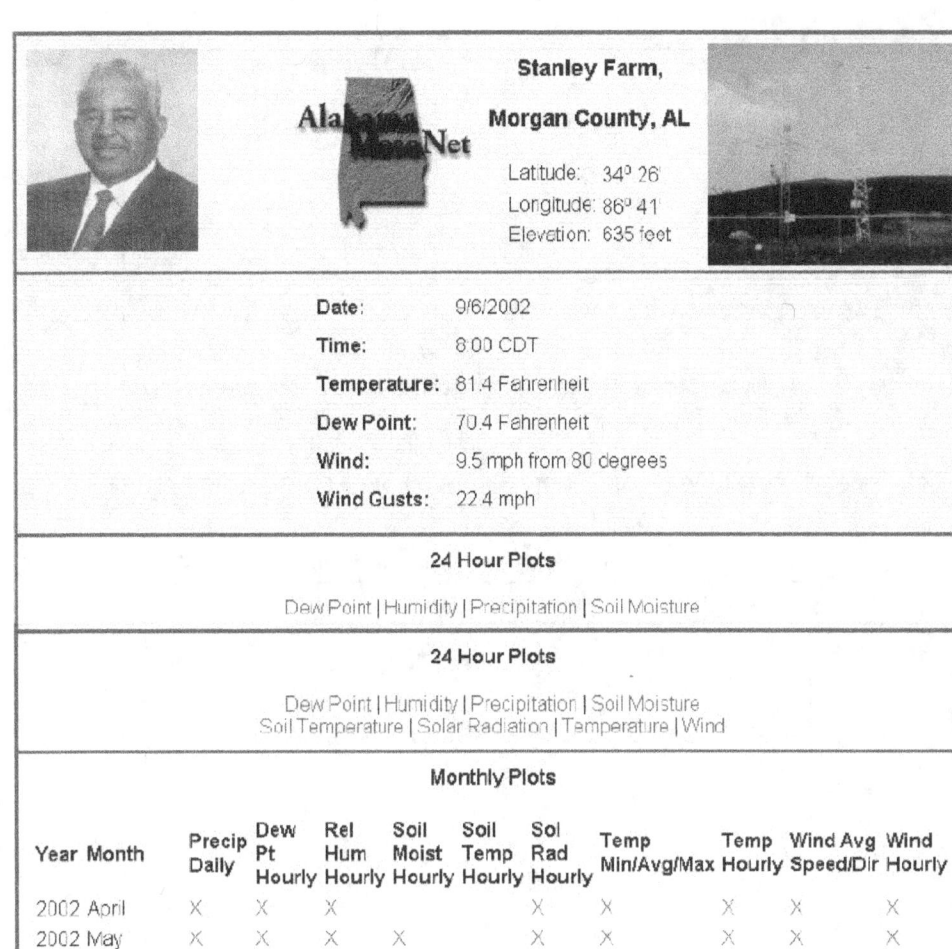

Stanley Farm,

Morgan County, AL

Latitude: 34° 26'
Longitude: 86° 41'
Elevation: 635 feet

Date:	9/6/2002
Time:	8:00 CDT
Temperature:	81.4 Fahrenheit
Dew Point:	70.4 Fahrenheit
Wind:	9.5 mph from 80 degrees
Wind Gusts:	22.4 mph

24 Hour Plots

Dew Point | Humidity | Precipitation | Soil Moisture

24 Hour Plots

Dew Point | Humidity | Precipitation | Soil Moisture
Soil Temperature | Solar Radiation | Temperature | Wind

Monthly Plots

Year Month	Precip Daily	Dew Pt Hourly	Rel Hum Hourly	Soil Moist Hourly	Soil Temp Hourly	Sol Rad Hourly	Temp Min/Avg/Max	Temp Hourly	Wind Avg Speed/Dir	Wind Hourly
2002 April	X	X	X			X	X	X	X	X
2002 May	X	X	X	X		X	X	X	X	X
2002 June	X	X	X	X	X	X	X	X	X	X
2002 July	X	X	X	X	X	X	X	X	X	X
2002 August	X		X	X	X	X	X	X	X	X
2002 September	X	X	X	X	X	X	X	X	X	X

Records / Averages

January | February | March | April | May | June | July
August | September | October | November | December

For more information about this station click here. This site is part of the USDA NRCS SCAN network, and is operated in cooperation with the Alabama A & M University HSCaRS Center ALMNET.

Current | ALMNet | Forecast | Hydrology | Links | Radar | Satellite | Wind

Figure 4—Website of the Stanley Farm SCAN site.

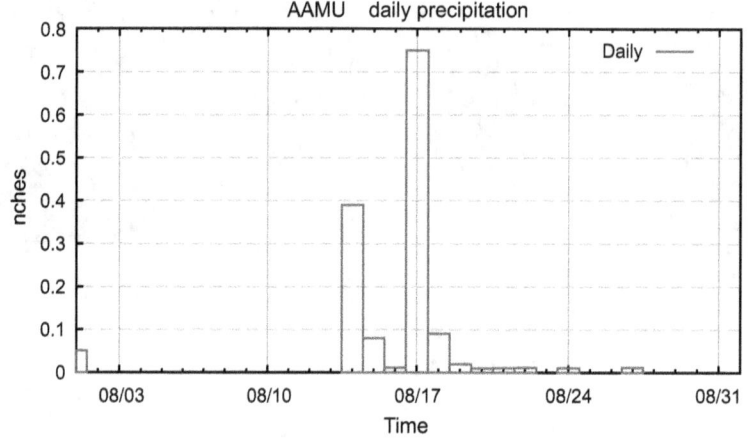

Figure 5—Plot of August 2002 monthly precipitation at the Stanley Farm SCAN site.

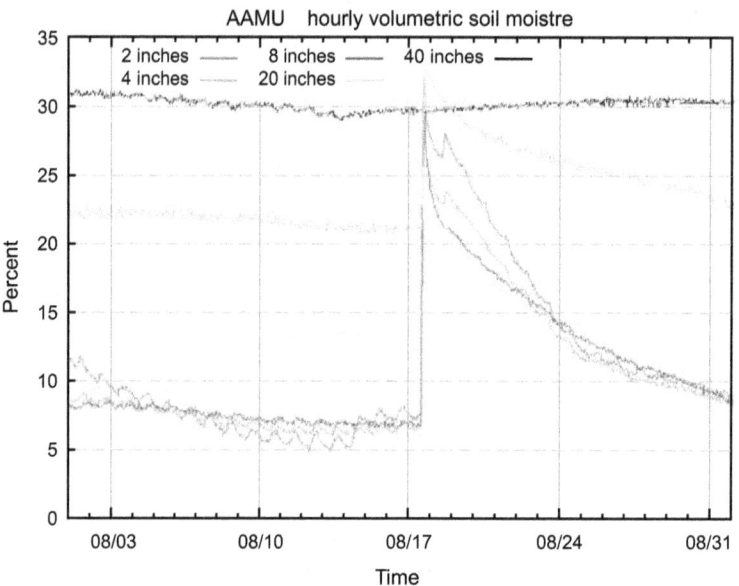

Figure 6—Plot of August 2002 hourly volumetric soil moisture at the AAMU Campus SCAN site.

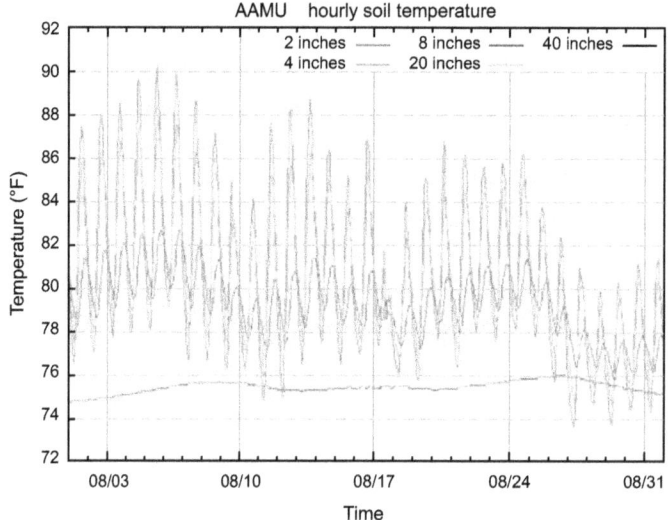

Figure 7—Plot of August 2002 hourly soil temperature at the AAMU Campus SCAN site.

Uses of the Program

Since the initial introduction of GIS instruction at AAMU in the early 1980s, a number of students have taken advantage of this technology to enhance their job opportunities with industry and Federal and State agencies. The expansion of the HSCaRS Research Center in 1995 provided a unique opportunity for students to gain hands-on experience with the use of GIS and RS technology tools applicable to their scientific field.

The initiation in 1996 of the annual HSCaRS' Summer Enrichment Program (SEP) that is designed to attract high-quality minority and female students has proven to be highly successful in introducing students to this technology. Since 1996 over 100 undergraduates have gained experience in the use and application of GIS and remote sensing technology as SEP interns. Our graduate students have also benefited from HSCaRS by receiving financial assistance and opportunities for a more in depth study of GIS and RS applications. Since 1996, we have supported 25 graduate students at the Master and Doctoral levels.

The establishment of the minor in RS/GIS technology has afforded HSCaRS and AAMU faculty an opportunity to train a greater number of students in the use of GIS and RS technology tools. The resources of the on-campus facilities in HSCaRS are extensively used by students and are upgraded annually to enable students to be trained on current versions of the industry's leading software.

The data collected by ALMNet are used to fulfill several research and teaching objectives of HSCaRS: validate data recorded by satellite and aircraft sensors that monitor the Earth's surface, support classroom instruction and graduate student activities by providing data for student projects, support the outreach activities of HSCaRS by providing data for students who participate in our annual Summer Enrichment Program and professional development short courses in RS and GIS.

SUMMARY

Urban and Community Forestry is one such area where decisionmakers can effectively use GIS tools in their work environment and gain enormous benefits. Today, communities are challenged with trying to accommodate new growth while maintaining the integrity of the existing neighborhoods and protecting the environment. A well designed and comprehensive GIS developed for these communities will afford planners and decisionmakers opportunities to test their plans before implementation. The GIS allows for smart growth of communities, better placement of urban trees, and transportation networks, as well as designing drainage and excess water flow from paved and densely populated areas. The GIS allows for a landscape-scale approach to planning thus enabling individuals to see the entire picture and the interrelationship of urban areas, rural communities, and our natural environments.

ACKNOWLEDGMENTS

The authors acknowledge the assistance of the HSCaRS faculty and staff. Acknowledgement is also extended to Dr. Rory Fraser for the information on urban and community forestry, the Department of Plant and Soil Science, and the Agricultural Experiment Station, AAMU Journal No. 503. Support was provided by NASA Grant No. NAG5-10721. Any use of trade product or firm name is for descriptive purposes only and does not imply endorsement by the U.S. Government.

REFERENCES

Alabama A&M University Undergraduate bulletin (2003-2005). 4900 Meridian Street, Huntsville, AL 35762.

Marshall, D.D.; Johnson, D.L.; Hann, D.W. 1997. A Forest Management Information System for Education: Research and Operations. J. of Forestry, 95 (10):29-30.

Wenger, K.F., ed. 1984. Forestry handbook, second edition. Urban forestry-section 16. John Wiley & Sons. New York: 887-906.

FOREST SERVICE'S APPROACH TO URBAN FORESTRY

Ed Macie[1]

Abstract—The U.S. Forest Service's role in Urban and Community Forestry is examined, starting with the program's enabling legislation, traditional activities, and delivery through the agency's many partners. Future challenges to urban forestry resulting from demographic changes and urbanization of the Southern landscape are addressed, using the Wildland-Urban Interface as a case study. Conclusions suggest research and information needs, opportunities in working with the public to address complex resource management issues, and leadership challenges for urban forestry practitioners.

INTRODUCTION

Urban Forestry, broadly defined, is the establishment, maintenance and improvement of trees where people live, work, and play. The traditional underpinnings of this profession have been focused on individual trees under public ownership, such as trees along public streets and within city parks, an emphasis on planting and maintenance, and with the objective towards beautification. A general increase in awareness of the benefits of urban trees, supported by urban forestry research, has resulted in a shift in the focus of urban forestry towards the management of ecosystems for a broad range of economic, social, and environmental benefits to society. The U.S. Forest Service has played a critical role in promoting these urban forestry values through the agency's broad Urban and Community Forestry Assistance program authority. This paper describes this authority and the Forest Service delivery of urban forestry programs, then further describes by way of case study, emerging needs and opportunities, which will define the future of urban forestry.

URBAN FORESTRY AND THE FOREST SERVICE

The Forest Service was first given the authority to deliver urban forestry programs in the late 1970's with an Urban and Community Forestry Assistance subtitle in the Cooperative Forestry Assistance Act of 1978. This authority was expanded in the 1990 Farm Bill to better define the agency role in urban forestry, to better enable the Forest Service to contribute to the evolution of the profession, and to better prepare for and work with State Forestry Agencies to address emerging issues related to urban natural resource.

Findings and General Authority and Purpose

The findings of Congress in establishing this Forest Service program authority showed their recognition and awareness of the multiple benefits urban forests offer to society, as well as the importance and need for society to actively maintain and improve the value of these resources. By paraphrasing these findings, the intent of Congress to provide the Forest Service a broad authority to work in urban forestry can be reduced to two simple points: (1) trees in our cities are good; they improve our environment, social well being, quality of life, sense of community, and put money in our pocket; and (2) trees in our cities are in decline, we need to learn more about them, teach and inform people, and get people involved. By establishing a national program, Congress granted the Forest Service authority to encourage tree planting and protect existing open spaces in urban areas and to strengthen research, education, technical

assistance, and public information programs which promote urban forestry. This authority further established an agency role to provide financial, technical, and related assistance to state forestry agencies so states could provide the same assistance to local units of governments and others, such as nongovernmental or nonprofit organizations.

The Urban and Community Assistance Act established a financial assistance program with the primary purpose of building capacity, at the state and local level. This assistance is intended to (1) improve the understanding of the benefits of tree cover in urban areas; (2) encourage the maintenance and expansion of tree cover on private properties; (3) provide education programs and technical assistance to state and local organizations and schools to encourage maintenance and expansion of forest cover in communities; (4) provide assistance through competitive matching grants awarded to local units of government, nonprofit organizations, and volunteer tree groups for urban and community forestry projects; (5) implement a tree planting program; (6) promote the establishment of demonstration projects in urban and community settings to illustrate the benefits of forest cover; (7) enhance technical and understanding of sound tree maintenance and arboricultural practices including practices involving the cultivation of trees, of individuals involved in the planning, development, and maintenance of urban forests; and, (8) expand existing research and educational efforts intended to improve the understanding of tree growth and maintenance, and the economic, environmental, social and psychological benefits of trees and forest cover in urban environments.

Urban Forestry Program Partners

The Urban and Community Forestry Assistance Act establishes State Forestry Agencies as primary partners in the delivery of the program. In the southern United States the Forest Service works closely with the individual 13 states of the Southern Region and with all the states collectively through the Southern Group of State Foresters. Through this partnership the States and Forest Service establish program priority and direction. Urban and Community Forestry Assistance funds are distributed through the states, to expand state capacity for urban forestry program delivery, and for grants to local units of governments or nongovernmental organizations.

Many other partner organizations participate and benefit from the Urban and Community Forestry Assistance Program. These include colleges and universities, State cooperative extension programs, regional and national nonprofit

---

[1]Regional Urban Forester, U.S. Forest Service, Southern Region, Atlanta, GA.

organizations, professional and trade organizations, and state urban forestry councils.

Beyond working with these traditional partners, the Forest Service is elevating the stature of the Urban Forestry Program within the agency. In the South two centers have been established to coordinate technology transfer efforts. The Southern Center for Urban Forestry Research and Information, in Athens, GA, focuses urban forestry on issues, while the Southern Center for Wildland Urban Interface Research and Information, in Gainesville FL focuses more on issues related to human influences on forest landscapes. Some urban forestry research is being conducted by way of cooperative agreements through these centers, and these programs of research will hopefully be expanded. Many of the National Forests in the South are also addressing urban forestry issues as urbanization near and adjacent to the forests are placing pressures on how these forests are managed. These pressures include recreation demands, conflict and impacts, law enforcement issues, forest health issues, communities risk issues, and special use permits (particularly with respect to infrastructure demands from adjacent communities. It is these types of challenges that introduce the very complex future for urban forestry.

THE LONG VIEW

The population in the South has increased dramatically over the last 10 years and is expected to grow to over 114 million people by the year 2020. This dramatic growth, coupled with economic and land use policy in the region, has resulted in heavy urbanization. Along with this urbanization comes a physical change to the landscape, challenges to how we manage natural resources, challenges to how the natural resource community works with people, and finally, the emergence of knowledge gaps and scientific uncertainties.

These challenging issues create a strong mandate for urban forestry programs at all levels, from grass roots up to the federal level. Practice in urban forestry will require work with a broader constituency because the population is becoming more diverse and older, and this diversity represents different interests with respect to natural resources. These multiple interests will also become evident through a greater number of landowners, particularly in the interface between cities and the rural communities, owning smaller parcels of land and managing (or not managing) this land with multiple ecological objectives. There will also be a greater emphasis on conservation programs to offset the consequences of urbanization. With conservation occurring at the state and local level will also come a demand for land managers who understand the balancing act required to work with so many stakeholders, for multiple objectives, with ecological intent, and across multiple jurisdictions.

HUMAN INFLUENCES ON FOREST ECOSYSTEMS

Many of the emerging issues related to the future of urban forestry and the management of natural resources were documented in a recent assessment of the Wildland Urban Interface, conducted by the U.S. Forest Service Southern Region and the Southern Research Station (Macie and Hermansen 2002). Wildland urban interface can be defined as an area where increased human influence and land use conversion are changing natural resource goods, services, and management. This area is where forests are becoming urban forests.

The assessment of the interface in the South was conducted from a cause and effect perspective across disciplines, with a focus on why interface was occurring in the region, what the implications of rapidly changing land use patterns and urbanizations are, and what our future information and research needs are to begin addressing these issues.

Common Themes
While conducting the assessment, major themes emerged which best describe the complicated nature of future issues.

The first theme is that wildland urban interface issues are about people. A rapidly growing population and how this population is transforming the landscape profoundly affects natural resources in the South. This increase in population is in part due to migration from other parts of the country, immigration from abroad, and by an aging (longer living) population. People are simply living longer. With more people comes a greater diversity of attitudes and perceptions, and priorities, even with respect to how the landscape is used or managed. What results is a "value gradient" across demographics and across the landscape from the city center to the rural hinterlands.

Public policy is an expression of people's values, and this becomes the second theme. In the wildland urban interface we see public policy both creating problems and providing solutions. There is a broad range of policy issues at various levels of government, which affect natural resources in the wildland urban interface. These issues could include transportation and land use policy, economic and taxation policy and a broad array of environmental policy at the federal, state and local level. At the local level it is not uncommon for the same jurisdiction to establish and work with policy that promotes development while also having policy that encourages conservation. It is also possible for policy to exist in conflict; for example a policy to conduct prescribed burns on federal land to reduce hazardous fuels may be in conflict with federal clean air standards. As the South becomes increasingly urbanized, public policy will begin to reflect the values, attitudes, and perceptions of urban constituencies. The policy arena is certain to create professional demands for the natural resource manager who will need to sit at the policy table to articulate policy needs and impacts related to resource management.

The third theme is that resource management challenges occur across multiple ownerships, multiple jurisdictions, and at various landscape scales. This results in part from changing land ownership patterns, land use change and urbanization. There are many more private landowners in the South than there were in the past, and the average size of private nonindustrial forest land ownership is increasingly smaller. Managers are faced with very limited small-scale management options. Across the landscape the land ownership mosaic is also made up of industrial forest and nonforest holdings, federal, state, and local public lands, developed land, institutional land, among others. This mosaic results in risks and concerns at the landscape or watershed scale. The environmental quality of a region or the management needs of a forest don't stop at property boundaries, yet not every property owner holds the same management objective, nor do they hold the same value, attitude, or priority. As risks to communities and forest health increase, the need to manage across policy units and ownership boundaries will create opportunities for the resource manager to work with multiple stakeholders through collaborative processes.

The final theme is that wildland urban interface issues should be addressed from an interdisciplinary perspective. No single issue can be understood without also understanding relationships. The following example illustrates this point. A community recognizing the need to diversify their economy embarks on establishing a developmental highway system to stimulate economic development. This results in migration of people from other parts of the region, new subdivisions, and urban sprawl. The rapid land conversion results in forest fragmentation, and loss of prescribed burning as a management tool because of fire-highway smoke conflicts. These changes subsequently result in increasing risks to forest health. These conversions are also ultimately resulting in the loss of ecosystem goods and services, most notability, increases in storm runoff and decreases in water quality. The community ends up raising taxes to build infrastructure to address the water quality issues. The loss of ecosystems services and higher tax rates become quality of life issues that make it difficult to attract more industry. While this scenario is an oversimplification, it does point out how connected issues are in the wildland urban interface, as well as the need to take a long view in understanding how policy decisions might affect natural resources.

CONCLUSION

The future presents many challenges for the natural resource manager in urban and urbanizing areas. These challenges call for a greater diversity in the urban forestry workforce, a greater ability for the urban forestry manager to work with people, more research, science based management, a greater use of technology, management for multiple objectives, and programs to address multiple scale and jurisdictional issues.

The general intent and specific purposes, as well as the flexibilities and partnerships written into the authority given to the U.S. Forest Service to deliver the Urban and Community Forestry Assistance Program, are highly consistent with the critical natural resource needs and emerging issues resulting from demographic shifts, changing land use patterns, and urbanization. By working with the State Forestry Agencies and other critical partners, the Forest Service is better equipped to enable natural resource managers to do their job. Through the Urban and Community Forestry Assistance Program, an integrated approach to addressing resource issues can be taken. This includes conducting research and technology exchange to put the best available information in the hands of decisionmakers and managers, conducting demonstration projects through The Urban and Community Forestry Assistance grants program, supporting grass roots participation and ownership in influencing local natural resource participation by establishing communication networks, and by building a broad based awareness and expertise to address urban natural resource issues.

REFERENCES

Macie, E.A.; Hermansen, L.A. 2002. Human influences on forest ecosystems: The Southern Wildland Urban Interface Assessment. Gen Tech. Rep. SRS-55. Asheville, NC: U.S. Department of Agriculture, Forest Service, Southern Research Station. 159 p.

THE ROLE OF GEOGRAPHIC INFORMATION SYSTEMS AND REMOTE SENSING IN URBAN FORESTRY EDUCATION AT SOUTHERN UNIVERSITY

Fulbert Namwamba[1]

Abstract—Southern University, Baton Rouge (SUBR) was the Nation's first program offering the 4-year B.S. degree in Urban Forestry. The role of Geographic Information Systems (GIS) and Remote Sensing (RS) in Urban Forestry was incorporated into the curriculum right from the beginning and has grown into a vital component. The program has fully fledged GIS/RS laboratories and initiatives, which have resulted into the leading GIS initiative at Southern University. This paper outlines the role of GIS and RS in Urban Forestry, and traces the historical perspective of GIS development in 1890 land grants schools and historically black colleges and universities (HBCU) as a whole. The paper explores advantages of mapping trees and the entry of data into GIS programs. Finally the paper describes the facilities available at SUBR Urban Forestry program, and spells out the vision, challenges and future of GIS at Southern University and forestry sciences related programs at 1890 land grant schools.

INTRODUCTION

Urban Forestry Program History

The Urban Forestry program at Southern University is the first 4-year Urban Forestry BS degree-granting program in the Nation. It was established in 1992, with $650,000 seed money and a 5-year grant from the U.S. Forest Service. Keeping with the land-grant mission of the university, the program has 3 areas namely (1) education (2) research, and (3) outreach. Geographic Information Systems (GIS) plays a major role in all three pivotal roles. The program has 6 full time faculty, a post-doctoral associate and 4 staff. The undergraduate program offers a Bachelor of Science in 2 options, Urban Forestry Science, and Urban Forestry Management and Policy. The graduate program offers a Masters of Science degree in Urban Forestry.

The teaching projects have focused on the innovative use of computers and modern equipment to enhance teaching and recruitment while the research projects have focused on using state-of-the-art technology to develop technological-based forest management methods from innovative scientific techniques. This technology-based approach has good potential for contributing to economic development.

What is GIS?

GIS is a set of computer hardware, software and databases for the capture, storage, analysis, and display of spatial data. Godfrey (2001) reports that unlike a CAD map, a GIS map has the power of a database behind it; with GIS, the database can be queried. For example, with tree survey information attached to a GIS map that includes tree points, it could be queried to find out how many trees are in poor condition or any other attribute that is recorded in the database. The trees in question will highlight in color. Visualizing the tree data is easier, making GIS a very powerful tool for the management of urban forestry data.

What is Remote Sensing?

The Earth is continuously monitored from dozens of satellites orbiting the planet collecting data. Other responsible imaging vehicles are airplanes and space shuttles. This process is called remote sensing (RS). The ability of satellites to image the earth is well known but there are some limitations to this process, like the effects of rain and cloud cover. These two atmospheric conditions cause problems with topographic photography of the Earth's surface, especially with forestry applications, since the majority of the world's forests are in tropical areas where cloud cover is almost year around.

GIS at SUBR Urban Forestry Program

As an education tool, GIS is critical as a training tool in all aspects of urban forestry. GIS fulfills the role of a vital computer skill required for maintaining urban forestry inventories and databases. Because of this, Southern University's Urban Forestry graduates are acquiring the required computer skills to compete in the job market, as well as being able to perform complex tasks required of a 21st century forestry sciences professional. SUBR Urban Forestry graduates will have basic skills in desktop GIS, spatial analysis, image analysis and the basics of remote sensing. The research at the Department involves the following areas, Global Change, Climate Change Assessment, Air Pollution Study, Hydrology and GIS, Pathology, Urban Forest Eco-physiology, and Urban Forest Assessment. Even though GIS is defined as a research area, in reality GIS is also a useful tool in all other research areas. GIS is useful for preparing inventories and databases for Urban Ecosystem Analysis models useful in Global Change, and Climate Change assessment. GIS has also been a critical tool for hydrology and air pollution research, as well as urban forest assessment. In the outreach initiative, GIS has been utilized in Green Infra Structure projects in the city of Baton Rouge, LA as well as with Baton Rouge Green, a nonprofit nongovernmental organization. The question is why is GIS so important in Urban Forestry?

STATUS OF GIS EDUCATION AT HBCU

GIS Development at HBCU

The 2002 White House Initiative on HBCU/U.S. Department of Education emphasizes the development of GIS in the HBCU education curricula. GIS development at the SUBR Urban Forestry program can be put into context by considering the development of GIS at other HBCU. Roach (2001) reports that recent surveys of information technology resources at HBCU have yielded not only valuable information technology inventories but have provided the basis for new funding and equipment made available to black campuses by government agencies and black college organizations, such as the United Negro College fund. Padgett and Crayton (2001), reports that by the year 2000, a number of historically black institutions employed GIS tools and technologies in their academic departments. In addition to Tennessee State, Clark-Atlanta University, Alabama A&M University and Southern University-Baton Rouge are among a small group of historically black institutions that make extensive use of GIS tools and techniques. Of the HBCU

---

[1]Assistant Professor, Urban Forestry Program, Southern University, Baton Rouge, LA.

offering forest sciences curricula, Alabama A&M, Florida A&M, and SUBR all have fully fledged GIS programs. At Alabama A&M, the GIS program is centered at the university's center for Hydrology, Soil Climatology and Remote Sensing (HSCRS) and its predecessor, the Alabama Center for Applications of Remote Sensing (ACARS) is the oldest of the Centers within the department. It is currently involved in research related to hydrology, soil climatology, and RS. Its objectives are: to develop a comprehensive research program investigating hydrologic processes with emphasis on RS measurements and modeling of soil moisture utilizing microwave and multispectral radiometric data, and utilization of airborne and space-borne platform data in surface soil classification, land use classification, environmental assessment, nutrient stress detection, and natural resource inventory and management. Howard University has been carrying out a HBCU GIS training workshop for 20 years. From the Southern Food Systems Education Consortium (SOFSEC) initiative, North Carolina A&T University has published materials (in Microsoft PowerPoint) for GIS instruction.

At the 18th annual HBCU GIS summer faculty workshop, Dr. David Padgett announced that he had administered a survey of GIS utilization to nearly 50 HBCU faculty members. The conference, hosted by the Howard University Continuing Education Urban Environmental Institute in July, was held in Washington, D.C. and Silver Spring, MD. In a study carried out by Padgett (2001) preliminary findings of the 85 schools surveyed by Tennessee State University include the following: (a) 6 percent offer degrees in geography, (b) 60 percent offer geography courses, (c) 12 percent offer courses with the words "GIS" in the course title, (d) 20 percent offer courses that use GIS in their content, (e) 20 percent are actively using GIS in research, (f) 19 percent have some presence of GPS and/or RS technology. The intention of the survey and its publication is to spread awareness of GIS technology and curriculum within the HBCU community, according to Padgett. Padgett (2001) added that GIS is quite popular in agriculture programs at HBCU. "GIS is something that farmers can utilize to improve cultivation of their fields. They can pinpoint through satellite imagery how to efficiently spread fertilizer and to conduct other tasks," he says. Detailed information was available at a Web site. Padgett stated that the Website survey would be updated periodically.

GIS/RS AND URBAN FORESTRY RELATIONSHIP

GIS and Land-Use Planning
Holden (2000) reports that in recent years GIS operations have assumed an increasingly large role in North American land-use planning. A good example is an application of GIS-aided modeling at an area in South Florida implemented by Tsihrintzis and others (1997). GIS was interfaced with a nonpoint source pollution model to facilitate data storage, management and display, derivation of model input parameters, and effective presentation of results.

RS and Urban Forestry
Myeong and others (2000) outline the role of digital, high resolution aerial imagery in urban cover classification using RS techniques. There are many forestry applications that RS can be used for. Some of these applications include terrain analysis, forest management, recultivation, updating of existing forest inventories, forest cover type discrimination, the delineation of burned areas, and mapping of cleared areas.

GIS, RS and Urban Forestry
Godfrey (2001) explains that in Urban Forestry, GIS software works by joining together tree information data to the tree point location. RS allows one to identify tree or timber stands. In most tree inventories, the information data tables come from tree management software, and the tree point location is entered into the GIS via digitization or the use of Global Positioning Systems (GPS). Most GIS programs work on similar principles: data tables are joined together on a common field. The common field is usually a unique ID number generated by the tree management software when the tree is surveyed. This number is assigned to the tree point when it is collected. The advantage to this system is the easy revision of the data. When the information data is updated in the tree management software, the change can be reflected easily in GIS.

Traditional Urban Forest Surveys Versus GIS
Godfrey (2001) reports that traditional survey inventories were limited to counting trees and recording their address, condition, d.b.h., genus, species, and maintenance needs. State-of-the-art tree management software packages like GIS allow for entry of tree information, tracking of work requests and work histories, and facilitating the creation of custom reports for urban forest resource management purposes. Utilization of GIS allows municipal arborists to take inventories one step further—they can map trees and work with their information.

Hence, GIS programs allow municipal arborists to: (a) map trees while allowing quick visual surveys, (b) make it easier to locate a tree in the field when a map is provided to indicate its location, (c) utilize maps as powerful tools to illustrate needs and situations, (d) utilize a GIS capability to excel at powerful queries with visual results, and (e) enable them to do process modeling.

Urban Forestry Data Entry with GIS
Godfrey (2001) recommends that in order to effectively incorporate a GIS program into an urban forestry management program, several questions have to be addressed. The first question is whether the trees are already in a management software program. Secondly, one has to consider whether an institution already has a GIS program. Thirdly, one has to consider what kind of system it is and what kind of base map it uses. Even more critical is its coordinate system. Finally the last question to be considered is how accurate and how old the base maps are.

With good organization in municipal authority information technology or planning departments can provide the answers to some of these questions. This information is crucial because it can have a profound effect on how tree location data can be handled. The data must be collected in the most cost effective manner, so it is important to know what is already available.

Global Positioning Systems (GPS) and Tree Inventories
A popular method of tree position entry is to locate the trees using Global Positioning Systems. GPS is a network of satellites. Their ground station receivers are used to triangulate positions on the earth. Trees can be located to within a meter with proper data handling. Inexpensive GPS units can locate a tree to within 10-20 feet. To obtain data accurate enough for practical forestry map use, higher-end GPS hardware and software is necessary. Many urban

forestry consulting firms will provide a qualified urban forester to evaluate the tree and collect the GPS data with proper processing for accurate locations.

It is to the urban forester's advantage to collect this data in a tree management program for future use in generating reports and queries, and handling maintenance and resident calls. In a typical survey, the forester evaluates the tree and enters the information into the tree management software. The software assigns a unique identifying number to the tree. The forester then collects GPS data and assigns that same unique ID number to it. The tree data and the tree location are imported into the GIS software and their data tables joined together on the field they have in common—the identifying number.

A very efficient method for surveying the urban forest is to map the tree at the same time it is being inventoried. The tree location can be recorded using GPS while the tree data is collected. A forester will have to inspect each tree in order to inventory it and can map the tree at the same time.

When developing a new urban forest inventory to include a GIS by using GPS, one has to examine all the options. After reviewing available tree management software for compatibility with desired aims and goals, one has to consider these urban tree inventory options. The first option is how the tree management software deals with GIS programs. The second issue is whether it is compatible with current municipal tree software. The third issue is how tree GPS data would be collected and how accurate its position would be. And finally the larger question is how tree GPS data and tree information would be moved into the GIS software.

These steps should allow for the use of resources already available within the system, getting more out of the municipality's software investment.

ESTABLISHMENT AND PRESENT STATUS OF SUBR GIS LAB

Issues Considered when Creating an Urban Forestry GIS

The process of creating an urban forestry education GIS, is essentially the same, whatever institution is in question (Godfrey 2001). This process requires the examination of five criteria that centers on the users of the proposed system. These are: (1) needs/requirements of the end users (2) hardware/software requirements (3) requirements of the GIS (4) database design requirements, and (5) system maintenance/updating requirements.

The needs and requirements of the end users are usually the first criteria to be examined when creating SUBR's urban forestry GIS. It is important to outline and understand exactly the type of information the faculty, staff and students put into the system and utilize on a regular basis. The needs are identified through the use of a questionnaire and personal interviews that help identify the needs. Many times the specific conditions of urban forests in Baton Rouge and Louisiana as a whole, play a role in defining the characteristics of the required GIS. The GIS and RS curriculum at SUBR is offered at both undergraduate and graduate levels.

SUBR Urban Forestry GIS/RS Laboratories Hardware

SUBR's Urban Forestry program presently has three GIS/RS laboratories. The nucleus of hardware was acquired from a USDA capacity building grant. From the initial grant the initial SUBR's GIS facility was set up with a Gateway AL-9200 server, hosting a network of eight Gateway E-520 workstations. Data acquisition is through two Calcomp III digitizers. The laboratory is networked with the rest of Southern University's internet network. The laboratory has a Hewlett-Packard network printer, coupled with a HP 1220 Inkjet color printer for class exercises. For high quality laser publishing, the laboratory has a Canon CLC 900 color printer that also serves as a color copier. High quality maps and photo-glossy posters are produced using a wide format Colorspan DM 4200 plotter. The Agricultural Center GIS laboratory has 4 high performance computers, including an SGI-Octane workstation for high quality graphics. It also houses the GIS library (with about 50 volumes and manuals) and 4 Trimble GPS units. In addition to the Trimble GPS units the laboratory houses a Red-Hen Video GPS unit. SUBR's latest GIS/RS laboratory is under development. It is Southern University's CCZARS's GIS/RS laboratory and will house a computer server with 20 Dell-Precision workstations.

GIS/RS Software

SUBR's Urban Forestry GIS program uses the popular ESRI's suite of GIS products. Software used presently includes 20 ARCVIEW 3.2 licenses and ARCGIS software. The university has site licenses from ESRI. For Remote Sensing, SUBR Urban Forestry program has 15 ERDAS Imagine licenses from ERDAS Inc. The program will also soon host and Intergraph Geo-media GIS laboratory, as well as host Micro-Station GIS.

GIS IMPACT ON OUTREACH PROJECTS

GIS and SUBR Urban Forestry Program Mission

The GIS curriculum at SUBR's Urban Forestry program has been designed to fulfill the requirements of the program's mission. Not only does the GIS serve the technology needs in Urban Forestry education but the research and outreach initiatives are also related to the role of HBCU's and minority population issues in the country. Padgett and Imani (2001) emphasize the need for qualitative and quantitative assessment of land-use management as concerns the question of environmental justice. At the moment, the GIS classes at SUBR are popular and students from other colleges take GIS classes. Students from Environmental Science, Public Policy, Civil Engineering, Environmental Toxicology and Science Mathematics education programs have been taking Urban Forestry's GIS and RS classes.

Bayou Bodcau Dam and Reservoir Project Operational Management Plan

SUBR faculty and graduate students worked on a comprehensive operational management plan for the Bayou Bodcau Dam and Reservoir Project. The exercise was a contract by the Army Corps of Engineers on 35,000 acres of Federal property. GIS was used to map, archive, update, and display natural resources and park facilities. The operational management plan has been published as a book—SUBR faculty and graduate students developed a database of at least 60 GIS map layers to assist Bayou Bodcau staff to manage the project land and resources.

Baton Rouge City as Laboratory Project

The project involves a partnership of students, educators, businesses, and government officials in a cooperative effort to implement a student curriculum for urban forestry. A program funded by the U.S. Forest Service places students as interns with the City of Baton Rouge Department of Parks and Forestry. The urban forestry, geographic information, and global positioning skills that the students learn at SUBR aid in identifying and maintaining a healthy urban tree population. Students conduct field inventories and work together to find constructive solutions to manage their urban forest's growth and identify key areas where they find significant problems.

SUBR's GIS curriculum trains students to CityGreen software from American Forests. This GIS application calculates dollar benefits based on natural systems, including the economic value of tree growth. American Forests is the Nation's oldest citizen-based conservation organization and a leader in the urban forestry movement. American Forests sponsors several programs including Urban Ecological Analysis, Global ReLeaf, and Cool Communities. This modeling software has been used by graduate students to examine environmental justice issues in the Scotlandville subdivision close to the SUBR campus.

Working with Citizen Action Groups and Nongovernmental Organizations
Urban Forestry's GIS facilities have been used for environmental justice studies of neighborhoods around Southern University. These are participatory research initiatives with Baton Rouge Green and Community against Drug and Violence (CADAV) organizations. CityGreen has been applied to studies at Bayou Duplantier, in collaboration with teachers and students at Lee High School. In the summer of 2004, SUBR graduate students mapped a street-tree inventory, the Old South Baton Rouge area, in collaboration with Baton Rouge Green. CityGreen has been used before to evaluate the public policy aspects of Southern University's tree inventory. SUBR's graduate students are updating the inventory and recently carried out an evaluation of the impact of green spaces around SUBR campus.

THE FUTURE
Southern University was recently awarded a 5-year $6 Million grant from NASA to set up a center for Coastal Zone and RS (CCZARS). Four of the principle investigators are from the Urban Forestry faculty. The grant has helped to set up a state-of-the-art GIS/RS lab with 20 powerful workstations, and the latest hardware and software required for spatial analysis. Recently ESRI has granted SUBR's application for a learning center. The learning center will offer ESRI certified training for GIS professionals. In addition to this, CCZARS will also offer training for Trimble GPS training, while RS training will be offered for ERDAS Imagine software. The new facility indicates the future direction of Southern University's GIS initiatives related to the Urban Forestry program.

SUBR faculty and graduate students worked on comprehensive operational management plan for the Burden center in Baton Rouge, LA. The exercise was a contract by Louisiana State University Agricultural center. GPS units were used to develop a tree inventory for the center. GIS was used to map, archive, update, and display natural resources and park facilities. SUBR faculty and graduate students developed a database of at least 20 GIS map layers to assist Burden center management to manage the project land and resources.

ACKNOWLEDGMENTS
The authors express their gratefulness to Dr. Oghenekome Onokpise of Florida A&M University and the Ford Foundation.

REFERENCES
Godfrey, C.G. 2001. GIS and GPS in urban forestry. City Trees, Journal of The Society of Municipal Arborists. Vol. 37, Number 3.

Holden, M. 2000. GIS in democratic and sustainable land use planning: lessons from critical theory and the Gulf Islands. Journal of Planning Education and Research 19(3): 287-296.

Myeong, S.P.; Hopkins, R.H.; Brock; Nowak, D.J. 2001. Urban cover classification using digital, high resolution aerial imagery. In: Proceedings of the American Society for Photogrammetric and Remote Sensing Annual Conference: 2001 April 23-27; St. Louis, MO. Bethesda, MD: American Society for Photogrammetric and Remote Sensing: (published on cd).

Nowak, D.J. 1992. Remote sensing and urban forestry. Proceedings of the American Society for Natural Conservation. Bethesda, MD: The Society, 1985 1992 103-108 p.

Nowak, D.J. 1993. Remote sensing and urban forestry. In: Proceedings of the 1992 Society of American Foresters National Convention, October 25-28, 1992; Richmond, VA: Society of American Foresters: 103-108.

Nowak, D.J.; Walton, J.; Myeong, S.; Hopkins, P.F. [and others]. 2001. Chapter 2: tree cover in Syracuse. In: Nowak, David J.; O'Connor, Paul R.; comps. 2001. Syracuse urban forest master plan: guiding the city's forest resource into the 21st century. Gen. Tech. Rep. NE-287. Newtown Square, PA: U.S. Department of Agriculture, Forest Service, Northeastern Research Station: 6-8.

Padgett, D.; Crayton, C. 2001. Historically black college and university (HBCU) Geographic Information Systems utilization status. http://gislabtsu.freehomepage.com/hbcugisweb2.htm.

Padgett, D.; Imani, N.O. 1999. "Qualitative and Quantitative Assessment of Land-Use Managers' Attitudes Toward Environmental Justice". The Environmental Professional, December 1999.

Roach, R. 2001. Taking stock of GIS technology at HBCUs. Black issues in higher education, www.blackissues.com and http://gislabtsu.freehomepage.com/BIhbcugis01.html.

Tsihrintzis, V.A.; Fuentes, H.R.; Gadipudi, R.K. 1997. GIS-aided modeling of nonpoint source pollution impacts on surface and ground waters. Water resources management. June 1997. v. 11 (3) p. 207-218.: Dordrecht: Kluwer Academic Publishers.

SESSION IX

Agroforestry Systems and International
Forestry

Presiding Moderator:

Harriet Paul
Florida A&M University

INTEGRATING HIGH VALUE HORTICULTURAL CROPS INTO AGROFORESTRY SYSTEMS IN THE TROPICS WITH FOCUS ON ALLEY CROPPING

Manuel C. Palada, Stafford M. Crossman, and James J. O'Donnell[1]

Abstract—Alley cropping systems have been developed primarily as an alternative to traditional slash and burn/bush fallow farming systems in the tropics. The goal is to improve long-term soil fertility and productivity, thereby sustaining crop production levels. While these systems have benefited most agronomic crops, their application to high value horticultural crops such as vegetables, herbs and fruits has not been studied extensively. As a technology, alley cropping has both negative and positive effects depending on crop and tree species, cropping pattern, soil type, climate and other ecological factors. Studies in the humid tropics of West Africa indicated that with fertilizer application, yield of vegetables such as pai-tsai (*Brassica chinensis*), amaranth (*Amaranthus cruentus*), celosia (*Celosia argentia*), okra (*Abelmoschus esculentus*) and tomato (*Lycopersicon esculentum*) grown in alley cropping systems with nitrogen fixing leguminous tree (*Leucaena leucocephala* Lam de Wit) were similar to yield in control plots (without alley cropping). With no fertilizer applied, yield of alley-cropped vegetables was higher than the control. Yield of vegetable crops responded more to fertilizer in control plots than in alley-crop plots indicating that alley cropping can reduce fertilizer requirement for vegetable production. In the semi-arid tropics of eastern Caribbean, alley cropping vegetable crops such as bell pepper (*Capsicum annuum*), eggplant (*Solanum melongena*) and sweet corn (*Zea mays*) with pigeonpea (*Cajanus cajan*), Moringa (*Moringa oleifera*), Gliricida (*Gliricidia sepium*) and Leucaena indicated both negative and positive effects. The presence of hedgerows in alley cropping resulted in reduced evapotranspiration, lower wind turbulence, slightly higher soil moisture, and lower surface soil temperature. In spite of supplemental drip irrigation, yields of vegetable crops were reduced in alley cropping systems. Alley cropping with pigeonpea reduced bell pepper yield by 50 to 60 percent, mainly the result of partial shading and reduced pepper growth due to inhibitory effect of pigeonpea residues. Alley cropping had no significant and beneficial effect on sweet corn yield during the establishment period. Marketable yield decreased 40 to 60 percent and Moringa hedgerows significantly reduced yield by 55 to 60 percent. Leucaena and pigeonpea had lower (17 to 20 percent) yield reducing effect on eggplant. For both crops (sweet corn and eggplant), plant height, yield and dry matter decreased as distance of rows to hedgerows decreased. Alley cropping with Leucaena maintained relatively higher soil moisture than with other species. Among the hedgerow species, Moringa and Gliricidia were more competitive than Leucaena and pigeonpea in terms of their effects on plant height, yield, and dry matter. Leucaena and Moringa exhibited the fastest regrowth after pruning and produced the highest total biomass. In terms of total nutrient contribution, Leucaena and Gliricidia produced the highest NPK yield. Growth and yield of medicinal plants and culinary herbs varied according to species in both hedgerow and no hedgerow treatments. Lemongrass (*Cymbopogon citratus*) and blue verbena (*Stachytarpheta jamaicensis*) were the most productive traditional species in both treatments while culinary herbs basil, and sweet marjoram were more productive than other species. In general, yield of medicinal plants and herbs was reduced under hedgerow intercropping although competition for light and soil moisture was minimal.

INTRODUCTION

High value horticultural crops are sources of food, medicine, and income to small-scale farmers in the tropics. These crops are important components of agroforestry systems and play significant roles by contributing to biological stability, enhancing crop diversity, conserving soil properties and increasing total productivity. According to Nair (1993), agroforestry with horticultural crops can be in various systems which include alley cropping or hedgerow intercropping, multilayer tree garden, home gardens, multipurpose trees in croplands, plantation crop combination, and taungya. This paper focuses on alley cropping systems involving high value vegetable crops, herbs and medicinal plants in the tropics.

ALLEY CROPPING

Alley cropping is a form of agroforestry wherein food crops are grown in alleys between hedgerows of trees or shrubs. The hedgerows are periodically pruned to prevent shading of associated food crops. Prunings are spread as mulch and green manure (Kang and others 1984). Continuous cultivation of annual food crops is possible in alley cropping systems, when fast growing, N-fixing leguminous species with large biomass and nutrient yields are incorporated in the system (Kang and others 1990). Alley cropping has been widely studied in the tropics for the past three decades, although

farmers have been using contour hedgerows of perennial woody legumes for erosion control for several decades (Kang and Shannon 2001). Early investigations on alley cropping were carried out in Nigeria during the 1970s to assess the potential of intercropping woody species with food crops as a land use system (Kang and others 1990). This system was originally developed to manage fragile uplands in the humid and sub-humid zones for continuous crop production and to improve the traditional bush-fallow cropping system (Kang and others 1981).

Throughout the tropics, nitrogen-fixing trees and shrubs are being utilized in agroforestry systems. Growing food crops with tree crops is known to be a stable and sustainable system. The benefits derived from these systems include: (1) improved soil fertility (Kang and others 1981, 1984; Young 1986, 1987), (2) increased nutrient supply particularly N (Kang and others 1981, 1984), (3) reduced soil erosion (Lal 1975, 1987; Pacardo 1984), (4) wind protection (Baldwin 1988, Norton 1988, Schaefer 1989), (5) increased soil organic matter content (Kang and others 1981, 1984; Nair 1983), and (6) sustained yield levels (Kang and others 1984, 1990).

While alley cropping systems benefit associated food crops, there are also limitations that can negatively affect crop production. Among the limitations are hedgerows of trees

---

[1]Manuel C. Palada, Research Associate Professor, Stafford M. Crossman, Extension Program Supervisor, and James J. O'Donnell, Agricultural Experiment Station, University of the Virgin Islands, Kingshill, St. Croix, U.S. Virgin Islands.

or shrubs that compete with food crops for soil moisture, light and nutrients, take a portion of land out of production, become a potential weed problem, and require extra labor for pruning and no immediate or short term benefits (Kang and others 1984).

Most studies with alley cropping were designed for agronomic field crops. There is little information on the effect of alley cropping on growth and yield performance of horticultural crops. The objective of this paper is to summarize studies on alley cropping involving vegetable crops and herbs conducted in the humid tropics of west Africa and semi-arid tropics of the eastern Caribbean.

ALLEY CROPPING WITH VEGETABLE CROPS IN HUMID TROPICS OF WEST AFRICA

The influence of alley cropping Leucaena (*Leucaena leucocephala*) on vegetable production was investigated in field studies conducted in southwestern Nigeria.

Study 1—Alley cropping Leucaena leucocephala with vegetables in sequential planting

To determine the feasibility of alley cropping vegetable crops with woody legumes such as Leucaena, a trial was carried out at Ibadan in southern Nigeria. Leucaena hedgerows were established using 3-month-old seedlings. Seedlings were planted at an inter-row spacing of 0.25 m in the hedgerows and 4 m spacing between hedgerows. The main plot treatments were the control (without hedgerows) and Leucaena hedgerows (alley cropping). Main plot size was 20x16 m, and for the alley cropping, treatment consisted of five hedgerows making four alleys of 20 m long each. The subplot treatments consisted of four vegetable cropping patterns as follows: (1) sweet pepper (*Capsicum annuum* L.), vegetable cowpea (*Vigna unguiculata* L. Walp.), Chinese cabbage (*Brassica campestris* L.), amaranthus (*Amaranthus cruentus* L.), and pai tsai (*Brassica chinensis* L.); (2) Chinese cabbage, okra (*Abelmoschus esculentus* L.), cucumber (*Cucumis sativus* L.), amaranthus, and pai tsai; (3) cabbage (*Brassica oleracea* L.), tomato (*Lycopersicon esculentum* Mill.), amaranthus, vegetable cowpea, and pai tsai; and (4) broccoli (*Brassica oleracea* L.), amaranthus, mungbean (Phaseolus radiatus L), lettuce (Lactuca sativa L), and pai tsai.

Each of the cropping patterns was planted in sequence in one of the subplot alleys and the corresponding control subplots. All treatments were replicated three times in a randomized block design. Various N, P, and K fertilizer rates were applied to each of the vegetable crops, except for the last pai tsai crop, which was not fertilized.

The Leucaena hedgerows were pruned to a height of 0.25 m above ground. First pruning was done 145 days after planting, and subsequently at 8- to 10-week intervals. Weight of prunings was determined and subsamples were taken for dry weight and nutrient yield determination. Prunings were spread in the alley-cropped plots as surface mulch.

During the 14-month growing period, total accumulative dry weight of the prunings from the hedgerows was 5.3 t ha⁻¹. This was equivalent to a nutrient yield of 223, 13, 157, 59, and 38 N, P, K, Ca and Mg in kg ha⁻¹, respectively. The various cropping patterns did not have any distinct effect on soil nutrient levels. Addition of Leucaena prunings in the alley-cropped plots resulted in slightly higher nutrient

status, particularly organic carbon level (data not shown). There were no significant (P>0.05) differences in yield of various vegetable crops in alley-cropped and in control plots, despite the better growth of the alley-cropped vegetables. Total yield for the various cropping patterns with and without alley cropping also showed no significant difference. Yield differences may have been masked by fertilizer application. It was decided not to fertilize the last test crop pai tsai. Rain splash and surface soil erosion resulted in very poor plant stand with direct-seeded pai tsai in the control plot. Average plant stand in alley-cropped plots was 76 percent compared to 31 percent without alley cropping. The presence of Leucaena hedgerows and mulch minimized the effect of soil erosion. With no fertilizer applied, alley cropping with Leucaena significantly (P<0.05) increased yield of pai tsai and nutrient status of the crop (table 1).

This study showed that various vegetable crops can be successfully grown in alley cropping systems with Leucaena. Alley cropping maintained higher soil and plant nutrient status, reduced soil erosion, and gave better plant stand of direct-seeded pai tsai compared to control (no alley cropping). Without fertilizer application, alley cropping increased yield of pai tsai.

Study 2—Alley cropping Leucaena leucocephala with vegetables in sole cropping

Studies were conducted on the same plots as in Study 1 to determine the effect of alley cropping and fertilizer application on yield of four vegetable crops grown in monoculture (sole cropping).

A randomized block design with three replications and four treatments were used for each of the following four vegetable crops: amaranthus, celosia (*Celosia argentia* L.), okra, and tomato. The four treatments were: control (no hedgerows) and alley cropping (with Leucaena hedgerows) without and with fertilizer application. Leucaena hedgerows were maintained at 4 m spacing. Fertilized plots received 30N-13P-24K in kg ha⁻¹ applied in split dosages (half at planting and the remainder 25 days after planting). Plot size measured 4x10 m. Seeds of amaranthus and celosia were direct-seeded at 0.5 inter-row and 5 cm intra-row spacing. Okra was directly seeded at 0.5 m inter-row and 0.5 m intra-row spacing. Seedlings of tomato were transplanted at the same spacing as okra. All plots were hand-weeded twice.

Leucaena hedgerows were pruned 25 cm above ground three times during the growing season. Prunings were evenly spread in the alleys as mulch. Prunings were weighed and subsamples dried. Dried samples were analyzed for N, P, K, Ca and Mg contents to estimate yields in the prunings. Yields of vegetable crops were determined from multiple harvests. To minimize border effects in yield assessment, a sample area of 3x4 m across the plot width and in the center

Table 1—Pai tsai yield and crop nutrient status as affected by alley cropping with *Leucaena leucocephala* (adapted from Chen and others 1989)

Cropping system	Fresh weight t ha⁻¹	Nutrient content (%)				
		N	P	K	Ca	Mg
Conventional	2.15	2.59	0.56	2.85	1.21	0.47
Alley	4.63	2.56	0.76	1.46	1.28	0.51
LSD, 5%	1.73	NS	0.15	0.39	0.02	0.04

of the plot was used to determine crop yield. The study was conducted over a period of 2 years.

Dry matter of Leucaena prunings was smaller in year 1 than in year 2 (fig. 1). Biomass yield was higher with the first pruning, which produced more than one-half of the total dry matter. This is due to the longer fallow period between croppings. Fallowing with Leucaena hedgerows also resulted in higher soil fertility (data not shown). In year 1, Leucaena prunings contained 133, 5, 64, 31, and 10 N, P, K, Ca and Mg in kg ha^{-1}, respectively, and in year 2, prunings contained 311, 11, 150, 73, and 23 N, P, K, Ca, and Mg in kg ha^{-1}, respectively. Assuming a 20 percent nutrient use efficiency of N from prunings as observed with maize crop, Leucaena prunings could have contributed a total of 37kg N ha^{-1} in year 1 and 62kg ha^{-1} in year 2.

Amaranthus—Plants grown in alleys with fertilizer treatments were taller than in any other treatments (table 2). Faster growth rate in alley cropped and fertilized plots resulted in early harvest. In year 1, yield in the alley cropped plots with and without fertilizer application were not different from yield in the fertilized control plots. The largest yield was observed from the alley cropped plot with added fertilizer and the lowest yield was obtained from control plot without fertilizer. In alley cropped plots without fertilizer application, yield was slightly lower than in control and fertilized plots. This would indicate that prunings from the Leucaena hedgerows could partially substitute for N fertilizer requirement. In year 2, yields from the alley cropped plots with or without fertilizer were higher than those in control plots (table 2). A significant response to fertilizer application was only observed in the control treatment. Lower yield was observed in the second year, which may be due to greater cloud cover.

Celosia—Plant height and days to first harvest were not affected by alley cropping or fertilizer application in both years (table 3). Alley cropped plots with fertilizer produced the largest yield but it was similar to alley cropped plots without fertilizer and control with fertilizer treatments. The control plot without fertilizer yielded less than other treatments. In the second year, largest yields were produced in fertilized alley cropped plots, while yields in alley cropped plots with no fertilizer applied were similar to that in the fertilized control plot. These results suggest that prunings from Leucaena provided N equivalent to fertilizer N in the control plot.

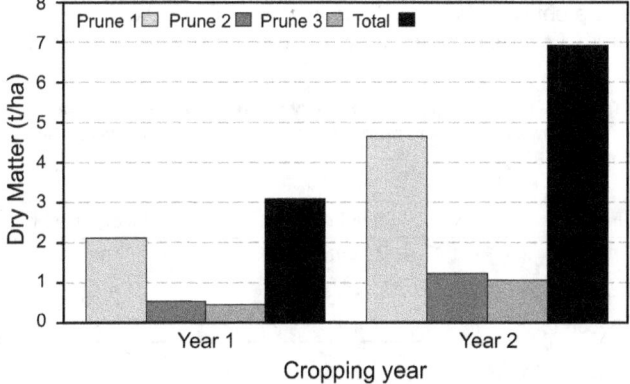

Figure 1—Dry matter production of Leucaena in alley cropping system.

Table 2—Growth and yield of amaranthus in alley cropping system (adapted from Palada and others 1992)

Year	Treatment	Plant height	Days to 1st harvest	Yield
		cm		*t ha^{-1}*
1	Alley (+F)	58	36	10.1
	Alley (-F)	45	37	7.4
	No alley (+F)	41	40	8.9
	No alley (-F)	35	50	2.5
	LSD (5%)	7	5	2.3
2	Alley (+F)	47	45	7.6
	Alley (-F)	40	47	5.6
	No alley (+F)	39	56	3.0
	Non alley (-F)	35	40	0.3
	LSD (5%)	13	3	2.6

+F = with fertilizer; -F = without fertilizer.

Table 3—Growth and yield of celosia in alley cropping system (adapted from Palada and others 1992)

Year	Treatment	Plant height	Days to 1st harvest	Yield
		cm		*t ha^{-1}*
1	Alley (+F)	54	44	20.3
	Alley (-F)	54	48	16.6
	No alley (+F)	53	51	18.1
	No alley (-F)	48	57	4.8
	LSD (5%)	NS	NS	2.3
2	Alley (+F)	78	51	24.0
	Alley (-F)	72	51	18.5
	No alley (+F)	76	51	17.5
	Non alley (-F)	61	51	8.7
	LSD (5%)	8	NS	4.6

NS = not significant.
+F = with fertilizer; -F = without fertilizer.

Okra—In year 1, fruit size was similar for the alley cropped plots with and without fertilizer applied and the fertilized control (table 4). In year 2, fruit size in fertilized treatments was larger than in treatments with no fertilizer (table 4). Fruit number did not differ between alley cropped and fertilized control treatments, although these treatments produced significantly more fruits than the control without fertilizer in year 1. The local cultivar grown in year 2 produced more fruits and required more harvests than the cultivar grown in year 1. In year 2, yield also did not differ among the alley cropped with and without fertilizer treatments and the control treatment with fertilizer (table 4).

Tomato—Alley cropping and fertilizer application increased the number of tomato fruits (table 5). Fruit size was not affected by alley cropping. Yields of control plot without fertilizer application were the lowest. More fruits were harvested in year 2 than in year 1, which may be the result of staking of the plants in year 2. Total number of fruits in year 2 was similar in alley cropped and control plots with fertilizer. The least number of fruits were harvested in the control plot without fertilizer (table 5). Alley cropping resulted in fruit sizes similar to those in fertilized control plots. Addition of fertilizer in alley-cropped plots in year 2 resulted in larger fruits. A similar result was also observed in fruit yield. In both years, yield of tomato with fertilizer application was significantly higher than in the control plot without fertilizer. The data indicate the combined effects of staking and alley cropping in increasing tomato yield.

Table 4—Fruit size and yield of okra in alley cropping system (adapted from Palada and others 1992)

Year	Treatment	Fruit size	No. of fruits	Yield
		g	x 1000 ha^{-1}	t ha^{-1}
1	Alley (+F)	15	266	4.0
	Alley (-F)	15	281	4.2
	No Alley (+F)	15	273	4.1
	No Alley (-F)	12	274	2.6
	LSD (5%)	2	50	1.0
2	Alley (+F)	8.7	503	4.3
	Alley (-F)	7.3	458	3.8
	No Alley (+F)	8.1	492	4.0
	No Alley (-F)	7.1	401	2.9
	LSD (5%)	0.7	97	0.7

+F = with fertilizer; -F = without fertilizer.

Table 5—Fruit size and yield of tomato in alley cropping system (adapted from Palada and others 1992)

Year	Treatment	Fruit size	No. of fruits	Yield
		g	x 1000 ha^{-1}	t ha^{-1}
1	Alley (+F)	73	191	13.9
	Alley (-F)	73	219	15.7
	No Alley (+F)	76	169	12.9
	No Alley (-F)	68	99	6.8
	LSD (5%)	NS	72	5.6
2	Alley (+F)	67	430	29.1
	Alley (-F)	60	326	20.2
	No Alley (+F)	65	430	28.2
	No Alley (-F)	58	246	14.4
	LSD (5%)	9	126	9.4

+F = with fertilizer; -F = without fertilizer.

This study has shown that alley cropping with Leucaena can benefit vegetable crop production in the humid tropics. Better yield of vegetable crops in alley cropped plots is in part due to the effect of fallowing with Leucaena, which resulted in higher soil fertility as observed at the beginning of the trial and from addition of prunings from Leucaena hedgerows which produced large amounts of mulch and green manure. Prunings provide significant amounts of N, P, K and Ca. Addition of prunings can reduce fertilizer, particularly N requirement for vegetable production.

ALLEY CROPPING WITH VEGETABLE CROPS IN THE SEMI-ARID TROPICS OF THE EASTERN CARIBBEAN

Studies were conducted in water-limited environment of Virgin Islands to investigate the influence of alley cropping various species of trees and shrubs on growth and productivity of selected vegetable crops.

Study 1—Effects of pigeonpea hedgerows on soil water and yield of intercropped pepper

Alley cropping experiments were conducted to determine the effects of pigeonpea [*Cajanus cajan* (L.) Millsp.] hedgerows on soil water and yield of intercropped bell (sweet) pepper (*Capsicum annuum* L.). Pigeonpea hedgerows were established using 2-month old seedlings planted at 4 m row spacing and 0.25 m in-row spacing. Hedgerows were allowed to grow for 4 months before intercropping with peppers. Hedgerows were pruned to 50 cm stubble height 5 and 7 months after planting. The prunings were applied as green manure mulch in 4 m wide alleys between hedgerows.

Pepper seedlings (45-day-old) were transplanted at 1.0 m row spacing and 0.61 m plant spacing in the first year. In the second year, row spacing was 0.67 m and plant spacing was 0.57 m. Pepper plant population in the first year was 12,500/ha for alley cropped plots and 18,750/ha for monoculture plots. Plant population in the second year was similar (26,048/ha) for alley cropped and monoculture plots. Peppers were fertilized with 200N-100P-50K kg ha^{-1}. N was applied in two splits, 1/3 at 17 days after transplanting and 2/3 at 52 days after the first application. All of the P and K were applied together with the first N application. Drip irrigation was applied at various regimes corresponding to soil water tensions of -20, -40 and -60 kPa.

Data were taken for soil water content (0 to 15 cm depth) using the gravimetric method. Soil moisture content was determined from pepper rows adjacent to hedgerows and from the middle rows. Evapotranspiration (ET) by pepper plants was estimated using the pan evaporation method integrated with crop coefficient values (Doorenbos and Pruitt 1977). To obtain a rough estimate of wind velocity in hedgerow and control plots, wind speed was measured using a hand-held wind speed indicator (Wind Wizard, Davis Inst., Hayward, CA). The indicator was held 50 and 100 cm above-ground level and measurements were made only during days when there were strong gusty winds. For each harvest, pepper yield samples were taken from four middle rows in the hedgerow plot and five middle rows in the control plots. The sample size (9m^2) in the hedgerow plot included an area occupied by the middle pigeonpea hedgerow. Pigeonpea biomass production was determined from dry weights of two prunings. Biomass included woody stem and leaves.

Pigeonpea hedgerows attained a height of 1.95 m at first pruning. Total dry matter produced from first pruning was 2.06 t ha^{-1}. The second pruning produced 1.71 t ha^{-1} dry matter giving a total of 3.77 t ha^{-1} for two prunings (table 6).

During the first year, pigeonpea hedgerow suppressed growth of peppers resulting in shorter and smaller plants relative to the control. Similar result was obtained in the second year. The reduced growth was attributed to partial shading by pigeonpea hedgerows.

Hedgerow intercropping significantly reduced pepper yield (table 7). In the first year, marketable yield in alley cropping was only 46 percent of the control, a yield reduction of 54 percent. In the second year, yield reduction averaged 59 percent even under equal plant population. Irrigation water regime did not influence pepper yield, but the lowest yields were obtained from treatment with lowest irrigation rate (-60 kPa). Low yield in hedgerow intercropping can be attributed

Table 6—Plant height and total dry matter yield of pigeonpea hedgerows in alley cropping system (adapted from Palada and others 1992)

Pruning	Plant height	Total dry matter
	cm	t ha^{-1}
First	1.95	2.06
Second	1.41	1.71
Total	3.36	3.77

Table 7—Marketable yield of bell peppers in alley cropping system with pigeonpea (adapted from Palada and others 1992)

Year	Irrigation regime	No hedgerow (no alley)	Hedgerow (alley cropped)	Yield reduction
	kP	*t ha⁻¹*	*t ha⁻¹*	%
1	-20	22.7	10.0	56
	-40	19.8	10.2	48
	-60	18.7	7.9	58
	Mean	20.3	9.4	54
2	-20	17.8	9.0	49
	-40	18.0	6.8	62
	-60	18.5	6.6	64
	Mean	18.1	7.5	59

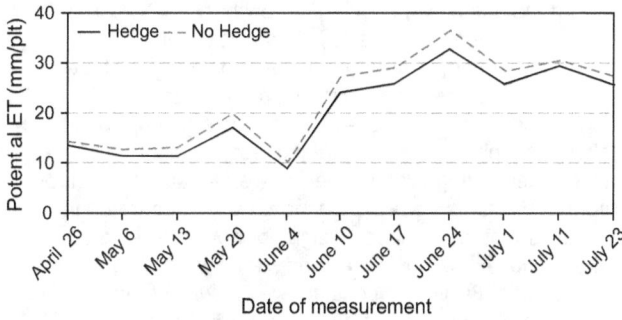

Figure 2—Potential evapotranspiration of bell peppers in alley cropping system with pigeonpea.

to lower plant population in the first year and crop-hedgerow competition. Partial shading of plants especially in rows adjacent to hedgerows and competition for soil water depressed plant growth. In the second year, low yield can be attributed to inhibitory effect of pigeonpea crop residues, which persisted from the previous season.

In both years soil water content in hedgerow plots was generally higher than the control. This could be explained by the effect of mulch from prunings and shading by hedgerows. Small differences in soil water content were observed between irrigation regimes. This result is consistent with the findings of Lal (1989) who reported higher soil moisture content in the top 0-15 cm layer in agroforestry system than in monoculture. Furthermore, hedgerows essentially served as windbreaks, which prevent rapid soil moisture evaporation. Wind speed in hedgerow plots was lower than the control (table 8).

Hedgerow intercropping significantly reduced ET of pepper plants (fig. 2). There were no significant differences in ET between irrigation regimes. The high ET of plants in the control can be explained by larger plant canopy and higher leaf area index compared to plants between hedgerows. Low ET in hedgerow intercropping may also be the effect of lower wind speed and turbulence. Thus, the combined effects of reduced wind speed and low ET may have led to higher soil water retention in hedgerow intercropping. This result support the report of Houreau (1980) where potential ET under a tree canopy is considerably reduced compared to unprotected open field.

For a given irrigation regime, water use by plants in hedgerow intercropping was higher than the control (table 9). As expected, total water use for the 4-month period was highest under irrigation regime which maintained soil water tension at -20 kPa and lowest at -60 kPa. Low ET in hedgerow intercropping should have reduced water use, but maintenance of high soil water content required increased

water use. Also, roots of pigeonpea may have utilized some water applied through the drip system. Ong and others (1990) reported that total water use as measured by transpiration in intercropping system was higher than that in pure stands of either pigeonpea or groundnut.

This study showed that under drip irrigation, hedgerow-intercropping pigeonpea with sweet pepper did not reduce soil water at 0-15 cm depth. ET of pepper plants in hedgerow intercropping was generally lower than plants in monoculture and was attributed to smaller crop canopy, lower leaf area index and reduced wind speed. In spite of higher soil water and low ET, total water use of pepper in hedgerow intercropping was higher than in monoculture. Hedgerow intercropping pigeonpea with pepper reduced marketable yield up to 60 percent due to lower plant population, partial shading, soil moisture competition, and inhibitory effect of pigeonpea residues.

Study 2—Influence of four hedgerow species on yields of sweet corn and eggplant in an alley cropping system

The performance of four hedgerow species, planted as alley crops were evaluated for their influence on growth and yield of eggplant (*Solanum melongena*) and sweet corn (*Zea mays*). The hedgerow species consisted of pigeonpea, Gliricidia (*Gliricidia sepium*), Moringa (*Moringa oleifera*) and Leucaena. Seeds of four species were sown in polyethylene bags and grown for 19 weeks prior to planting in field plots. Each plot consisted of three hedgerows 12 m long with 5 m between hedgerows. Trees were planted 30cm apart within hedgerows. The plants were drip-irrigated for 4 weeks to ensure good establishment.

Table 9—Total irrigation water use of bell peppers in alley cropping system with pigeonpea (adapted from Palada and others 1992)

Treatment	Irrigation regime	Irrigation water use (liters/plant)	
		Year 1	Year 2
Hedgerow	-20	35	56
	-40	29	33
	-60	17	21
	Mean	27	37
No hedgerow	-20	37	50
	-40	26	26
	-60	14	19
	Mean	26	32

Table 8—Wind speed (m sec⁻¹) at 50 cm aboveground in pigeonpea hedgerow and no hedgerow plots (adapted from Palada and others 1992)

Treatment	Date of measurement				
	February 24	March 6	March 13	March 18	May 14
Hedgerow	1.00	0.33	0.0	3.29	3.75
No hedgerow	3.46	2.83	2.34	4.33	4.42

During the establishment phase growth (plant height) of hedgerows were measured every 4 weeks with the initial measurements made at 8 weeks after planting. At the end of the establishment period measurements of total plant height and stem diameter at 50 cm above ground were taken. The initial cutting of the hedgerows was at 40 weeks after transplanting. All four species were cut at 50 cm above ground. Prunings (except pigeonpea) were separated into leaves and stem and fresh weight for both components taken. Subsamples of leaves and stems were weighed, and then dried at 80°C until constant weight was obtained. The dried samples were ground and analyzed for N, P and K. After the initial cutting, hedgerows were pruned periodically in preparation for planting the alleys or, as needed, to lessen the competition with vegetable crops. At each pruning the hedgerows were cut to 50 cm height and weight data recorded as described previously. Moringa, Gliricidia, and Leucaena were pruned seven times, and pigeonpea twice. All data were collected from the middle hedgerows.

Pigeonpea had the fastest growth rate during the first two prunings. In the later measurements, Leucaena and Moringa had the fastest rate of growth. Overall, Leucaena had the greatest height growth (341 cm), followed by Moringa and Pigeonpea (287 cm). Moringa had the largest stem diameter (3.8cm) at the end of the establishment period. Mean plant survival for all species was 97 percent. In the initial cutting of four hedgerow species, leaf biomass ranged from 3.7 t ha^{-1} for pigeonpea to 0.6 t ha-1 for Moringa. Leucaena produced the largest amount of total (leaf + stem) biomass (8.5 t ha^{-1}). Leucaena also produced the greatest stem biomass (5.4 t ha^{-1}).

Leucaena and Gliricidia consistently produced the greatest amount of leaf biomass annually from pruning. Leucaena responded well to pruning although its yield was somewhat suppressed due to defoliation by Leucaena psyllid (*Heteropsylla cubana*). Gliricidia was slower to establish and required a longer recovery time in the early prunings. In the later prunings, Gliricidia produced as much leaf biomass as Leucaena and Moringa. Moringa produced the largest amount of total biomass from prunings (23 t ha^{-1}). Moringa also produced the greatest stem biomass from the prunings, 15 t ha^{-1} compared to a mean of 5.25 t ha^{-1} for Gliricidia and Leucaena. It also responded well to pruning and in the second and third years produced as much leaf biomass as Leucaena and Gliricidia. Pigeonpea did not respond well to pruning, produced the smallest quantity of total biomass (1.5 t ha^{-1}) and many plants died after the second pruning.

Total leaf biomass production from all cuttings (initial + prunings) over the 3-year period ranged from 13.6 t ha^{-1} for Leucaena to 5.2 t ha^{-1} for pigeonpea. Leucaena and Moringa produced the largest total biomass (fig. 3). Moringa also produced the greatest amount of stem biomass (17.3 t ha^{-1}). There were no differences in the foliar-N concentration of Leucaena, Gliricidia and Moringa (mean=37.5 kg N ha^{-1}). Leaf concentrations of K and P varied between species. Concentrations of K in the leaf biomass were highest in Gliricidia (20.5 g K kg^{-1}) and lowest in pigeonpea (9.9 g K kg^{-1}). Moringa had the highest concentration of foliar-P (2.3 g P kg^{-1}). Calculated from leaf nutrient concentrations and biomass production, the incorporation of prunings or their application to the soil as mulch resulted in the equivalent

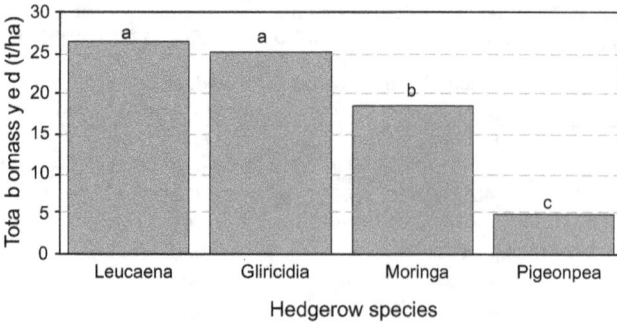

Figure 3—Biomass yield for hedgerow species in alley cropping.

nutrient yield of 558, 26 and 235 kg NPK ha^{-1} for Leucaena; 389, 20 and 220 kg NPK ha^{-1} for Gliricidia; 301, 16 and 158 kg NPK ha^{-1} for Moringa; and 138, 10 and 52 kg NPK ha^{-1} for pigeonpea, over the 36-month study period.

It appears that the two hedgerow species with potential for alley cropping are Leucaena and Gliricida. Leucaena can establish a hedgerow quickly, produces large quantities of high-N leaf biomass and withstands frequent prunings. Gliricidia required a longer time to establish, but proved a good biomass producer once established. It is tolerant to frequent prunings, is high in N and its low spreading growth habit lessens competition for light with the vegetable crops. Moringa's foliar-N concentrations were equal to both Gliricidia and Leucaena, which is surprising since Moringa does not fix N as do Gliricidia and Leucaena. This may indicate that Moringa is an efficient scavenger of soil nutrients. Moringa's rapid growth and upright form caused excessive shading on the vegetable crops. Pigeonpea initially grew the fastest, produced a hedgerow rapidly and in the first cutting had the greatest leaf biomass, but its inability to withstand pruning makes it a poor choice for use as a hedgerow.

Sweet corn—One month after the first pruning of hedgerows, sweet corn was planted in alleys between hedgerows. Plants were spaced 1m between rows and 30 cm between plants in the row. In hedgerow plots, sweet corn was fertilized with prunings from hedgerows, pruning + 100 kg N ha^{-1}, and pruning + 200 kg N ha^{-1}. In the control plots (no hedgerows), sweet corn was fertilized with N at rates of 50, 100, and 200 kg ha^{-1}. All plots received 100 kg ha^{-1} of P and K. The experiment used a split plot arrangement with three replicates. The main plots were the hedgerow species and the fertilizer treatments were the subplots.

In general, results showed no significant differences in plant height among the hedgerow species and the control. However, the shortest plants were observed in Moringa hedgerows. Plants in rows adjacent to hedgerows (rows 1 and 5) were shorter than plants in middle rows (rows 2 to 4). This was attributed to the competitive effect of hedgerows for moisture and light. A similar pattern was observed for plant dry matter. No significant differences were observed between hedgerow species. Generally, sweet corn yields were low and can be explained by poor germination and low stand count, in spite of the fact that plots were re-seeded. Also, early tasseling was observed as a result of varietal response to a shorter photoperiod. This resulted in reduced plant height and vegetative growth. There were no significant differences among treatments (hedgerow species and control, and between fertilizer rates) in terms of total ears harvested, total ear weight, number of marketable ears and weight of marketable ears. Highest corn yield (total ear weight) was obtained from the control (2.05 t ha^{-1}) followed by Leucaena (1.57 t ha^{-1}) and Gliricidia (1.48 t ha^{-1}).

In the second cropping, the effect of N levels on marketable yield was not significant, but the main effect of hedgerow species was significant. Among the hedgerow species, yield of marketable ears ranged from 10.3 t ha^{-1} for Moringa to 16.4 t ha^{-1} for pigeonpea (table 10). Differences in yield of marketable ears between hedgerow species were not significant, but all yields were significantly lower than the control (no hedgerow). On a row-by-row yield, it was generally observed that sweet corn yield increased as row distance from hedgerow increased; however, yield reduction was greatest (40 to 90 percent) in rows adjacent to the hedgerows (table 10). Similar trends were also observed on plant height and plant dry matter yield. Differences in yield reducing effect among species were not significant, but all yields were significantly reduced in alley cropping system as compared to the control. Yield reduction ranged from 40 percent in Gliricidia hedgerows to 61 percent in Moringa hedgerows. Moringa and Leucaena were more competitive than Gliricidia and pigeonpea in terms of their effects on yield a dry matter production of sweet corn. Corn plants in Moringa and Leucaena hedgerows suffered severe moisture stress early in the season. This was also observed until tasseling stage and plants in rows adjacent to hedgerows were severely affected.

Eggplant—The influence of hedgerow species on growth and yield of eggplant was evaluated for two seasons using similar treatments with that in sweet corn. Results showed that Leucaena hedgerows did not reduce eggplant height, whereas Gliricidia, Moringa and pigeonpea significantly reduced plant height. Generally, plants in middle rows were taller than plants adjacent to hedgerow indicating competition effect of hedgerows. Nitrogen levels had no influence on yield, but the main effect of hedgerow species was significant. Eggplant yield increased as row distance from hedgerows increased (table 11). Overall, alley cropping significantly reduced eggplant yield. Yield reduction in Gliricidia and Moringa hedgerows were 55 and 60 percent, respectively. Under Leucaena and pigeonpea hedgerows, yield reduction was 15 and 20 percent, respectively.

During the second season, yield response was almost similar with that obtained in the first season. Plants in middle rows were taller than plants in rows adjacent to hedgerows. The effect of N levels was not significant, but the main effect of hedgerow species on eggplant yield was significant. Eggplant yield increased as row distance from hedgerows increased. Differences in yield reducing effect among species were not significant, but all yields were significantly reduced in the alley cropping system. Yield reduction ranged from 22 percent in pigeonpea to 58 percent in Gliricidia hedgerows. Low yield reduction in pigeonpea hedgerows was attributed to very poor pigeonpea stand virtually eliminating any competition effects.

Study 3—Yield performance of medicinal plants and culinary herbs in hedgerow intercropping with Moringa during early establishment
An on-farm experiment was established to evaluate agronomic and economic potentials of medicinal and culinary herbs grown with medicinal trees in an agroforestry system. Indigenous medicinal herbs included in the evaluation trial were 'Inflammation Bush' (*Verbersina alata*), 'Japana' (*Eupatorium triplinerve*), and 'blue verbena' or 'worrywine' (*Stachytarpheta jamaicensis*). Culinary herbs evaluated were basil (*Ocimum basilicum*), chamomile (*Marticaria recutita*), lemongrass (*Cymbopogon citratus*), sweet marjoram (*Origanum majorana*), rosemary (*Rosmarinus officinalis*), sage (*Salvia officinalis*), and thyme (*Thymus vulgaris*). The medicinal plants and culinary herbs were grown in alleys formed by hedgerows of medicinal trees (*Moringa* sp.).

Germination and establishment of Moringa sp. hedgerows were excellent. Trees reached an average height of 4.26 m for *M. oleifera* and 2.99 m for *M. stenopetala* at 6 months. Biomass production from prunings 6 months after planting indicated that *M. oleifera* was superior to *M. stenopetala*. Total plant fresh and dry weights of *M. oleifera* were greater than *M. stenopetala*. *M. oleifera* growth rate was faster than *M. stenopetala*. This result indicates that *M. oleifera* is a fast growing tree, which attains a height of 2 to 3m after 6 months of growth. Establishment and growth of medicinal plants and culinary herbs varied according to species. Blue verbena and lemongrass established well compared to Japana and Inflammation Bush. Among the culinary herbs, basil, sage and thyme established better than chamomile and rosemary. Establishment of chamomile was very poor in that a majority of the plants did not survive 2 weeks after planting. Likewise, rosemary did not establish well and was sensitive to high-pH soil.

Table 10—Marketable ears of sweet corn by rows as influenced by hedgerow species (adapted from Palada and others 1994)

Hedgerow species	Row[a]					
	1	2	3	4	5	Total
	- - - - - - - - - - - - - - - - - Yield (t ha^{-1}) - - - - - - - - - - - -					
Gliricidia	2.09 b	3.17 a	2.71 a	6.25 a	1.58 b	15.8 b
Leucaena	1.79 bc	4.21 ab	2.25 b	3.40 a	0.75 b	12.4 b
Moringa	0.25 c	3.63 ab	3.33 b	2.38 a	0.71 b	10.3 b
Pigeonpea	1.67 bc	2.25 b	5.13 a	3.58 a	3.75 a	16.4 b
Control	3.80 a	4.88 a	5.96 a	7.54 a	5.84 a	26.3 a

Mean separation in columns by Duncan's multiple range test, P = 0.05.
[a] Rows 1 and 5 are adjacent to hedgerow, rows 2 and 4 are second rows from hedgerow, and row 3 is the middle row.

Table 11—Eggplant yield by rows as influenced by hedgerow species

Hedgerow species	Row[a]					
	1	2	3	4	5	Total
	- - - - - - - - - - - - - - - Yield (t ha^{-1}) - - - - - - - - - - - - - -					
Gliricidia	4.4 c	11.7 c	21.7 bc	11.0 a	4.9 c	53.9 c
Leucaena	10.2 b	23.7 ab	28.5 a	24.9 a	12.7 b	99.8 b
Moringa	4.9 c	13.2 c	18.8 c	8.8 b	3.2 c	48.5 c
Pigeonpea	8.3 b	21.5 b	25.9 ab	22.0 a	11.2 b	88.8 b
Control	20.5 a	27.3 a	28.3 a	26.1 a	18.3 a	120.0 a

Mean separation in columns by Duncan's multiple range test, P = 0.05.
[a] Rows 1 and 5 are adjacent to hedgerow, rows 2 and 4 are second rows from hedgerow, and row 3 is the middle row.

Growth and yield of medicinal plants and culinary herbs varied among species (table 12) and blocks such that differences in plant height and plant fresh and dry weights between treatments (hedgerow vs. no hedgerow) were not detected. However, in general yields (plant fresh and dry weight) of medicinal plants and culinary herbs were higher in the lower terrace (no hedgerow) compared with those in the upper terrace (hedgerow). The lower yield in the higher terrace can be attributed to competition (shading by hedgerow) and relatively lower soil moisture (data not shown). During the early stage of growth, severe drought was experienced and soils quickly dried up in spite of supplemental irrigation. This condition was apparent in the upper terrace as shown by severe plant wilting. Subsequent rainfall in October resulted in plant recovery.

This initial study indicates that integration of medicinal plants and culinary herbs into agroforestry systems involving medicinal trees is feasible in water-limited environments such as the Caribbean. The most productive species—lemongrass, basil, and blue verbena produced high yields in both the upper and lower terrace. Their growth and yield was slightly influenced by the presence of hedgerows. Thyme, sage, Inflammation Bush, and Japana were slow growing and were more influenced by hedgerow than other species including sweet marjoram. Traditional medicinal plants including lemongrass, blue verbena, Inflammation Bush, Japana as well as some culinary herbs such as basil, thyme, sweet marjoram, and sage can be grown in alleys formed by hedgerows of medicinal tree Moringa with minimal negative effect on growth and yield. Competition for light and soil moisture was not critical at the early establishment period of hedgerows. Additional studies are needed to determine the long-term effect of tree-crop interaction on total productivity of this system in the tropics.

These studies have shown the potential and limitation of alley cropping with vegetable crops in the semi-arid tropics. The evaluation on the performance of hedgerow species in terms of establishment, growth, biomass, and nutrient production and response to pruning and competitiveness showed that Gliricidia and Leucaena have potential. Although these species have high biomass and nutrient yield, their yield-reducing effect on eggplant and sweet corn is significant. Moringa is very competitive due to its rapid growth and upright architecture, which caused excessive shading on vegetable crops. Pigeonpea has the lowest biomass and nutrient yield and did not tolerate repeated prunings. In terms of their reducing on vegetable yield, Moringa has the greatest effect followed by Gliricidia and Leucaena. Pigeonpea has the least effect since the competitive effect was almost absent due to its poor regrowth after pruning. Thus, it can be concluded that although, alley cropping reduced vegetable yield significantly, the degree of yield reduction depends on hedgerow species. Future studies should investigate spacing and row arrangement to determine optimum arrangement between hedgerow species and vegetable crops for minimum competition.

The results of these studies suggest that for minority and small landowners and farmers who would integrate agroforestry system in the form of alley cropping or hedgerow intercropping into their farming system, careful selection of tree and crop species should be considered to minimize tree-crop competition at the same time maintain balance and compatibility.

Table 12—Growth and yield of medicinal plants and culinary herbs in hedgerow intercropping—St. Croix, Virgin Islands, 2002

Treatment	Herb species[a]	Plant height	Plant fresh weight	Plant dry weight
		cm	*g*	*g*
Hedgerow	Basil	46.6	270.0	57.0
	Sweet marjoram	30.8	48.0	8.8
	Thyme	27.4	39.3	8.3
	Sage	27.8	32.6	7.6
	Lemongrass	71.9	458.0	114.0
	Blue verbena	49.0	96.0	29.9
	Inflammation bush	40.6	13.8	2.0
	Hedgerow mean	42.0	136.8	32.5
No hedgerow	Basil	50.1	276.0	71.0
	Sweet marjoram	27.0	51.0	9.9
	Thyme	24.8	45.8	10.9
	Sage	27.3	40.8	9.5
	Lemongrass	77.9	564.0	140.0
	Blue verbena	53.9	139.0	32.6
	Inflammation bush	46.3	30.6	6.1
	No hedgerow mean	37.3	163.8	39.1

[a] For each species statistical analysis for all data indicated no significant differences between treatments. Yield data are based on one harvest for thyme, blue verbena and inflammation bush; and three harvests for basil, sweet marjoram, sage and lemongrass.

SUMMARY

In the tropics, the success of integrating high value horticultural crops into agroforestry system through the use of alley cropping or hedgerow intercropping is largely determined by agroecological conditions. In the humid tropics where soil moisture is not limiting, yield of vegetable crops was improved by alley cropping using nitrogen fixing leguminous trees. The presence of hedgerows did not result in soil moisture competition between vegetable crops and trees. In semi-arid tropics where water is limiting, alley cropping did not benefit vegetable crops due to severe soil moisture competition and shading effect. Alley cropping reduced yield, but enhanced microclimate by reducing evapotranspiration and wind speed. The potential of alley cropping high value horticultural crops with tree hedgerows is greater in the humid tropics compared to semi-arid tropics.

REFERENCES

Baldwin, C.S. 1988. The influence of field windbreaks on vegetable and specialty crops. Agriculture, Ecosystems and Environment 22/23:191-203.

Chen, Y.S.; Kang, B.T.; Caveness, F.E. 1989. Alley cropping vegetable crops with Leucaena in Southern Nigeria. HortScience 24: 839-840.

Doorenbos, J.; Pruitt, W.D. 1977. Guidelines for predicting crop water requirements. Irrigation and Drainage Paper No. 24. Food and Agriculture Organization, Rome, Italy.

Houerou, H.N. 1980. Le role des legneux fourragers dans les zones sahelienne et soudanienne. Colloque international fourragers legneux Afrique. Addis Ababa, Ethiopia.

Kang, B.T.; Wilson, G.F.; Lawson, T.L. 1984. Alley Cropping: a stable alternative to shifting cultivation. International Institute of Tropical Agriculture, Ibadan, Nigeria.

Kang, B.T.; Reynolds, L.; Atta-Krah, A.N. 1990. Alley Farming. Advances in Agronomy. 43:315-359.

Kang, B.T.; Sipkens, L.; Wilson, G.F. 1981. Alley cropping maize (Zea mays L.) and Leucaena (Leucaena leucocephala Lam. de Wit) in Southern Nigeria. Plant and Soil. 63:165-179.

Kang, B.T.; Shannon, D.A. 2001. Agroforestry with focus on alley cropping. p. 197-224 In: Sustaining Soil Fertility in West Africa. SSSA Special Publication no. 58. Soil Science Soc. of America and American Society of Agronomy, Madison, WI.

Lal, R. 1975. Role of mulching techniques in tropical soil and water management. Tech. Bull. No. 1. IITA, Ibadan, Nigeria.

Lal, R. 1987. Managing the soils of Sub-Saharan Africa. Science 236:1069-1076.

Lal, R. 1989. Agroforestry systems and soil surface management of a tropical alfisol. I. Soil moisture and crop yields. Agroforestry Systems 8:7-29.

Nair, P.K.R. 1983. Agroforestry with coconuts and other plantation crops. In: P.A. Huxley (ed.). Plant Research and Agroforestry. ICRAF, Nairobi, Kenya. 79-102

Nair, P.K.R. 1993. An Introduction to Agroforestry. Kluwer Academic Publishers, Dordrecht, The Netherlands. 499 p.

Norton, R.L. 1988. Windbreaks: Benefits to orchard and vineyard crops. Agriculture, Ecosystems and Environment. 22/23:205-213.

Ong, C.K.; Singh, R.P.; Khan, A.A.H.; Osman, M. 1990. Agroforestry for the drylands: recent advances in measuring water loss through trees. Agroforestry Today. 2:7-9.

Pacardo, E.P. 1984. Soil erosion and ecological stability. In: E.T. Craswell, J.V., Remeny, J.V. and Nallana, eds. Soil Erosion Management. ACIAR Proc. Series No. 6. Australian Center for International Agric. Research: 82-87.

Palada, M.C.; Kang, B.T.; Claassen, S.L. 1992. Effect of alley cropping with Leucaena leucocephala and fertilizer application on yield of vegetable crops. Agroforestry Systems 19:139-147.

Palada, M.C.; Crossman, S.M.; Collingwood, C.D. 1992. Effects of pigeonpea hedgerows on soil water and yield of intercropped pepper under drip irrigation. Proc. Caribbean Food Crops Soc. 28: 517-532.

Palada, M.C.; O'Donnell, J.J.; Crossman, S.M.A.; Kowalski, J.A. 1994. Influence of four hedgerow species on yield of sweet corn and eggplant in an alley cropping system. Agronomy Abst.1994: 7.

Schaeffer, P.R. 1989. Trees and sustainable agriculture. Amer. J. of Alternative Agric. 4:173-179.

Young, A. 1986. The potential of agroforestry for soil conservation. Part I. Erosion control. Working Paper No. 42. International Center for Research in Agroforestry, Nairobi, Kenya.

Young, A. 1987. The potential of agroforestry for soil conservation. Part II. Maintenance of soil fertility. Working Paper No. 43. International Center for Research in Agroforestry, Nairobi, Kenya.

AGROFORESTRY TO ENHANCE LAND PRODUCTIVITY AND ENVIRONMENTAL PROTECTION

James L. Robinson[1]

Abstract—Agroforestry is the intentional, interactive, integrated and intensive blending of agricultural and forestry production and conservation practices. Agroforestry technologies can be readily incorporated into most farm and ranch operations and are also useful to many communities. These practices provide cost-effective ways to diversify production and increase income, while simultaneously enhancing natural resource conservation.

INTRODUCTION

The National Agroforestry Center (NAC) in Lincoln, Nebraska had its origins in the 1990 Farm Bill. It began as a USDA Forest Service effort in 1992 and expanded into a partnership with the USDA Natural Resources Conservation Service (NRCS) in 1995. The mission is to accelerate the development and application of agroforestry technologies to attain more economically, environmentally, and socially sustainable land-use systems. To accomplish its mission the Center interacts with a national network of partners and cooperators to conduct research, develop technologies and tools, establish demonstrations, and provide useful information to natural resource professionals.

Agroforestry is the intentional, interactive, integrated and intensive blending of agricultural and forestry production and conservation practices. Agroforestry technologies can be readily incorporated into most farm and ranch operations and are also useful to many communities. These practices provide cost-effective ways to diversify production and increase income, while simultaneously enhancing natural resource conservation.

Research and Development

The NAC has a small research staff funded through the U.S. Forest Service that conducts research primarily on the design and installation of forested buffers to protect water quality. We partner with other research institutions in a coordinated effort to develop the most complete, readily available research on buffers possible to help implement an effective program that includes tree-based buffers.

We also partner with Agricultural Research Service (ARS), land grant universities (1862 and 1890) and other institutions of higher learning to develop research and demonstration sites for many of the agroforestry practices utilized in the United States.

For the past several years, the NAC has been contributing matching dollars to the Sustainable Agriculture Research and Education Grant Program (SARE) for approved agroforestry projects.

It is apparent that to further knowledge of agroforestry, the relationship with our conservation partners and cooperators are an essential and valued part of our conservation program.

Technology Transfer and Applications

The NAC has 7.5 agroforesters and technology transfer specialists whose main responsibility is the development and the delivery of agroforestry technology on a broad suite of agroforestry practices that fall in six major categories:

1. Alley Cropping—the growing of an annual or perennial crop between rows of high value trees. The agricultural crop generates annual income while the longer-term tree crop matures. Examples are walnut and soybeans, pecan and a hay crop, or pine and milo.

2. Forest Farming—the cultivation of high-value specialty crops under a forest canopy that has been modified to provide the correct shade and microenvironment for the crop. These specialty crops usually fall into three categories; medicinal, culinary, or ornamental.

3. Windbreaks—trees planted to prevent soil erosion and to protect crops, livestock, buildings, work areas, roads, or communities from wind or snow. Living snowfences primarily protect roads, but can also harvest snow to replenish soil moisture or fill ponds and reservoirs in arid parts of the country.

4. Riparian Forest Buffers—natural or planted streamside vegetation of trees, shrubs and grasses. They are designed to buffer non-point source pollution, such as excess nutrient and pesticide runoff generated from adjacent land use. They are also extremely important to the aquatic and terrestrial habitat of many southeastern streams.

5. Special Applications—many opportunities for utilizing trees and shrubs for specific agricultural or rural community concerns. These special applications include the disposal of community wastewater or farm animal waste in poplar or pine fiber plantation, visual screening, noise abatement, and odor control.

6. Silvopasture—systems combine growing of timber with forage and livestock production. The trees provide longer-term returns while livestock grazing of the managed understory generates an annual income and cash flow. This combination of trees and forage often reduces stress on animals and provides a high level of forage production while still providing comparable wood production to a plantation.

[1]Agroforester, USDA-NRCS National Agroforestry Center, Fort Worth, TX.

Silvopasture is the agroforestry practice that has received the most emphasis in the southeast during the past couple of years. It is a natural for the Southern pine forest in terms of both economic and environmental benefits. However, in order to be successful, it must become socially acceptable and technically defensible. When many of us went to forestry school, we were taught that cows in the woods were bad. The examples shown to us were of overgrazed stands where soil erosion and or browsing damage were severe and wildlife habitat destroyed. Obviously the prevalent thought was cows were bad. Grazing specialists were taught about "brush" control. Brush (read that trees) was considered undesirable competitors for sun, water and nutrients and significantly reduced forage production. Obviously trees were bad in a forage production system.

In the late seventies and early eighties, Dr. Cliff Lewis with the U.S. Forest Service began researching the feasibility of growing grass and southern pine on the same acreage. His work was followed by Dr. Henry Pearson also with the U.S. Forest Service and later with ARS. The most recent work was done by Dr. Terry Clason, Louisiana State University. Their work became the foundation for silvopasture in the South. Silvopasture has developed into a management system that maximizes the potential production of both timber and forage. Others have taken on the challenge and continued work in silvopasture systems is being carried out through many of our colleges and institutions across the South including Florida A&M University.

This past year, the NAC has sponsored and carried out training sessions with support from many partners in the South to provide technical silvopasture training to NRCS, extension personnel, State forestry and wildlife agencies, conservation districts and private NGO's and consultants. Over 400 technical people have received training this past year in Florida, Alabama, Georgia, and South Carolina. Several presentations have also been made to landowner groups across the South and an effort is being proposed to conduct landowner workshops beginning this next year.

In addition to those training sessions, the NAC held a three day silvopasture workshop for all 1890 institutions at Alabama A&M University. Twelve of the 1890 institutions were represented plus individuals from the Alabama Forestry Commission outreach foresters, and the Alabama Farmers Federation.

Silvopasture has become institutionalized as an agroforestry system not only through the NAC, but also our many partners such as the Center for Subtropical Agroforestry, the University of Florida; the University of Missouri Center for Agroforestry; CINRAM, the University of Minnesota; Grazing Lands Technology Institute; NRCS; The National Grazing Lands Conservations Initiative; USDA Agriculture Research Service; Cooperative Research, Education, and Extension Service, especially SARE and our many cooperators at 1862 and 1890 institutions, federal and state agencies; and nongovernmental organizations.

CONCLUSION

Agroforestry is "social forestry". Its' purpose is sustainable development. Practices are focused on meeting the economic, environmental, and social needs of people on their private lands. Agroforestry practices are intentional combinations of trees with crops and/or livestock that involve intensive management of the interactions between the components as an integrated agro-ecosystem. These key characteristics are the essence of agroforestry and are what distinguish it from other farming or forestry practices.

While silvopasture is the agroforestry system receiving the most attention today, it is not the only agroforestry practice applicable to the South. What it will take to be successful is a partnership with state and federal agencies, conservation and farm organizations, and the educational institutions working together to bring the research and technical information to the land. Landowners will ultimately judge the viability of the systems and if it meets their goals and objectives, agroforestry systems will become a part of the landscape.

The NAC remains committed to exploring the potential of agroforestry in the South and working with willing cooperators and partners to further our knowledge and expertise on a system designed to aid the sustainability of our land for today and the future.

REFERENCES

Byrd, N.A.; Lewis, C.E.; Pearson, H.A. 1984. Management of southern pine forests for cattle production. USDA Forest Service. General Report R8-GR 4. 22 p.

Clason, T.R. 1999. Silvopastoral practices sustain timber and forage production in commercial loblolly pine plantations of northwest Louisiana, USA. Agroforestry Systems 44: 293-303.

Garrett, H.E.; Rietveld, W.J.; Fisher, R.F., ed. 2000; North American Agroforestry: an integrated science and practice; ASA; 402 p.

OPPORTUNITIES AGROFORESTRY PROVIDE MINORITY AND LIMITED RESOURCE LANDOWNERS

Rory Fraser[1]

Abstract—Minority landowners are not perceived by land management agencies to be engaged in land stewardship. An innovative research and outreach project aimed at increasing minority landowners' participation in land stewardship is presented in this paper. Landowners and faculty, staff and students of Alabama A&M University are trying to determine if goat rearing and tree growing, together, provide a viable land management alternative for landowners and an effective strategy for combating wildfire and its associated problems. This example of agroforestry is presented as an alternative for engaging minority landowners in land stewardship.

INTRODUCTION

Forests are becoming of greater social and economic importance in the South, and the integration of farming and forestry is increasing in importance to farmers and rural economies. In Alabama, forestry has gone from 10 percent of farm agricultural and forestry cash receipts in 1978 to 22 percent of receipts in 1998. Timber ranked second among farm sources of income (Bliss and Muehlenfeld 1995). Schelhas and Zabawa (2000) make the point that minorities and poor people are in danger of being left behind in these changes, and careful attention must be paid to their interests in forestry research, outreach, and management. They cite the Zabawa (1991) study informing us that during the 20th century, black land ownership and farming have declined at rates exceeding those for whites, and black farm size has continued to substantially lag behind white farm size. This is consistent with Dismukes and others (1997) and the USDA Civil Rights Action Team (1997) who concluded minority and limited resource landowners have historically been underserved by extension and assistance programs in the South. Joshi and others (2000) pointed out that, despite statewide and regional economic benefits of the forestry industry, there are continuing shortfalls in human capital development in many forest dependent communities, which, they contend, threaten the long-term economic and social well being of these communities. Schelhas and Zabawa (2000) conclude that there has been insufficient research, outreach, and education on minority and limited resource landowners and their forests in the South. If government and private forestry programs are to provide an equitable distribution of benefits to all segments of society in the South, we need to fill the gaps in our knowledge through systematic research on the relationships between people and forests with special attention to those populations who have been traditionally underserved because of race/ethnicity, gender, or resource limitations. In this paper, we present an innovative research and outreach agroforestry project aimed at increasing minority landowner participation in land stewardship by providing them an opportunity for improved short-term viability.

FOCUS AREA

The area chosen for this study is Alabama's Western Black Belt, which derives its name from its soil as well as the ethnicity of the population. These eight counties are among the 10 (the others are Macon and Bullock) with over 50 percent black populations in the 2000 census. Poverty is endemic in this region, with poverty rates (34.9 percent) almost twice the State's average of 18.8 percent. The disparity between black and other farmers is most poignant in the USDA 1997 Census of Agriculture data for the region. Blacks own 21 percent of the farms; make up 21 percent of the people who identify farming as their principal occupation and report 19 percent of the farms with harvested croplands. However, they only own 5 percent of the land, operate 6 percent of the harvested croplands and generate 2 percent of the value of agricultural products sold. The major difference between the two groups is the size of farms. Others own farms that are five times the size of their black counterparts. At the same time, the average value of sales from black farms is $3,476 or one-fifteenth the average sale ($50,841) from all farms in the region. Ownership of harvested cropland seems to be a major problem for black farmers; the average size for the 280 operations is 40.4 acres. Sixty percent (359) of the farmers are full owners of their properties but they only average 9.5 acres of harvested cropland. On the other hand, one-third of the farmers are part owners and they operate the majority 70 percent (average 40.4 acres) of harvested cropland. The 43 tenant farmers operate 373 acres, an average of 8.7 acres per farm. These small operations do not yield very high levels of return. So, despite 230 blacks reporting farming as their principal occupation, only 83 reported more than $10,000 of agricultural products sold. More than half sell less than $2,500 worth of products in a year. However, harvested croplands only account for 13 percent or 182,232 of the 1.37 million acres farmland in the 8-county region. The rest of the 486,897 acres of total croplands makes up another 22 percent of the farmland. Twenty-eight percent (385,974 acres) of the farms are wooded areas, 9 percent are pastured woodlands, and the other 27 percent (375,096 acres) are idle lands or lands subscribed to special programs such as Conservation or Wetland Reserves (118,587 acres).

NEEDS ASSESSMENT

Limited resource landowners on small acreages have to develop income-earning alternatives in order to keep their land. Recent landowner workshops (held by Alabama A&M University (AAMU), in Normal, AL, and the Alabama Forestry Commission (AFC) and the Federation of Southern Cooperatives (FSC) in Epes, AL) provided anecdotal evidence suggesting that many alternatives tried in the past required high labor inputs, close monitoring, or special skills. Limited resource landowners expressed a need for land use

[1]Associate Professor, Center for Forestry & Ecology, Alabama A&M University, Normal, AL.

activities that generate income, require little time, are socially and culturally consistent, and are accomplishable given the time required for a full-time job, family, and religious activity. Timber growing is something they had all done, usually without a plan, and tree farming has the desired attributes. However, the income generated from this activity is too long term. They need activities that also generate income in the short term, i.e., semi-annual or annually to help defray short-term expenses, such as maintenance and taxes. Some alternatives such as row and specialty crops require periods of intense activity or highly specialized knowledge in order to be successful. Goat herding, however, is an activity that generated a great deal of interest among black farmers in Alabama. Farmers seem to be intrigued by the efficiency with which guard animals handled and protected the herd. They liked the fact that these animals are hardy, graze on most vegetation (especially kudzu), and graze well among established tree stands. More importantly they were excited by the current and growing demand for goat meat both in Alabama and in the region. The landowners see this as an opportunity to retain trees while generating short-term income. In turn, the goats graze the ground vegetation in the forest and keep the underbrush relatively clean. In other silvopastoral systems, such as cattle-tree systems, trees have been shown to grow even faster. Similar benefits may also occur in goat-tree systems. As a result of these workshops, at least four landowners have acquired goats. Others were intrigued, but lacked the resources to become involved. These potential benefits aside, goat-tree management systems offer a new opportunity for a creative solution to wildfire management. Goats have been shown to be very effective—an environmentally friendly as well as an inexpensive way to control brush and grass in three fire-prone California locations: Los Altos Hills, Beverly Hills, and Menlo Park. Goats may be especially effective when vegetation control is of critical importance in areas sensitive to: chemicals, e.g., riparian areas; and smoke, e.g., urbanized areas. But, despite goats being wonderful defoliants when managed properly, they are not natural and have to be managed to minimize environmental damage and economic loss.

The Research Problem
The question of interest to many of these farmers is: does goat rearing and tree growing provide a viable alternative for landowners? For many foresters the question is: do goats provide an effective strategy for combating wildfire and its associated problems without negative impact to preferred trees and plants?

Landowners Input
The 12 landowners discussed this problem and opportunity on the Outreach Advisory Council of the AFC. As a result, they organized a meeting in Camden, AL of landowners, AFC staff, AAMU and Tuskegee University (TU) faculty, FSC and Wilcox County High School (WCHS) staff, Wilcox County extension and Alabama Department of Agriculture staff in October 2001. The members of this group raised the following questions: What special knowledge, time and resources are required for landowners to develop the knowledge needed to manage the goats? What are the costs/benefits involved in rearing a goat herd in the forest? How does goat herding and tree growing activities complement/detract from each

other? How must forest management practices be modified to accommodate goat rearing? How effective are goats in reducing wildfire risks and smoke hazard/pollution? Finally, there was a great deal of interest in: How can landowners be involved in researching these questions, themselves? At the conclusion of the meeting, AAMU and TU faculty were tasked to develop a proposal that addresses these questions. The project design was required to incorporate participatory on-farm research, peer teaching, start-up funding, technical support, and networking opportunity for participants. And, an advisory committee comprised of landowners, AFC staff, AAMU and TU faculty, FSC, and WCHS staff, was established to review the proposal and give direction to the project if or when it was funded. This project is the outcome of a successful proposal to the U.S. Forest Service Title IV Fire Plan: Economic Action Program Community Assistance Category.

Project Objectives
The primary objective of the project is to evaluate a goat-tree agroforestry system on privately owned lands. However, other objectives of the project were:

- Participatory Research—by engaging underserved landowners in the research process and by conducting the research on their property

- Human Capital Development—by providing training and learning experiences to participating landowners. They, in turn, were expected to assist other underserved landowners who have been inspired by their efforts

- Economic Development—by providing start-up funds as well as technical assistance in record keeping and marketing to participants

- Technical Support—by facilitating interactions between university faculty, state and federal agencies' staff and extension personnel and the participating landowners

PROCEDURE
The project proposed pilot testing the establishment and management of agroforestry systems on private properties by actively engaging landowners, academics, and institutions. Faculty, staff and students of AAMU and TU helped to establish 10 herds of goats: two as demonstration projects (FSC lands at Epes, AL and a WCHS school farm Camden, AL) and eight from a list of landowners who had attended an AFC, AAMU or FSC workshop and expressed an interest in actively participating in the project. The criteria used to select the eight landowners were: (a) members of the underserved landowner population with established tree stands on their own properties, (b) landowners willing to purchase a herd of goats and actively participate in the study for at least 3 years, and (c) landowners who were prepared to invest time and effort in attending training sessions/meetings and recording data.

Each established herd is to be treated as a case study and is a variant on a range of: land areas, cover types, and grazing intensities. Initial training of the landowners, by a successful goat breeder/instructor, is to be followed by other training/ meeting sessions at AAMU, TU and FSC. Collaborators from the AFC, FSC, and TU, provided the farmers assistance in: (a) establishing a herd, (b) maintaining the herd, (c) devising a time-management scheme, and (d) establishing and maintaining a record-keeping system. The breeder/instructor acts as a telephone consultant to landowners and provides technical assistance advice to the herders. An AAMU Ph.D. student provides technical assistance and keeps track of landowners' activities by maintaining a log for each herder. A telephone help service is provided to the rancher/instructor and landowners in the project.

Information maintained by the landowners and retained as project records are the following:

- Time—required by new herders to: (a) develop the requisite training, acquire a herd of goats and guard animals, (b) prepare the farm for the herd, (c) complete the routine daily activities associated with maintaining the herd, (d) breed and cull the herd, and (e) engage in other herd maintenance activities

- Cost—associated with goat rearing, i.e., the activities listed above and the opportunity cost associated with time spent on these activities

- Critical information needs of the goat herders—determine the assistance available to them both in terms of references as well as sources

- Complementarities of goat rearing and tree growing—identifying, assessing and quantifying the mutual benefits, e.g., protection of property by dogs and maintenance of under bush by goats

- Financial returns of the goat-tree systems

- Effectiveness of goats in fuel reduction—evaluate vegetation control and fire-reduction

- Impacts of goats on vegetation—positive and negative effects on trees and plants in the forest

RESULTS AND CONCLUSIONS

To date, eight farmers have been identified. They were provided some start-up funding and two workshops on starting and managing a goat herd, and encouraged to attend three other workshops provided by AAMU or the FSC. The group is multi-cultural with one Hispanic, one White, six Black families in seven different counties (Sumter, Fayette, Tuscaloosa, Crenshaw, Marengo, Pickens, and Wilcox). Two of the landowners have no previous experience with goats, and all the others have had goats but they either pastured them or allowed them to free range without management. All of the landowners had some history of trying alternative uses for their land: some had tried cattle, sheep, bees, row crops, etc. with varied levels of success. None of the participants had managed their goats or alternatives based on current science. They either left it to nature or done it the old way.

The FSC have also started their herd and is using it as a training and demonstration project for landowners in and around Sumter County, their home-base. They have identified five landowners whom they are training and supporting. At the same time, they have started training these five and other landowners in the formation of a goat-herders marketing cooperative.

WCHS has not launched its project as yet. The forested area suitable for the project has been reallocated for a major construction project, a football stadium. However, an agreement was struck with a neighbor (of the school property) who is interested in the project. The proposed location meets all criteria and allows easy access for the students at WCHS. The project will be supervised by an advisory committee of parents, instructors, foresters, and agriculturalists who are interested in promoting hands-on agroforestry education at WCHS.

There has been a lot of interest generated by this project. Other landowners who have heard of the project have expressed an interest in joining. At least 10 of these landowners have attended training sessions or visited a participant's herd. At the same time there has been a great deal of sharing among the participants. Some have even provided direct assistance in fencing construction, buying, breeding, transporting, and birthing of others goats. Participants talk to each other in meetings, during visits, and on the telephone about their problems and how to resolve them.

We have learned a great deal from this experience. On the positive side, we learned that there is a wealth of knowledge and resources in the community. For example, the "goat lady" (Mrs. Doris Smith of Catherine, AL), an avid goat breeder, is the inspiration and advisor for all the participants. We have also learned about inspiration. At least 15 people have been influenced to be involved in agroforestry just from the enthusiasm of partners and early participants in this project. We have seen the development of a fledgling network with people sharing experiences, learning from each other, helping out, giving moral support, and looking out for each other. Participants are beginning to appreciate their market power and are engaging in collective selling and collective buying.

On the other side, we have learned that there are a number of hurdles to overcome. For example, institutional support for projects like this could be a major obstacle—they can be very inefficient. Collaboration is also challenging because communication, commitment, and follow up with other institutions are not easy. At the same time, these projects are time consuming, and there is a level of inconsistency and inconstancy about keeping an agenda and keeping everybody apace with that agenda.

What can we share from this experience? It is too early to tell. But, we think that this project could be a model for: participatory research, on-farm research, peer sharing/learning, and alternative land management practices.

This modified tree-farming system could provide a profitable solution to an ongoing problem with wildfire and bring about economic development in rural communities. Underserved landowners have expressed a very high level of interest in this land-use activity since it is culturally acceptable, the cost of start-up is relatively low, there is a ready market that is under supplied, and the time and effort required seem to be less than what is required for alternative activities. By direct engagement in researching this problem, underserved landowners may rediscover an interest in tree farming and land ownership, thereby reversing past and current trends. The AFC outreach activities and efforts with underserved landowners could be enhanced, while one of the expressed needs of the underserved is being addressed.

ACKNOWLEDGMENTS

This project would not have been possible without the support of Arione Irby and Rosalind Peoples of the AFC Outreach Advisory Council, Tim Boyce, Alabama State Forester and his Executive Assistant, Gus Townes. Charles and Doris Smith (goat lady), AFC staff Lakedra Byrd, and FSC staff Derek Wilkerson and Amadou Diop all provided immeasurable support for the project. Funding was provided by the AFC through the U.S. Forest Service Title IV Fire Plan funds.

REFERENCES

Bliss, J.; Muehlenfeld, K. 1995. Timber and the economy of Alabama. Alabama Cooperative Extension System, ANR-602, Auburn University, Auburn, AL.

Dismukes, R.; Harwood, J.L.; Bentley, S.E. 1997. Characteristics and risk management needs of limited resource and socially disadvantaged armers. Agriculture Information Bulletin No. 733. Commercial Agriculture Division, Economic Research Service, and Risk Management Agency, U.S. Department of Agriculture.

Joshi, M.L.; Bliss, J.C.; Bailey, C. [and others]. 2000. Investing in industry, underinvesting in human capital: forest-based rural development in Alabama. Society and Natural Resources 13(4): 291-296.

Schelhas, J.; Zabawa, R. 2000. Minority and limited resource landowners and forests in the South: developing a research agenda. Southern Research Station, USDA Forest Service, Tuskegee University, AL.

USDA Civil Rights Action Team. 1997. Civil rights at the United States Department of Agriculture. Report 14. Civil Rights Division, U.S. Department of Agriculture.

Zabawa, R. 1991. The black farmer and land in South-Central Alabama: strategies to preserve a scarce resource. Human Ecology 19(1): 61-81.

PROTECTING THE ECOSYSTEM THROUGH RELIGION: THE CASE OF RELIGIOUS GROVES IN ONDO, NIGERIA

Olugbemi Moloye[1]

Abstract—Many African cultures belong to societies that have always had an environmentalist ethical consciousness as integral aspects of their overall ethical system. Preserving the environment was a necessary part of these cultures in ensuring the inviolability of the ecosystem. The objective of this paper is to demonstrate the extent to which eco-consciousness pervades every aspect of the African life and the place of awe which the ecosystem is enshrined as it is conspicuously manifested in religious practices. For example, Yoruba children in West Africa were taught through folklore early in life to perceive the environment as a place where demons with ten thousand heads as well as one-eyed creatures live, hence the forest ecosystem is treated with respect and sometimes, trepidation.

INTRODUCTION

Many commentators on the development of environmentalist ethics in Africa have observed that the level of industrial development in sub-Saharan Africa has not risen to the level that has made the emergence of environmentalism an integral aspect of the post-industrial society of the West. William Slaymaker ascribes the slow development of eco-criticism and eco-literature in Africa to the low level of industrialization in most of the countries of Africa (Slaymaker 2001). He argues that many of the conditions that generate eco-consciousness in writers and critics in the industrial countries of the West are relatively absent or underdeveloped in Africa. These conditions, according to Slaymaker, range from literary and critical traditions that assume the presence of natural history in human history to opening of spaces for the interests of the nonhuman dimension of nature.

While Slaymaker acknowledges the mention of nature in African poetry, he is able to identify Niyi Osundare's The Eye of the Earth (1986) as the only major poetic work that is concerned with the environment. It is conceivable that the palpable effects of overuse of the environment could have led to the surge in environmentalist ethics in the West, but, like so many other aspects of human behavior, it is conceivable that non-Western societies have a different tradition in which the environment, often seen as nature, is viewed and represented as intrinsically indispensable to human flourishing, and thus worthy of special consideration at all times. Several of the cultures in Africa show convincing evidence that they belong to societies that have always had an environmentalist ethical consciousness as integral aspect of their overall ethical system. The aim of this paper is to demonstrate the extent to which eco-consciousness pervades every aspect of the African life and the place of awe which the ecosystem is enshrined as it is conspicuously manifested in religious practices. It will also demonstrate that despite the absence of placard-carrying, crowd-shouting environmentalists in Africa as in Western societies, the Yoruba and indeed, African societies have devised ways of preserving the sanctity of the environment. In pre-colonial Africa, preserving the environment needs neither Government legislation nor ecology police before the inviolability of the ecosystem is maintained and upheld. Yoruba children were taught through folklore early in life to perceive the environment as a place where demons with ten thousand heads as well as one-eyed creatures live, hence the environment is treated with respect and sometimes, trepidation.

It may be appropriate to criticize contemporary African scholars for not paying sufficient attention to the current environmental degradation to which African societies have been subjected to in recent times, but any measure of familiarity with pre-colonial cultural and social practices ranging from myth, ritual and oral poetry will reveal the ubiquity of eco-consciousness in the oral traditions of several African communities of nature as the source of human flourishing. To the African, the forest carries both symbolic and cultural values in the physical as well as in the metaphysical realm. Any attempt to make a distinction between the two will amount to a futile exercise as the forests feature holistically in the culture, language, history, art, medicine, politics, social structure and most importantly, the religion. The point is that the African world is not easily reduced to compartments as religion is hardly separated from daily life.

It is appropriate to point out that the centrality of nature and of nature-culture tension to people of African descent was acknowledged in ancient times in different forms of ritual and poetic performances. Among the Yoruba of Nigeria, for example, the month of Oro or Orele (among the Ondo-Yoruba of the rainforest area) is one dedicated to rituals of respect and commitment to the vitality and veneration of nature. Prayers and sacrifices are made for the continuation of the bounty and scarcity of nature. This tradition of chanting of images and metaphors of utmost respect for both human and non-human nature is more evident in a poetic genre called Ijala or Are Ode (Babalola 1977). In this poetic performance, all units of nature, from the little plant to the biggest animal in the forest, and from the smallest stream to the mighty Niger River and the Atlantic Ocean, and from the rolling flat savannah to the high mountains serve as the target of panegyrics or praise poetry.

In recent years, African writers in European languages, particularly English and French, have also focused in different ways on the importance of nature and the environment to the survival of humanity. The most cited poet of nature in recent times is Leopold Senghor, the Negritude poet, whose contrast between green (nature) in Africa and brown

[1] Professor, Department of Anthropology and Sociology, Florida A&M University, Tallahassee, FL.

(construction of steel and brick edifices in New York) was a very popular poem in the 1960s. The present paper is designed to provide a rigorous discussion of how Africans have imagined and imagine nature in both oral traditional and religious practices before contact with Europeans.

Land Use Before Colonialism

Before contact with Europeans, indigenous African peoples lived in close proximity with their environment through time. No doubt the arrangement might be encysted in mysticism, nonetheless the perfect synergy between man and nature facilitated a flourishing ecosystem. With the introduction of legitimate trade, the land that was once collectively owned and managed by family members underwent balkanization as the seed of individual ownership was planted through the introduction of cash cropping. The transformation of Africa's forest economy from subsistence to cash economy was in large part designed to satisfy the insatiable appetite of European needs for tropical crops. It was also made to institutionalize a capitalist middle-class cadre capable of maintaining a European way of life, which had been created through colonialism. In line with the goals of a cash economy, chemicals were indiscriminately poured into the African flora and fauna in order to maximize productivity. The institutionalization of legitimate trade abolished the traditional sacredness of land use, owing to the fact that cash crops became permanent features, which led to the destabilization of collective family land ownership. In the name of profits no natural phenomenon is beyond defilement and de-sacralization as rivers and trees, most especially those considered sacred, came under the hammer of "legitimate" trade, profit and inordinate greed. In the words of Calame-Griaule (1970), forest trees in Africa are seen as the links between the spiritual world of ancestors and its people on earth. Rituals and ceremonies which draw on forest symbols often serve to link people with their cultural heritage, as well as their ancestral past. All over Africa trees are traditionally seen as material symbols. It is under the trees people seek to escape from the scotching mid-day tropical sun. It is the African tree that provides material as well as therapeutic nourishment as the herbalist doctor relies on it for medicaments. Many African myths depict the tree as an ancestral wisdom, authority and custom, it is no wonder why village elders meet under shaded trees at the village square to deliberate on public policy and arbitrate social conflicts. The tree does not only provide shade but a bond between the dead and the living as those before the current generation of elders also sat under the trees at the village square.

Incidentally these were practices European colonialists thought were foolish and anti-development. For the sake of "development" therefore, the African flora and fauna were defaced as the tall trees that were once considered sacred were felled and shipped to Europe. It must be pointed out that colonialism in Africa had its contradictions like other forces of external imposition. While timbers were being felled and shipped to Europe, there was a gathering in London in 1900, dubbed the "Convention for the Preservation of Animals" which was later to become the colonial wildlife legislation in Anglophone Africa. If there is any truth to that convention, it was designed to provide Europeans with a "Garden of Eden"

in Africa, which Europeans already had lost to indiscriminate environmental despoliation in the name of development. Consequent to the Convention, land was demarcated as national parks as well as game reserves, which was meant for the protection of large animal species and their habitat. Incidentally these were decisions taken in European capitals without consultation with the natives whom the decision was meant to benefit. No doubt such a decision affected the lives of subsistence farmers and fishermen as it deprived them access to their means of livelihood. Had the Europeans taken time to understand traditional land use policy in Africa, they might not have overlooked the traditional role the environment plays in the lives of the people.

There is probably no cultural group in Black Africa, without allusion to the mysticism of the environment. To the African, the forest is the home to invisible principalities. It is the place where the ancestors reside and ritually journey home to meet with their descendants during such ritual performance as the rites of rebirth and intensification. The forests are viewed in both positive and negative lights. They have the potential to provide sources of evil if violated as well as power and benefit if treated with care. The herbalist doctor relies on the forest to provide him with therapeutic medicaments, hence, the environment is treated with veneration and trepidation most especially the area of the forest that is allocated for worship and consequently considered beyond defilement. In many African societies, forest area and specific trees such as the Iroko or Akoko trees (among the Ondo-Yoruba for example), are protected and valued for particular cultural occasions and historic symbols. Historically Africans are known to conserve biodiversity by:

1. Protecting particular ecosystem or habitats (such as sacred groves, royal burial grounds, sacred rivers)

2. Protecting particular animal or plant species (such as totem and tabooed species)

3. Regulating exploitation of natural resources (such as banning of harvesting or hunting in religious forests)

SACRED RELIGIOUS GROVES

Sacred groves are the site of ritual and secret society initiations with tremendous essence in traditional Africa. It is in the scared groves that puberty rites take place. It is also a place where social and political values, morals, secrets, and laws are passed on to the younger generation. Sacred groves house the most important and social relics of antiquities. In some communities, the groves are the sites of ancestral burials or sacred places where communication between man and nature take place. This is due to the fact that the sacred trees and forests are believed to house the spirits of the past and the covenant of the future for the community. Hence it is only the initiates that are allowed in the groves. For example Igbo Ora among the Ondo-Yoruba land is believed to be the place where the Ondo people were brought back from extinction after a number of cataclysmic events had threatened their very existence, hence its sacredness.

Traditional religion in Africa is best described as the religion of nature because of its cosmic orientation. It demonstrates a holistic perspective of reality as it ascertains the interdependence between man and nature. Accordingly nature is accorded ultimate respect as equal partners and this is what the Yoruba do to a fault. Igbo Ora at Ondo in South Western Nigeria contain trees and animals considered sacred. Resultantly, animals found in Igbo Ora are not to be killed neither are the trees to be felled. This is due to the role Igbo Ora had played in the history of Ondo community.

There was a time in the mythical past of the Ondo community when three kings had died in quick succession within 6 years. As it is the fashion in Yoruba tradition, it became imperative to identify the root cause of the tragedy through oracular consultation. Emissaries were sent to Ile-Ife which is acknowledged to be the spiritual home of the Yoruba for consultation with a diviner. While at Ile-Ife, the emissaries met with Chief Sora, a renounced diviner, who after divination told them to bring a myriad of 201 different items. After the Ondo people had assembled these items, Chief Sora was invited back to Ondo in order for him to preside over the sacrificing of these items, which was done at Igbo Ora. Legend indicates that as Chief Sora was coming back from Igbo Ora, upon getting to the front of the King's palace, he erected his Oyeren sword at a place that has since become a place where the King washes his hands traditionally. There were other symbolic rituals performed, all of which were designed to put to an end to the abridged lives of Ondo kings. Indeed the Oba's palace was formerly moved from one part of the town to a newly designated area.

Three years later, the Ondo community experienced a cataclysmic pestilence as livestock and poultry died in their thousands. To compound the disaster, the Ondo community experienced a long drawn out drought, which led to a massive death by hunger, an anathema in farming community. Once again, the Ondo king sent for Chief Sora to help come arrest the misfortune. On arrival, Chief Sora consulted the oracle as he did the first time only to be told that a sheep should be sacrificed in order to end the cataclysm. At this juncture, the Ondo king demanded that Chief Sora should not return to Ile-Ife where he had come but should stay put in Ondo. After due consultation, the Chief decided to stay permanent. Chief Sora's relocation was not without conditions. It is taboo for subsequent Soras to pass the spot where the Oyeren sword was erected the first time he came to save the Ondo people. In light of the contributions of Chief Sora to the Ondo people, it has become a tradition for the Ondo people to set a day aside in the year to commemorate their re-birth through the re-enactment of Oranfe. The Oranfe festival has come to symbolize a ritual drama of social rejuvenation and reawakening, which brought back the Ondo people from the jaws of extinction.

CONCLUSION

Its annual re-enactment symbolizes the creative power of sacrifice, which is performed in the Igbo Ora sacred grove. Having accomplished the task of preempting societal disaster through sacrifices and libations, it became imperative that Igbo Ora would attain deification status, hence the non-defilement of its sacred ground through hunting and felling of trees. No doubt the annual celebration of Oranfe has become a ritual re-enactment, which in the eyes of the Ondo people, gave them a new lease on life. It is a ritual commemorated by the people in their finest splendor and gaiety.

REFERENCES

Adams, A.; Mayes, J., eds. 1998. Mapping intersections: African literature and Africa's development. Africa World Press, Trenton, NJ.

Adamson, J. 2001. American Indian literature, environmental justice and ecocriticism: the middle place. University of Arizona Press, Tucson, AZ.

Alaimo, S. 2000. Undomesticated ground: recasting nature as feminist space. Cornell University Press, Ithaca, NY.

Babalola, S.A. 1977. Form and content in Yoruba Ijala. Oxford University Press, Oxford, UK.

Branch, M.P. 1998. Reading the earth: new directions in the study of literature and environment. Moscow, University of Idaho Press, Moscow, Idaho.

Brown, S.G. 2000. Words in the wilderness: the U.S. environmental movement from a critical perspective. MIT Press, Cambridge, MA.

Buell, L. 1995. The environmental imagination: theory, nature writing, and the formation of American culture. Harvard University Press, Cambridge, MA.

Buell, L. 2001. Writing for an endangered world: literature, culture, and environment in the U.S. and beyond. The Belknap Press of Harvard University Press, Cambridge, MA.

Coussy, D. 2000. La Litterature Africaine Moderne au Sud du Sahara. Karthala, Paris, France.

Dann, K. 2000. African earthkeepers: a wholistic interfaith mission. Orbis Books, Mary knoll, NY.

Godfelty, C.; Fromm, H., eds. 1996. The ecocriticism reader: landmarks in literary ecology. University of Georgia Press, Athens, GA.

Grove, R.; Green, H. 1994. Imperialism: colonial expansion, Tropical Island Edens, and the origins of environmentalism. Cambridge University Press. Cambridge, MA 1660-1860.

Harvey, D. 1996. Justice, nature, and the geography of difference. Blackwell, Oxford, UK.

Hochman, J. 1998. Green cultural studies: nature in film, novel, and theory. University of Idaho University Press, Idaho, Moscow.

Huttermann, A. 1999. Ecological message of the Torah. Scholars Press, Atlanta, GA.

Kahn, P.H. 1999. The human relationship with nature: development and culture. MIT Press, Cambridge, MA.

Kerridge, R.; Sammells, N., eds. 1998. Writing the environment: ecocriticism and literature. Zed Press, London, UK.

Krebs, A. 1999. Ethics of nature. Walter de Gryter, New York, NY.

Krech, S. 1999. The ecological Indian: myth and history. Norton, New York, NY.

Kroeber, K. 1994. Ecological literary criticism: romantic imagining and the biology of mind. Columbia University Press, New York, NY.

Landry, D. 2001. The invention of the countryside: hunting, walking, and ecology in English literature. Palgrave, New York, NY 1671-1831.

Martinez-Alier, J.; Guha, R. 1997. Varieties of environmentalism. Essays North and South. Earthscan, London, UK.

Marshall, P. 1992. Nature's web: an exploration of ecological thinking. Simon and Schuster, London, UK.

Mazel, D., ed. 2001. A century of ecocriticism. University of Georgia Press, Athens, GA.

McCagney, N. 1999. Religion and ecology. Blackwell, Oxford, UK.

McGregor, R.K. 1997. A wider view of the universe: Henry Thoreau's study of nature. University of Illinois Press, Urbana, IL.

McKusick, J.C. 2000. Green writing: romanticism and ecology. St. Martins Press, New York, NY.

Milton, K. 1996. Environmentalism and cultural theory: exploring the role of anthropology in environmental discourse. Routledge, London, UK.

Murphy, P., ed. 1998. Literature of nature: an international sourcebook. Fitzny, Chicago, IL.

Nelson, B. 2000. The wild and the domestic: animal representation, ecocriticism, and Western American literature. University of Nevada Press, Reno, NV.

Oruka, O.H., ed. 1994. Philosophy, humanity, and ecology: philosophy of nature and environmental ethics. ACTS, Nairobi, Kenya.

Osundare, N. 1986. The eye of the earth. Heinemann Press, Ibadan, Nigeria.

Preece, R. 1999. Animals and nature cultural myths, cultural realities. University of British Columbia Press, Vancouver, BC, Canada.

Rooney, C. 2000. African literature, animism, and politics. Routledge, London, UK.

Sarver, S.L. 1999. Uneven land: nature and agriculture in American writing. University of Nebraska Press, Lincoln, NE.

Saro-Wiwa, K. 1986. A forest of flowers. Saros Press, Port Harcourt, Nigeria.

Schipper, M. 1989. Beyond the boundaries: African literature and literary theory. Allison, London, UK.

Scigaj, L.M. 1999. Sustainable poetry: four American ecopoets. University Press of Kentucky. Lexington, KY.

Sekoni, R. 1993. Folk poetics: a socio-semiotic study of Yoruba trickster tales. Greenwood, Westport, UK.

Slaymaker, W. 2001. "Ecoing the other(s): the call of global green and African responses."PMLA 116: 120-144.

Thones, S.; Recheleau, B.; Recheleau, D. 1995. Gender, environment, and development in Kenya: a grassroots perspective. Rienner Press, Boulder, CO.

Tichi, C. 1979. New earth: environmental reform in American literature from the Puritas through Whitman. Yale University Press, New Haven, CT.

Voros, G. 1997. Notations of the wild: ecology in the poetry of Wallace Stevens. University of Iowa Press, Iowa City, IA.

Welker, M. 1999. Creation and reality. Fortress Press, Minneapolis, MN.

Wylie, H.; Lindfors, B. 2000. Multiculturalism and hybridity in African literature. Africa World Press, Trenton, UK.

Onokpise, Oghenekome U.; Rockwood, Don L.; Worthen, Dreamal H.; and Willis, Ted, eds. 2008. Celebrating minority professionals in forestry and natural resources conservation: proceedings of the symposium on the tenth anniversary of the 2 + 2 Joint Degree Program in Forestry and Natural Resources Conservation. Gen. Tech. Rep. SRS–106. Asheville, NC: U.S. Department of Agriculture, Forest Service, Southern Research Station. 111 p.

The 22 papers in this symposium highlight the program and its contribution to increasing minority professionals in forestry and natural resources conservation. The tenth anniversary symposium brought together graduates of the program, current students and officials from the universities, the U.S. Forest Service, other agencies, and private industry. The theme of the symposium was "Education, Training, and Diverse Workforce."